THE NATURE OF POLITICS

Selected Essays of Bertrand de Jouvenel

Edited and with
an Introduction by
Dennis Hale
and Marc Landy

Boston College

Foreword by
Wilson Carey McWilliams

Rutgers University

SCHOCKEN BOOKS / NEW YORK

First published by Schocken Books 1987
10 9 8 7 6 5 4 3 2 1   87 88 89 90

Library of Congress Cataloging-in-Publication Data
Jouvenel, Bertrand de, 1903–
    The Nature of Politics.
    Bibliography: p.
    Includes index.
    1. Political science—Collected works. I. Hale,
Dennis. II. Landy, Marc Karnis. III. Title.
JA42.J68 1987   320   86-21909

Design by Cassandra Pappas
Manufactured in the United States of America
ISBN 0–8052–4023–3

In Memoriam

JULIUS S. GLASER
(1916–1986)

*President of
Schocken Books
1982–1984*

Contents

Foreword

Marc Landy and Dennis Hale deserve to be thanked for making the work of Bertrand de Jouvenel more accessible to Americans. Twenty-five years ago, I was privileged to study with de Jouvenel, who was then a visiting professor at the University of California. A gracious teacher, puckish toward academic mores—"Do professors in America really assign their *own* books?"—de Jouvenel encouraged us to risk the step from the study of theories to engagement in theorizing. Master artisan that he is, de Jouvenel also helped us to see that, in political theory as in all the arts, the craft is inseparable from the work, and that political science is an art precisely because it has a duty to be artful.

He told us, for example, that when he submitted *On Power* for publication, he was told that the work was unacceptable because it lacked footnotes. According to the story, de Jouvenel immured himself in a library, emerging with a long list of references, only to be told that he now had too many. Consequently, de Jouvenel said, he was compelled to make a political decision: which footnotes to discard and which to keep. In the end, as he told it, he decided to keep "the most obscure, because they should be remembered." Whether this account was strictly true or not, it offered a vital lesson: that questions of justice are involved in intellectual practice, that justice entails claims on our memories as well as our conduct, and, above all, that a political writer must proceed on the assumption that words matter.

One of the great themes of de Jouvenel's work is the contemporary ascendancy of power over words, in intellectual life as well as in political practice. Classical political theory held that words *define* power, pointing out that power is extrinsic, given meaning only by the ends it serves. The whole world is not power to someone who would save his soul, just as kingship does not empower, but burdens a philosopher. Classical theory, consequently, was engrossed with substantive restraints, ends which distinguish distracting energies from those which truly empower.

By contrast, early modern theorists—Machiavelli and his inheritors—argued that words can channel power. They were inclined to regard power as objectless and limitless—"in the first place," Hobbes wrote, "I put for a generall inclination of all mankind, a perpetuall and restlesse desire of Power after power, that ceaseth only in Death"[1]—but they maintained that law, informed by science, can guide and direct power toward ends we choose. From them, we derive our concern for procedural restraints, the "due process" of law. Even in the nineteenth century, theorists, now overawed by history and its forces and disposed to speak of inevitabilities, still retained enough of the earlier modern faith to believe that words can *reveal* power, showing us the direction in which power must go and allowing us to pick the winning side.

In the twentieth century, however, technology and total war seem to condemn such frail confidence. Intellectuals, captivated, have been tempted to regard words as no more than the *creations* of power. The same fascination is evident in the claim that the meaning of terms is "operational," and in the modern notion that language itself is only a "construction" built by power. Orwell carried that logic to its conclusion in *1984;* de Jouvenel has seen its workings at first hand.

Yet, although de Jouvenel does hope that words may regain their authority over power, he is no counterrevolutionary. He envisions an instauration, not a restoration. Like Theseus who slew the Minotaur, de Jouvenel would bring the old gods to a new city.

De Jouvenel's most important work presumes a political world in which action is equal, if not preeminent, in relation to speech, a position which is the starting point for his "Pseudo-Alcibiades."[2] Under modern conditions, theory cannot lead practice simply by *prescribing* what is best, as de Jouvenel believes classical political philosophy tried to do. The force and pace of events is too great; the politics of the age seem to call for leaders who are "pure act," like Henry Adams's Theodore Roosevelt, free from the distractions of reflection. But "Pseudo-Alcibiades" also brings praxis

---

1. *Leviathan,* part 1, chapter 11.
2. "The Pseudo-Alcibiades: A Dialogue on Political Action and Political Responsibility," *Yale Review,* 50 (December 1960):161–171

into dialogue with theory; it presents the "contestation" in speech, shifting the conflict onto ground where words are ascendant.[3]

Political practice—and the political science created in its image—has its own fatal weakness. Action is tied to description: it is epimethean, bound to what has been or, at best, to what is. The creature of past and present, political science is constantly outrun by change, reduced to a desperate, often clever, but ultimately futile pursuit of happenings it failed to forsee.[4]

Like Henry Adams, de Jouvenel argues that power can be tamed only by a "quantum leap" of theoretical imagination, able to place political speech far enough ahead of events to enable deliberation to direct or turn the frightful energies of the time. For *demos* to rule *dynamis,* democratic government requires foresight and planning.

At the same time, de Jouvenel, an anguished witness to totalitarian enormity, knows that prevision is too important to be left to visionaries. It demands a mantic political science, schooled in that disciplined "art of conjecture" to which de Jouvenel has devoted so much of his own thinking and writing.

De Jouvenel also reminds intellectuals of their own responsibility for the emancipation of power. Beginning with the proposition that freedom is doing what one wills, modern political thinkers, following Hobbes, maintain that what we want is infinite by nature. Hence, the problem of liberty is our chronic inability to do as we want; for practical purposes, freedom is power. Power is set free by the conviction that it will liberate us.

Despite ancient warnings, moreover, modern political theorists were persuaded that the growth of power would also be *safe.* In the historical view shared by Karl Marx and Herbert Spencer, progress—the advance of human power over nature—is associated with a decline in coercion (the movement from the "military" to the "industrial" stage of society), and with the waning of government (as the state "withers away").

The root of this error lies in the fact that, in modern politics,

---

3. Just as de Jouvenel's title, *Sovereignty: An Inquiry into the Political Good,* implies that the political good, not power, defines what is truly sovereign.

4. De Jouvenel, knowing the centrality of the automobile in the imagery of his American students, told an undergraduate class in 1960 that political science is "like a car with taillights into the past, and dashboard lights to help us classify and quantify the present, but no headlights to let us see into the future."

direct personal rule declines in favor of mechanisms of indirect
control, rule exerted by markets, mass persuasion, and the invisible politics de Jouvenel calls "polysynody." The contemporary
celebration of the "decline of bureaucracy" repeats this mistake,
seemingly oblivious to the fact that new "technologies of control"
are more efficient forms of mastery, without the creaky, relatively
human inefficiencies of bureaucratic rule. This century's experience ought to make clear the ghastly irony of the promise that the
"government of men" will be replaced by the "administration of
things."

Yet de Jouvenel's teaching also reminds us that resistance to
power is always difficult and rare. Liberal political philosophy
asks, "How can naturally free human beings be brought to obey?"
but for de Jouvenel, this is the wrong question. Political authority
is natural, and human beings have a high "propensity to comply."
Political science, consequently, should be more concerned with the
questions, "How do human beings *become* free? What prompts
them to resist a power which defies law?"

Freedom and right resistance, de Jouvenel indicates, derive
from a sense of what is fitting, a conviction that some things are
unseemly even when commanded by authority or power. In this
view, liberty's proper name is dignity. Even if we concede that
freedom is doing as one wants, it is also true that free people want,
and will strive for, control over their other wants. Human beings
are not free if they are merely automatons pursuing desires even if
that pursuit is successful. Freedom presumes the ability to evaluate
ends; even more, it requires the kind of courage which enables one
to do what is honorable and scorn what is shameful despite the
bribes and torments of power.

De Jouvenel locates the sources of such bravery in those associations which, unlike mere "interest groups," exert moral force in
the lives of individuals. Civic friendship, the feeling of affection
and obligation between citizens, is the strongest shield against
power. Up to this point, de Jouvenel's argument parallels Aristotle's, a likeness which is especially clear in *The Pure Theory of
Politics.* De Jouvenel, however, seeks to free civic friendship from
the "prison of the corollaries"—Aristotle's association of political
friendship with the *polis,* a regime which is small, stable, and
relatively austere. While de Jouvenel might concede that such
small polities *best* promote friendship, he is concerned to direct

our attention to the forms of friendship and of kindness possible in our times—lesser in quality and less likely to appear, and, for those reasons, more in need of cultivation.

Our governments are too clumsy and impersonal to promote friendship directly, but they can at least be friendly to friendship. Modern political thought tends to value human relationships only to the extent that they lead toward, or do not impede, desired *consequences*. Bonds and attachments which "stand in the way of progress" are regarded as "frictions," "hang-ups," or "fetters on the modes of production." Modernity reduces friendship to a means, preparing to sacrifice it on the altar of ends. De Jouvenel, by contrast, urges the claims of the great *configurations*—fraternity, friendship, and community—to be considered as ends in their own right.

De Jouvenel's practical judgment is elegantly balanced, and he recognizes that political life involves consequences as well as configurations, both Dux, the leader, and Rex, the king. De Jouvenel's theorizing, however, teaches the invaluable lesson that, just as foreign policy exists to protect domesticity, service to kings is the true office of leaders, and the edification of citizens is the true vocation of political science.

WILSON CAREY MCWILLIAMS

Rutgers University

Acknowledgments

We would like to acknowledge the assistance of M. de Jouvenel in this project. He was generous with his time, even though our project was a distraction from more important labors, and offered his help with unfailing humility and courtesy (and much skepticism about its reception by the publishing world).

His skepticism was unfounded; our editors at Schocken Books—Emile Capouya, Betty Gold, and Merope Lolis—have been most supportive of the project from the beginning.

Thanks are also due to Dan Cullen of Boston College and Acadia University, who used his fine scholarly gifts to aid us in amassing these essays and compiling the bibliography; and to Corinne Mellul, a graduate student at Boston College, who used her trips home to Paris to help with some difficult research problems.

Introduction

Bertrand de Jouvenel is the least famous of the great political thinkers of the twentieth century. He has few disciples, and although his books are often cited they are less often read. De Jouvenel has also been a prolific composer of essays, but these have received even less attention than his books. The essays published in this volume comprise a mere fraction of his total output. We have selected them because they serve to clarify, elaborate, and expand upon the themes of his three masterworks: *On Power* (1945), *Sovereignty* (1957), and *The Pure Theory of Politics* (1963).

What is the reason for de Jouvenel's obscurity? Partly it is a matter of nationality: de Jouvenel stands outside both of the main branches of twentieth-century political philosophy, the Anglo-American and the German. He is neither Lockean nor Hegelian, neither a liberal nor a Marxist. His voice belongs neither to the left nor to the right, and his writing has therefore the freshness and simplicity of the best teaching. The writer to whom he bears the greatest resemblance is probably Alexis de Tocqueville, but, like de Tocqueville, his fate has been to be misunderstood on both sides of the Channel and on both sides of the Atlantic.

De Jouvenel does, of course, share some common ground with the larger schools of thought which surround him. He shares with the left a deep concern for reducing human misery and ecological depredation, and he shares the left's belief in the need for government-directed economic planning. On the other hand, he shares the right's abiding suspicion of state power and its belief in the superiority of the market as the normal method for economic decision making. He is neither a romantic reactionary nor a celebrator of progress. He deplores the weakening of community solidarity that has accompanied the rise of industrialism and yet refuses to ignore or deprecate the extraordinary improvements in human health and well-being that industrialism has brought about. His freedom from ideological blinders makes him seem almost a gallic Orwell, pointing up inconvenient truths to those who would reduce the world's ills to "capitalism" or "the government." But his ambition stretches beyond Orwell in that he attempts to develop a theory of the good state which rests upon a clear-sighted understanding of the true nature of political behavior.

It is ironic that such a singular writer should see himself as part of a discredited generation. Yet in his memoir, *Un Voyageur dans Le Siècle,*[1] he describes his strong sense of identification with others who came to political maturity during the 1920s and who shared a passion for international reconciliation and a commitment to the institutional embodiment of that goal, the League of Nations. The rise of Hitler, the outbreak of war, and the capitulation of France were more than just tragedies for him. These events represented the failure of everything that he and his political brothers had most treasured, and forced him to consider that the basic conception of politics that they shared was fundamentally wrong.

But this same misunderstanding was shared by a much wider circle than the one to which de Jouvenel belonged. By the 1940s he came to see the disasters of the twentieth century in a wider context, as the culmination of many generations of delusion regarding the nature of politics. *On Power,* the first fruit of these speculations, was written in the midst of war and published in 1945. The political writing de Jouvenel has done since the war is a continuation of that first great effort to rethink the problem of the state by reexamining the fundamental nature of politics itself.

Edouard Bertrand de Jouvenel des Ursins was born in 1903. His parents epitomized the two faces of turn-of-the-century France. His father, Henri, was the son of a baron, Raoul de Jouvenel, from the southern region of Corrèze. Raoul identified strongly with the central elements of the French right: Catholicism, royalism, and nationalism. Bertrand's mother, Sarah Claire Boas, was the daughter of a wealthy industrialist, Alfred Boas, whose own cosmopolitanism was reflected in his calling himself an Israelite, not a Jew, and belonging to the Freemasons. The Dreyfus affair, which had so torn French society, was the very event responsible

1. *Un Voyageur dans le Siècle* (1978).

for bringing Bertrand's parents together. Henri had become an active supporter of the Dreyfusards and had become acquainted with the Boas family in that capacity.

Henri and Sarah divorced when Bertrand was still a child (the divorce was almost as shocking to Raoul as the marriage had been). Both parents became influential political figures during the 1920s and both provided Bertrand with important introductions to the political and literary haut monde. Henri served as France's representative to the League of Nations and was a prime mover behind the League's adoption of a mutual security agreement binding members to come to the aid of victims of aggression. He was also elected to the French Senate. Sarah made use of her wealth and social graces to preside over a salon of great prestige and importance. She worked tirelessly to convince the French government to champion the cause of an independent Czechoslovakia, the plans for which were largely hatched in her living room. In recognition of her service, Edward Beneš, the first prime minister of Czechoslovakia, gave the twenty-one-year-old Bertrand his first job, as Beneš's personal secretary.

After working for Beneš for a year, de Jouvenel began the journalistic career which he was to follow until the second world war. Throughout the 1920s and well into the 1930s he wrote for a variety of newspapers and magazines identified with the French left. He considered himself to be a progressive and stood for the national assembly as a candidate of the Radical Socialists, the most moderate of the parties composing the Popular Front. His allegiance to the left arose in part from his concern for international reconciliation (a strong theme of French left politics between the wars) and also from his deep concern over the problem of poverty—a theme that came to obsess him during the years of the Great Depression. Even during the prosperous twenties he detected a strong link between poverty and international conflict as he watched the effect which the impoverishment of the Germans, resulting from the Treaty of Versailles, had upon the popularity of extreme nationalist movements. He tried to convince the French left of the need to assist Germany in restoring prosperity, but to no avail.[2]

2. These themes can be found in two early works: *L'Economie dirigée* (1928) and *Vers les Etats Unis d'Europe* (1930).

De Jouvenel's years as a journalist are of the utmost importance for understanding his later work. To a degree unparalleled by any other chronicler of the rise of totalitarianism in the 1930s, even Orwell, de Jouvenel witnessed the key events and came to know the key individuals firsthand. He conducted long interviews with Benito Mussolini, Pierre Laval, Winston Churchill, Neville Chamberlain, and Adolf Hitler. He was in Germany in 1932, Spain in 1936, Austria during the Anschluss, Poland during the Blitzkrieg, and, most sadly for him personally, Czechoslovakia during the Nazi invasion. This firsthand experience gave him a respect for the stuff of politics as opposed to the abstraction of it. In *On Power* he would write approvingly of the gift which good politicians have for the "touch and feel" of politics, for the development of a tangible understanding which is not reducible to analytic categories. He also came to recognize the key role of timing in determining great events. The French chose to be severe toward Germany during the twenties and accommodating in the thirties. Had the sequence been reversed Hitler would have been stopped. Likewise, the British chose to appease Hitler (in Czechoslovakia) at a time when they might have been able to crush him, and to stand up to him (in Poland) when they had no chance of winning.

De Jouvenel's travels also taught him that possibilities existed for improving man's condition that had not occurred to the French. His trips to the United States (which included a stint as an extra in Hollywood playing the role of a Frenchman) convinced him that the energy and experimentalism of the New Deal offered more hope for ameliorating poverty than the timidity of the French Popular Front governments. While in the United States he interviewed figures as diverse as Huey Long and Rexford Tugwell in an effort to understand why the Depression had reached such depths, and how a government with as little ideological underpinning as F.D.R.'s could mount such a vigorous attack upon it.

Such active involvement in the events of his times left another indelible mark on de Jouvenel—an appreciation of the danger and difficulty inherent in political action. His statement "trouble is [the political scientist's] business"[3] contains more than a hint of personal chagrin, for he has had ample cause in his own life to discover that all political choices are risky and that the appearance of

---

3. "Political Science and Prevision," this volume.

misconduct is extremely hard to distinguish from actuality. Several of his actions, or at least the appearance that they created, caused him to be reviled by former friends and fellow journalists, to be castigated as a friend of fascism, and even to be accused of being a German collaborator.[4]

Like many other members of his generation, de Jouvenel had been active in efforts during the twenties and early thirties to improve relationships not only between the French and German governments but between their respective peoples as well. In this context he made friends with Otto Abetz, a young nationalist and francophile who would later serve as Hitler's ambassador to France at the time of the Occupation. In part, it was through the intervention of Abetz that de Jouvenel was granted the opportunity to interview Hitler in February of 1936.

Reading the interview today is an unnerving experience. Hitler is portrayed as a forceful if somewhat eccentric politician whose abiding passion is the reconstruction of Germany, and whose plans contain nothing to alarm the French. (This portrayal, it should be said, owes a great deal to the simple fact that Hitler lied to de Jouvenel about German intentions, just as he lied to everyone else.) De Jouvenel quotes Hitler's assurance that statements to the contrary in *Mein Kampf* are the excesses of a "first edition" writ-

---

4. The charge of having sympathized with fascism, and even of having collaborated with the Germans, has stuck to de Jouvenel ever since the 1930s, especially in his native country. There are apparently two major incidents that feed this misconception: de Jouvenel's brief membership in the Parti Populaire Francais and his association with Otto Abetz, the German ambassador to France during the Occupation, both of which are discussed below. In 1983, de Jouvenel brought a libel action in France against the author Zeev Sternhell for having repeated these accusations in print. Among those testifying on de Jouvenel's behalf was the French historian Raymond Aron, who left his hospital bed against doctors' orders in order to make his appearance in court. During his testimony, Aron called de Jouvenel "one of the two or three leading political thinkers of his generation." He totally rejected the idea that there was any justification at all for placing de Jouvenel among those who had aided and abetted the coming of Hitler. He called Sternhell's book "the most ahistorical book that I can conceive of. The author never places things in the context of events. He gives fascism a definition so vague and imprecise that it could refer to anyone. He loses sight of the fact that national socialism was, in the Thirties, a theme which spread throughout Europe. It is true that we, the men of that generation, we despaired about the weakness of democracy. We sensed that war was coming. So we dreamed. But it is inadmissible that this be used to defame people who are worthy of respect, even with regard to their mistakes" (*Le Monde,* October 19, 1983, p. 12 [editor's translation]). Leaving the courtroom, Aron collapsed and died.

ten at a time when French troops were still on German soil, occupying the Ruhr. Hitler goes on to say that he is not a writer preparing a new edition but rather a politician who will rectify those early mistakes through a policy of friendship with France.[5] Nowhere does de Jouvenel suggest any sympathy for Hitler. He simply allows Hitler to put the best face on German foreign policy.

The interview caused a furor. Apparently through the machinations of Joachim von Ribbentrop and Otto Abetz, its publication was delayed until February 28—one day after the French Chamber of Deputies voted to approve the Franco-Soviet Pact, a treaty Germany had opposed in a vigorous propaganda campaign. After the vote, and after the interview had finally appeared in print, the Germans pointed to its "delay" as evidence that the French "elite" was trying to mislead the masses by suppressing evidence of Germany's friendly intentions toward France. De Jouvenel came to believe that he had been used by Abetz in an elaborate propaganda scheme.

On March 7, 1936, one week after the interview appeared in print, Germany moved to reoccupy the Rhineland. Despite his long association with the Franco-German friendship movement, de Jouvenel called for a military response to this provocation.

The failure of France and Britain to move against Hitler at a time when Germany could have been easily defeated was a bitter disappointment to de Jouvenel, and it led to his break with the Radical Socialists. Looking about for new comrades, he found François Doriot and the Parti Populaire Français (PPF). Doriot had been a leader of the French Communist Party and mayor of the working-class city of Saint-Denis. He was purged by the Communists for defying Moscow and advocating an alliance with the Socialists, a line that Moscow would itself later endorse. De Jouvenel admired the working-class character of the PPF and hoped that it would develop into a popular democratic movement transcending the doctrinaire squabbles of the left. But, much to his dismay, the party drifted inexorably rightward as Doriot came more and more to view Communism as the sole evil to be addressed. Having just quit one party, de Jouvenel was reluctant to abandon another, especially when Doriot came under increasingly heavy attack. He

5. The interview with Hitler was published in *Paris-Midi*, February 28, 1936. It was conducted on February 21, 1936.

finally left the party in response to its failure to condemn the West's appeasement of Hitler at Munich.

Munich was the final turning point for de Jouvenel. His strong family commitment to Czech independence, combined with his contempt for the cowardice of both the British and French leadership, provoked him into personally undertaking the fight against Nazism. He secretly volunteered for service in the Intelligence Branch (Service Renseignement [SR]) of the French Army. His journalistic talents and his wide circle of friends abroad gave him the opportunity to function as an overseas journalist, relaying to the SR whatever information he could garner of military and/or strategic importance. In that guise he made trips to East Prussia and Poland and reported back on the status of German troop strength.

When France declared war on Germany, de Jouvenel volunteered for the infantry as an enlisted man and joined a regiment from his native Corrèze. He spent the next year training with the peasants and villagers who comprised his unit. His description of this period in his memoirs reveals a strong sense of camaraderie with these young men. Having spent his life in the drawing rooms of the literati and in the corridors of power, the decency, simplicity, and moral vigor of these amateur soldiers was refreshing and enlightening. He counts it as one of the gravest disappointments of his life that a severe training injury forced him to leave his unit and recuperate at Corrèze. By the time he recovered, the French had capitulated and his unit had been disbanded.

After the armistice was signed, de Jouvenel was recalled to service in army intelligence. He was asked to make use of his close friendship with Otto Abetz, now the German ambassador, to learn as much about Nazi intentions for France as possible. The task was onerous because it required that he conduct himself as a friend of the Germans. This was distasteful in itself, but it also meant that he would be viewed by his fellow Frenchmen as a collaborator; nonetheless he agreed. Since real journalism had ceased as a result of the Nazi takeover, de Jouvenel decided to continue his historical studies at the National Archives in Paris and to let that work serve as his excuse for taking up residence close to Abetz.[6]

6. Works of this period include a series of volumes on the coming of the war: *La Réveil de l'Europe* (1938); *D'une Guerre a l'Autre*, 3 vols. (1940–47); and *Après la Défaite* (1941).

Abetz (who was married to a Frenchwoman and openly admired French culture) was only too happy to see and talk with such a witty and charming French friend. For the next two years de Jouvenel continued to spend as much time as possible with Abetz and other officials and to report on those meetings to his army superiors. After the invasion of Russia, however, the intentions of Germany toward France no longer remained in doubt. In addition, de Jouvenel had come to believe that his information was of little value, especially since it was not clear that Abetz continued to enjoy the confidence of the Führer. In the summer of 1942 de Jouvenel decided to return to Corrèze and join the resistance.

De Jouvenel became an active member of the Corrèzean resistance, working to help downed Allied fliers evade capture. On September 21, 1943, sensing that the Germans were aware of his resistance work, and that he was being followed in order that his superiors might be exposed, de Jouvenel and his wife crossed the border to Switzerland where they remained for the duration of the war.

Thus did de Jouvenel's personal travails mirror those of the world around him. His decision to devote the rest of his life to scholarship was an effort to understand the roots of the naiveté that he had shared with his friends and of the evil perpetrated by their enemies. It was not long before this effort produced substantial results.

Even while he worked for army intelligence and for the resistance, de Jouvenel pondered the cause of the calamity into which the world had been thrown. In January 1943, "Of Political Rivalry" was published in the review *Suisse Contemporaine.* In this essay de Jouvenel asked what must seem, in retrospect, an odd question: "Is war alien to modern times?" What a question to ask in the middle of the most destructive war in history!

But de Jouvenel's generation had hoped that war *was* an alien spirit in modern times and that the first world war, an aberration, would be the last. To the best minds of the twenties and thirties the true spirit of modern times was summed up by two ideas: progress and popular sovereignty. The real story of history was not to be found in military engagements, but "in the integrated exploitation of the world's resources for the benefit of man in association with his fellows."[7] The best minds believed that "the spirit of conquest

---

7 *On Power: Its Nature and the History of its Growth* (1948), 6.

pertains, never to peoples, but only to their rulers."[8] As the sovereignty of the people spread across the globe, therefore, war could only recede to the remaining backwaters where superstition and absolute monarchy could fight their last battle with enlightenment.

This was the great dream of the twentieth century, shattered now for the second time. Why is it, de Jouvenel asked, "that we are retreating from civilization instead of advancing toward it. . . ?"[9]

One answer is political rivalry. Whenever any one state becomes powerful, other states are driven to imitate it in self-defense. In the past, states increased their power by adding territory—at first through adjoining provinces or nations and later by taking over territory far away, in the form of colonies.

But in modern times a more ominous method of increasing power has been found:

> [That is] the advance made by any one power in exploiting the natural resources of its own national domain. If it increases the draft which it makes on the strength and wealth of its people and contrives to get this increase accepted, it then changes the relationship between its own sinews of war and those of its neighbors; it becomes, if its capital is small, the equal of great powers, and if it is large it brings hegemony within its reach.[10]

This technique—extended to its farthest reaches by Hitler but in no way invented by him—made World War II possible, a war in which:

> Everyone—workmen, peasants, and women alike—is in the fight, and in consequence everything, the factory, the harvest, even the dwelling-house, has turned target. As a result the enemy to be fought has been all flesh that is and all soil, and the bombing plane has striven to consummate the utter destruction of them all.[11]

Although Hitler was its indirect cause, the unparalleled scale of the destructive force unleashed by World War II could, neverthe-

8. Ibid, 136.
9. Ibid, 139.
10. Ibid, 140.
11. Ibid, 1.

xxii   *Introduction*

less, not be explained as a consequence of Nazi barbarism. All Allied governments contributed to it, and what is more significant, they did so *easily*. All Allied governments competed enthusiastically in drawing deeply on the resources of society. Mass conscription, the commandeering of private property, the suspension of civil liberties, the relocation of entire populations, state direction of national economies—all of these practices were quickly adopted in the democracies with hardly a ripple of protest. They were, after all, necessary. "The most surprising feature of the spectacle which we now present to ourselves is that we feel so little surprise at it."[12]

Could it be that we are witnessing, de Jouvenel asked, a phenomenon more general, and more basic, than the rise of a madman to authority in a great state? To answer this question it was necessary to study the natural history of the one human institution without which modern life would be unimaginably different: the apparatus of the state—or, as de Jouvenel called it, "Pouvoir."

On Power

The title of this work is misleading to the English-speaking reader. In French the term *pouvoir* can have the specific meaning of governmental authority rather than the more general English meaning of "the ability to do something."[13] De Jouvenel's purpose in this work is not to discuss political power as an abstraction but rather to trace the evolution of governmental authority from its roots in primitive societies to modern times. By undertaking such a "natural history" of the beast he hoped to discover where we had acquired the demonic impulse and the herculean energy that enabled us to commit the horrors of both world wars and the Holocaust.

De Jouvenel's own depiction of totalitarianism is similar to that found in the works of its other great students, Orwell and Hannah Arendt. His great contribution is to give totalitarianism a genealogy. In doing so, however, he has demonstrated the embarrassing fact that the totalitarian state, black sheep though it may be, is a legitimate member of the modern family of nations: not only does it have the same ancestors, it has many of the same family charac-

---

12. Ibid.
13. This nuance is often missed in translation. Compare the definition offered in the *Petit Larousse* to that in the French–English edition of the *Larousse Dictionary*.

teristics, even if in a distorted or exaggerated form. Totalitarianism is the last step in a long journey that began when kinship ceased to be the exclusive source of group identification. The engine driving this evolution is the concept of mobilization. Unlike any earlier form of government, including the badly misunderstood "absolute monarchy," modern states have the capacity to achieve a total mobilization of the spiritual and material resources of their peoples. Perhaps the most telling image in the entire work is the contrast between the medieval king and the modern prime minister. The former, despite the grandiloquence of his title, had to go hat in hand to the castles of the barons to beg for funds and men with which to mount military campaigns. The latter, while a mere commoner, has access to the enormous tax revenues of the state as well as the right to conscript soldiers from among the populace at large.

The medieval king was constrained by the level of existing technology—collecting taxes is difficult without post offices, roads, or computers. But the more important constraint was the limited nature of his claim to authority. Ruling in God's name, he was also God's servant and he was pledged to maintain the order that God had created. In that order he was but the first among nobles, each of whom had clear title to lands and vassals. The expansion of power could come only from the expansion of the monarch's claim. He needed to set himself above the other nobles and for this he required the help of the people. He had to convince the masses that their own emancipation depended upon him. Thus an alliance between monarch and commoner was born in joint opposition to the intermediate authorities who served to obstruct the well-being of both.

The essence of this argument is borrowed from de Tocqueville's description of the ancien régime: the king seduces the aristocracy into foresaking its responsibilities and then turns the people against the now useless aristocracy in the name of progress and justice. De Jouvenel agrees with de Tocqueville that once the people have accomplished this task they recognize that they have no further need of the king. They choose to run the centralized state apparatus, which he has created, in their own name. Deposing the king is therefore the last, not the first step in the process of centralization and disintermediation that creates a modern government. Popular sovereignty thus replaces monarchic absolutism as the basis for the claim to govern. De Jouvenel improves upon de Tocqueville by describing just how much is gained for state power in this shift of claim. As long as the people believe that the government belongs to the king they feel limited in their obligation to obey and serve it. Those limits relax and later disappear once the people believe that they are governing themselves.

Borrowing from Jean-Jacques Rousseau, de Jouvenel points out the absurdity of a literal interpretation of popular sovereignty. Once the size of the polis expands beyond that which is governable by the direct participation of all citizens, people stop governing themselves. Whether or not they are able to exercise effective control over their government depends upon the effectiveness of the specific institutions which they develop for controlling the behavior of those who do govern. As the modern state becomes increasingly bureaucratized and therefore hierarchical and remote, it becomes difficult for the citizen to exercise such control. From the standpoint of power what matters is not the *truth* of popular sovereignty but its *credibility*. As long as it remains credible, the government can obtain credit. The populace will obey edicts, pay taxes, and allow its young men to be conscripted. In de Jouvenel's terms, it will be *mobilized*.

The extent of mobilization depends upon the depth of credit the people extend. Such credit is not obtainable simply through verbal trickery. For the people to believe that they are self-governing, they must see that their well-being is enhanced as a result of state action. The modern welfare state was created, therefore, so that the government could enhance its credit by providing economic stability and security for the populace.

For de Jouvenel, the importance of this bargain cannot be overstated. It is the determining event of modern history. Not only does this bargain make the modern state possible by vastly increasing the state's credit, it also makes modern life possible. By elevating the mass, power allows the creation of an enormous middle class—literate, energetic, and politically powerful—made up of descendants of subjects once doomed to penury and servitude. Economic security and improved living conditions also enable populations to grow to unheard-of dimensions, permanently altering the scale of modern life. In tandem with this growth is the emergence of industrial and commercial enterprises which power nurtures for their tax revenues and their military potential. In this way, the modern industrial economy is born—an economy which has made its own enormous contribution to the standard of living of the great majority of modern citizens. There is no turning back from this step. It is precisely this awareness that separates de Jouvenel from conservatives who in other ways share his alarm at the direction of modern life.

De Jouvenel, however, does not consider men to be mere economic creatures. They cannot be simply bribed into acquiescing to any and all forms of state power. To be effective, the government must persuade the people that it is advancing the cause of liberty as well. To establish its monopoly of authority, the Minotaur (as de Jouvenel calls the modern state) must eradicate the modern equivalent of the nobility; that is, all those intermediate institutions which also exert some claim on the loyalties of citizens and therefore serve as competitors for their credit.[14] The Minotaur, therefore, seeks to devour labor unions, churches, fraternal organizations, and all other such intermediate bodies. The specific tactics here changed but the strategy is essentially the same as that devised by renaissance kings. The people must be convinced that these intermediate bodies obstruct their liberty—that they are parochial, hidebound, and self-seeking. All too often these charges are easy to substantiate. One would have a difficult time rallying contemporary American citizens to save the American Medical Association, the Teamsters, or Union Carbide from government suppression. The lack of public spirit expressed by these "baronies" seals their doom as surely as it was sealed for the French aristocracy by their tax privileges and their decadent life-style.

By tracing the genealogy of power, de Jouvenel succeeds in putting the twentieth century back into the story of human history, from which it had been expelled by many of its students. De Jouvenel discovered that what is exceptional about the twentieth century is not the *nature* of power—which never changes—but its *scale,* which is subject to constant expansion. It expands because of its vitality—without which power sickens and dies and is re-

---

14. The destruction of intermediate institutions by totalitarian regimes is an important theme in Hannah Arendt's *Origins of Totalitarianism* (New York: Harcourt Brace and World, 1951). It is de Jouvenel's contribution to show that this is a tendency of power generally—not a unique attribute of totalitarianism (although it is carried farther in such a regime). This is one of the "family traits" totalitarianism shares with its more respectable cousins.

placed by a more vigorous power—and also because of its usefulness. Power grows because it accomplishes great tasks and it can
therefore make use of the most elemental human instinct: the
desire to live a better life. Knowing that this analysis would lead to
the charge that he was a reactionary, de Jouvenel wrote:

> I am not setting up as an enemy of the growth of Power and
> of the distension of the state. I know well the hopes that men
> have of it, and how their trust in the Power which shall be
> warms itself at the fire of the sufferings which the Power that
> was inflicted on them. The desire of their hearts is social
> security. Their rulers, or those who hope to become their
> rulers, feel no doubt that science now enables them to condi-
> tion the minds and the bodies of men, to fit each single
> person into his proper niche in society, and to ensure the
> happiness of all by the interlocking functions of each. This
> undertaking, which is not lacking in a certain grandeur,
> marks the culmination of the history of the West. If it seems
> to some of us that there is in this design rather too much
> confidence here and rather too much presumption there . . .
> —what is the good of being Jeremiahs? In my view,
> none. . . .[15]

Sovereignty: An Inquiry Into
The Political Good

"The problem stated, the mind moves on in search of answers . . ."
                                                    —*On Power*

On Power is a study in pathology. In describing the rise of the
modern state and its increased capacity to mobilize, de Jouvenel
does not establish the inevitability of totalitarianism. He can point
out the similarity between F.D.R.'s use of the radio and his ma-
nipulation of symbols like the Blue Eagle, and Hitler's use of the
tools of mass communication, without at all implying that Nazism
and the New Deal are the same. They are merely part of the same
human story. The large state, the rise of popular sovereignty, and
the advent of techniques of mass communication and control make
totalitarianism possible but do not render it inevitable. In *Sov-*

---

15. *Power*, 12–13.

ereignty de Jouvenel explicitly examines what the other alternatives might be.

Sovereignty's subtitle, "an Inquiry into the Political Good," is significant for what it reveals about the orientation of de Jouvenel's thought. It demonstrates his roots in a classical as opposed to a modern understanding of politics. He assumes that there is in fact such a thing as the political good which is a thing unto itself and not simply the sum of individual goods achieved through collective means. He accepts Aristotle's definition of man as a political animal. The legitimate purpose of state action, therefore, is not just the promotion of the material, or even the psychic, well-being of individuals. Because he is concerned with the well-being of the polity itself, he believes that policies must be shaped to produce good politics; that is, a set of conditions in which the citizenry thrives and improves its political understanding.

Because politics is natural to man it is also irremovable. Any society will have politics. In this sense de Jouvenel puts himself at odds with both liberals and Marxists. Man is neither so base as to be incapable of governing his affairs nor so perfect that he can create a perfect order in which politics would be unnecessary. The dynamism inherent in political life is ineradicable. This acceptance of continual political change places de Jouvenel at odds with all modern views of politics be they conservative, liberal, or radical. Conservatives conceive of society as being static. Radicals seek to overthrow the status quo and create a new order which, given its perfection, would also be static. Liberals accept change, but only that created by the perfect machine, the market. If politics cannot be removed, then the cure for the pathology of modern states lies in improving the quality of politics itself.

To understand what constitutes good politics, de Jouvenel begins by trying to understand the essence of all politics, authority. Again he begins by rejecting modern understandings. As the foundation of politics, authority is, perforce, natural. One need not invent the elaborate myth of the social contract to explain why men agree to obey other men. Such an inclination is as natural as a son obeying his father or a ballplayer heeding his coach.

The omnipresence of authority does not serve to eliminate disobedience which results from the conflict of competing authorities. The son disobeys his father to please his peers. The ballplayer goes against the coach's orders because a prestigious sportswriter favors another approach. These conflicts are the stuff of human misery because they undermine the invaluable service which authority performs. Authority is the basis of all organized activity and, thus, of all human achievement. Even the life of the marketplace is subsequent to a prior authoritative act of organizing the market and providing for the security and stability which it requires to operate.

The key step to understanding politics is to recognize that authority performs two vital but distinct functions. It builds and preserves, stirs and calms, aggregates and stabilizes. It is the root of all innovation and of all stasis. De Jouvenel provides names for these two often inimicable functions: the authority figure who innovates he labels *dux;* the authority figure who stabilizes he calls *rex.* A leader may well come to symbolize one or the other of these qualities: David is dux, Solomon is rex. More typically a leader will embody both qualities, emphasizing one or the other as circumstances require. (Contrast the F.D.R. who proposed "bold and persistent experimentation" with the F.D.R. who told Americans "we have nothing to fear but fear itself.")

Politics is animated by the paradox that rex and dux are both complementary and contradictory. No society can endure change that is all encompassing or stasis that is absolute. The very fact that most aspects of life will remain unchanged in the short run allows us to embark upon new ventures. An unfamiliarity with change renders us unable to adapt to new circumstances (when they inevitably occur) or to improve our lot.

While rex and dux represent essential qualities of our life in common, they also frame the principle lines of cleavage in any society. The interests of some—the poor, the young, the outcast— are best served by change. The interests of their opposite numbers are best served by adherence to the status quo. Somehow these paradoxical elements must be kept in a dynamic equilibrium, which is the task de Jouvenel assigns to the most all-encompassing form of authority, the sovereign.

> Public authority . . . acts as a more or less discriminating filter to innovation in behavior and diversions from the norm. Necessarily, it is on guard to remedy the resulting uncertainty. It is in this process of filtering and remedying, in this unceasing work of repair to an equilibrium that the question of the Political Good is most often posed.[16]

---

16. *Sovereignty: An Inquiry into the Political Good* (1957), 55.

Thus the political good is different from other forms of good. It stands behind them. It reconciles the fruits of change with the deep need which men feel for certitude, coherence, and continuity. The basic mission of the political good is to strengthen the social tie itself: to reinforce

> the friendship felt by one citizen for another and the assurance that each has of the predictability in another's conduct—all of them conditions of the happiness which men can create for each other by life in society.[17]

Once again de Jouvenel aligns himself with the classic understanding of politics. The purpose of politics is to perpetuate the good city, the city of mutual respect, trust, and affection. De Jouvenel, however, recognizes that the preconditions which have traditionally been relied upon for this task no longer exist. He cites four such corollaries for the sustenance of social friendship: small size, cultural homogeneity, resistance to innovation, and the banning of foreign ideas. These corollaries are both irretrievable and inimicable to other valued human goals. His aim is therefore to liberate the political good, conceived of as the maintenance of the social tie, from "the prison of the corollaries."

The gravest error of modern politics has been to ignore the vast differences between modern and ancient society and to try to govern the former as if it were the latter. Any effort to build walls around the city—to close it off from a world of change—is doomed to failure, and can only be attempted by using the most hideously coercive means. De Jouvenel's approach to escaping the "prison of the corollaries" is to adopt—and then *adapt*—the modern liberal conception of government as umpire rather than animator. The proper function of the modern state is to regulate, not to control or direct the nongovernmental institutions and activities which provide the life force of modern society. But unlike the classical liberal state, which enforces a neutral set of rules or protects the market from monopolists and thieves, the state in de Jouvenel's view must be (and can be) guided by a vision of the political good. What does this vision consist of?

Government should not try to create social friendship because it does not know how. It is too blunt and clumsy an instrument to perform such a delicate and creative task. This view reflects not

17. Ibid, 123.

only de Jouvenel's skepticism about governmental capacity, it also reflects his appreciation for the subtle nature of social friendship. In the modern context, social friendship is not reducible to mere similarity of background or outlook nor to the sort of idolatry embodied in modern nationalism. It is rather a framework of loyalties nurtured and sustained by common experience.

> It [social friendship] . . . must grow of itself by way of men's ordinary intercourse, always provided that the intercourse is so regulated that noxious activities are as far as possible restrained. By means of this regulation, which is the essential feature of the art of politics, mutual trustfulness grows apace among men. . . .[18]

De Jouvenel's notion of "noxious activities" which the state must restrain is far more expansive than that contained in the liberal notion of regulation. The latter is limited to the enforcement of promises and the redress of market failure. The protection of social friendship requires a good deal more. The state must be able to break up social logjams. As de Tocqueville recognized, sustaining social friendship requires preventing any particular social group from exercising outrageous privileges and/or blocking the advancement of other meritorious groups. Whatever its practical failings, the principles underlying antitrust legislation would jibe with these principles. The state must also facilitate the practice of group solidarity. One imagines that de Jouvenel would have been a vigorous supporter of the Wagner Act and similar efforts to promote free collective bargaining. For him the advantages inherent in enabling laboring men to join together in the fraternal pursuit of common improvement would far outweigh whatever limits on their liberty are imposed by compulsory membership and dues paying.

While the task ascribed to the sovereign is limited, it is extremely difficult to achieve. This is due in large measure to the dissatisfaction which people express toward all those institutions, especially government, which comprise "society."

> [People] have a tendency to classify as personal relations those which please them and convey an emotional warmth and as "social relations" any which they dislike and find a

18. Ibid, 132.

burden. It is often said nowadays: "I cannot dine with friends. I have a social engagement." Thus social relations means for us the unpleasing remnant of the complex of relations from which the pleasing ones have been extracted. For this reason society affects us as a burden even when it is in reality carrying us.[19]
Nothing is less natural than a concentration of authority which keeps it far away and out of sight . . . the natural thing is an immediate authority which is present bodily and asserts itself spontaneously in every human grouping.[20]

The facelessness of modern society and the abstract nature of governance is at odds with deeply rooted human desires for tangibility and communion. Human imagination delights in devising remedies for these defects. Given the diversity of human intellect, these remedies differ markedly. Hare Krishna and the Ayatollah are two of the many contemporary examples of this impulse at work, but so are labor unions, consciousness-raising groups, and neighborhood associations. The danger to the political good arises from the well-nigh irresistible impulse to make use of the vast resources of the modern state to implement a particular vision of a perfect social order whose very perfection requires that it be imposed on others. The mayhem and discord which results from competitive efforts to make use of government to promote justice is itself the greatest cause for the unraveling of the social tie.

De Jouvenel accepts the quest for justice as an inevitable, and on the whole laudable, attribute of the human soul. To ensure that the search for justice does not destroy liberty is the greatest of all of government's regulatory challenges. It must parry all the thrusts aimed at using government to install a perfect social order. Not only are such efforts destructive but the process of resisting them is itself educational. It can help the citizenry to learn that justice is an attribute of human character, not a feature of any particular social organization. No institutional blueprint can ensure that men will relate to each other justly. Instead each must develop those qualities of mind and soul which encourage and permit him to work out just solutions to the multitude of specific problems that confront him each day. The greatness of politics lies in its mundane applica-

19. Ibid, 138.
20. Ibid, 175.

xxxii   Introduction

tions; and the challenge is to make the state an asset rather than a
liability in this endeavor.

The Pure Theory Of Politics

If the taming of the state is the great task of modern politics, what
should be the contribution to this endeavor of the "science of
politics"?

Here again, de Jouvenel betrays his classical roots. The end of
political knowledge is the good city, but there are many pitfalls
along the way. Political knowledge is dangerous—in the wrong
hands it can as easily be used to destroy as to nurture the good life.
In fact, political knowledge is *more* apt to destroy than to create,
since the best citizens refrain from pushing themselves forward,
while the worst (as Yeats said) "are full of passionate intensity."
This is the theme of the third of de Jouvenel's great works, *The
Pure Theory of Politics* (1963). This work owes much to de Jouvenel's visits to Great Britain and the United States between 1958
and 1960, at which time he taught at Cambridge, Yale, and Berke-
ley, renewing an intellectual dialogue begun in the late 1940s. *Pure
Theory* was written in English, and in a number of places seems
designed for an English-speaking social science audience. Its
themes and concerns are those of the political science of the time,
especially in the United States. What is a science of politics? What
is theory? What is the mission of the political science discipline?
What should be its attitude toward "facts" and "values"?

But de Jouvenel's treatment of these questions is original and
refreshing, which should make this work of particular interest for
American political scientists. For de Jouvenel manages to go beyond the stale debate over what kind of "science" the study of
politics should (or could) become, by putting to the reader a
provocative question: Why is it that politics, the oldest of the
organized studies in our tradition, has not *already* produced a body
of accepted principles that form the core for the other, newer
sciences? Surely it is not because political scientists, ancient or
modern, were or are unequal to the task. There must be another
reason, and grasping it helps us to understand both politics itself
and the urgent mission of those who study it in modern times.

Politics involves both "configuration" and "dynamics"—it is
about "where different things stand in relation to one another"

(presidents and legislatures) and "how successive events arise from one another" (political cause and effect).[21] Configurations are static, at least in the short term: Congress and President have confronted one another from the same hills (both literally and figuratively) for nearly two hundred years. But it is otherwise with political dynamics: at any moment there will be an uncountable number of actions taken in the political realm that may or may not have consequences in the future, depending on whether those actions move others to the appropriate response. This "moving of others" to take certain actions is what de Jouvenel calls the "technology of politics."[22] It is what all practical men need to know, and what the most successful of them *do* know. Should it form part of the knowledge of the political scientist?

Certain objections arise immediately. Political technology (as those who follow American elections have reason to know) is very unreliable; of all the "promptings" that occur daily, very few take fire and result in genuine "events." How are we to found a "science" on such uncertainty? The other objection comes from the classical school of political philosophy: this kind of "knowledge" is the stuff of sophists, and not true knowledge at all. It is not wisdom; and wisdom is the only goal worthy of study and reflection.

These de Jouvenel concedes to be serious objections. *The Pure Theory of Politics* and much of the work he has done since constitute his response.

In the "Pseudo-Alcibiades," for example, ambition (Alcibiades) confronts wisdom (Socrates) with a challenge that must haunt de Jouvenel, as it must haunt anyone who has seen evil close up and been unable to forestall it: "Knowing and getting others to Know is your pursuit, Socrates. Doing and getting others to Do is mine."[23] And when Socrates points out that what Alcibiades wants Athens to do will probably turn out to be a disaster, the future tyrant responds: "If so, it is a disaster which your wisdom, Socrates, is unable to prevent, since you cannot get the people to do other than I recommend."[24]

The knowledge of how to move men to action—the fundamen-

---

21. *The Pure Theory of Politics* (1963), 3. See also "Political Configuration and Political Dynamics," this volume.
22. Ibid, 8.
23. Ibid, 26.
24. *Pure Theory*, 27.

tal ingredient in all "politics"—is a dangerous knowledge. For that very reason, centuries of political philosophy have been rightly concerned with constraining those who wield power by focusing on "ought" rather than "is." The function of political philosophy has been "to civilize power, to impress the brute, improve its manners, and harness it to salutary tasks."[25] The "factual science of politics" has always been seen as a source of danger, and only in very recent times has the discipline abandoned the "moral pulpit" for the laboratory.

On the whole, de Jouvenel approves of this change. Unlike many of his colleagues, however, he is deeply aware of its menace. "And [this awareness] might suffice to turn the scholar away from a quest for knowledge which may be ill-used, if the technology of politics awaited on his discoveries."[26] But it does not. The knowledge of how to move others has escaped the bottle in which it had been imprisoned for most of our history, with the greatest discoveries coming from those "who are least sensitive to the . . . appeal of traditional theory . . . while those with finer feelings are victims of processes which they cannot grasp."[27] The damage has been done; the task is now to repair it, and to prevent further disasters.

The multiple crises of the twentieth century are political in origin—they involve a grotesque distension of the state, an erosion of republican citizenship, a decline in civility. To understand our troubles means to deepen our understanding of "elementary political behavior," not for its own sake—the political scientist is no soulless collector of data—but for the sake of the political good whose definition has guided political inquiry for two thousand years. For politics, in the end, is not like other sciences—which is another reason for its lack of a set of agreed principles.

> We are inevitably more exacting when investigating human affairs than in the case of natural phenomena; regarding the latter we may be content to find an order, whatever it may be; in human society, however, we are not content to find some pattern, we want it to fit our idea of justice.[28]

25. Ibid, 35. See also "On the Nature of Political Science," this volume.
26. *Pure Theory*, 38.
27. Ibid.
28. Ibid, 33.

To guide this search, to inform it, to civilize it, to direct it away from the destructive fantasies of the modern political imagination, this is the proper role for political science—work enough for any lifetime. To have advanced this cause so far, in the face of so many tragic events, is the basis for de Jouvenel's claim to our attention and—we think the reader will agree—our affection as well.

Boston College
Chestnut Hill, Massachusetts
December, 1986

Born in a political milieu, having lived through an age rife with political occurrences, I saw my material forced upon me.

—*Bertrand de Jouvenel*

The Nature of Politics

Political Science must presumably be a *knowledge*. Of *what*, of which order of facts? Of political facts. How defined? In order to be a true science, it must seek regularities: in the behavior of which agents? And in what respects? To delimit the object of our study we may use one of two methods. We can start from the *amorphous* mass of facts which are loosely called political, and boil it down to the common denominator which earns these facts their qualification. Or we can start from a narrow and clear definition.

This latter course involves the considerable difficulty of finding a good definition, and the great inconvenience that some things termed political may happen to fall out of the limits of our definition. The former course, however, we have found impracticable, and the reasons are hereafter expounded.

The root word *politic* is currently employed with the function of an adjective. It does not clearly and definitely designate any distinctive thing; it has no frontiers, indeed, the word *nonpolitical* is used merely to denote another political attitude. The use of the word *politic* designates not a thing, but the relations of anything with government. This assertion can easily be illustrated. There is no natural affinity between the word *politics* and the word *meat*, but they come together as soon as it is proposed that the government should do something about meat. We call *political* the pressures started upon the public authorities to bring about this or that decision desired by this or that private interest, we also call *political* the stands taken on the matter by the parties, with a view to attaining or retaining popularity and power. Finally, the line of conduct adopted in the meat issue, is in most languages

"The Nature of Politics" was a lecture delivered at the London School of Economics, 1953. Reprinted from *The Cambridge Journal*, volume 7, no. 8 (May 1954). Used by permission of the publisher.

called a *politic:* this is a literal translation from the French: "une politique."

English has here an advantage over my own language which disposes only of a difference of articles to denote the difference existing between the tug-of-war over some decision, which comes under "*la* politique," and the line of conduct finally followed, which we call "*une* politique." The English are fortunate in being able to contrast "politics" and "policy."

With this duality, the root *politic* organizes its growths in a symmetrical manner upstream and downstream in relation to a waterfall of decision. *Politics* may be taken to denote the tussle which precedes the decision, and *policy* the course adopted. It is quite clear that each little group taking part in the tussle has its policy, its line of conduct to bring about the decision it desires, and the small group's policy at this stage is not to be confused with the policy it seeks to promote. No less clearly this ultimate policy is not beyond politics, for politics go on, and the policy adopted is a factor in them.

Are valuable results likely to be achieved by the method outlined above, which consists of the progressive breakdown into its elements of a vast mass of phenomena all falling under the word 'politics'? We do not think so: not a single science can be named which seeks to arrive at the simple by way of the complex.

We much prefer the opposite method, making our base a narrow meaning of the word *politics* and building on it.

The conduct of a private individual, operating on a very modest scale, is sometimes called "politic." When is it so called? Whenever his conduct has been apt to bring about the results desired by him, has been well conceived for its purpose, has been well calculated. But there is something more than that. No one would say that Robinson Crusoe, in using his intelligence to make himself comfortable on his island, had acted on wise political principles— but on wise economic ones.

The word *economy* is used to denote the good employment (or, more generally, just the employment) of the resources of which a man disposes. When, therefore, is it proper to speak of his private behavior having a "political" complexion? Whenever the help of other men is a necessary condition of his attaining his aim and object. Conduct which secures this help, and causes men to perform whatever is necessary to the realization of the mover's object, is "political" conduct, and "political" action is action which bends to the actor's will the wills of others.

It is this "politics of personal relationships" which is the great theme of Balzac. Critics have gone on saying ever since Taine (Balzac's own words authorizing this view) that Balzac's monument is the description of a society in its every part—and that is what Zola, with others after him, has tried to do again. But it is bad criticism: Balzac was not a painter of society as others were painters of battlescapes. What he has painted in various settings is essentially the individual's political conduct in society. In most of the novels of Balzac, a goal is set, very often some mundane situation, and the author unfolds the fullness of his genius in describing the maneuverings which tend to achieve this situation, and the blunders and counter maneuverings which tend to destroy it.

A man's "mundane situation" is analogous to his "political situation": both rest on a concurrence of sufficient assents to his importance; both are won by certain agents, whom he has been able to rally to himself, working actively in his favor. Balzac lays especial stress on some agents whose knitting and unraveling of reputations fascinate him: they are the grandes dames whose doings he paints with predilection.

Developing the implications of Balzac's vision, we will advance the proposition that we are in the presence of "politics" wherever a project calls for the favorable disposition of other wills, and insofar as the agent applies himself to enrol these wills. It is a significant fact that the word *campaign* covers strivings for very various objects, when the conditions necessary to the attainment of all these objects are similar. Whether it is a man aiming at a public office or at admission to a club, or Madame Turcaret seeking an entrée into someone's salon, or an industrialist trying to put a new product on the market, not one of them, different though these ends are, can achieve his own, except by disarming hostility, rallying popularity, winning support, conciliating wills.

Any action tending to rally and enroll foreign wills is political in form and, whatever the undertaking to be furthered, the pattern of the rallying action is the same. Whether it is a case of securing the support of several political groups for the formation of a ministry, or of several financial groups for the start of a business, or of several social groups for some philanthropic venture, the way of approach is the same.

Must we say, then, that every human undertaking has its politics? Certainly, just as each single one has its economy as well. The entrepreneur proves himself a good economist when he makes such allocation of his means as will best enable him to attain his end; he proves himself a good politician when he enriches his means with the help he wins from others. It is legitimate thus to word the epitaph of a *strategos:* He proved successful in the struggle, thanks to the adroit policy which brought him allies and to the prudent economy which gave him great superiority of force at the decisive point.

Economics and politics here appear as two complementary arts necessary to the efficiency of human action: economics is concerned with the use of resources already to hand, politics with increasing them. It also appears that, in any enterprise requiring for its accomplishment the energies of more than one man, the political aspect precedes in logic the economic aspect: how to extract the maximum of useful results from the forces assembled is a problem second to that of the assemblage of those forces. Take, for instance, an enterprise which is in substance economic, a matter of business: the first step in it must be action which is political in kind, a "campaign," namely, to assemble the financial backing.

We thus arrive at a first conception *very narrow* but very precise, of the art of politics: it is a technique for the addition of human energies by the union of wills.

And action political by its form can, we think, be usefully defined as that which makes for the addition of further energies borrowed from wills which have an independent existence. This definition is useful because what it gives us is a clearly delimited human phenomenon which occurs at all times and places and thus lends itself particularly to study.

The technique of addition is at its lowest when the addition to be brought about is a precarious one—when, that is to say, it is intended with a view to some once and for all action and one to which the human elements involved in it are naturally predisposed so that enthusiasm comes easily to the boil. As, for instance, when white men are incited to lynch black men whom they hate already. But, as the action in this example is morally low, we will take another one so that there may be no confusion between what is low morally and what requires only a low degree of political art. The action required to bring neighbors together to fight a fire is also a political action, but of quite a low degree, since the cooperation needed is only for a short time and meets with ready acceptance from the men called on. One difference, however, we may note between these two political actions (rallying for a lynching and rallying for fighting a fire): the predisposing factor is in the one case a passion and in the other a feeling of moral obligation.

The technique of addition is at its highest when the final cause of the addition is not some once and for all action but the establishment of some state of things *necessitating* the rallying in permanence of the human elements which bring it about.

The rallying of men will be found a more difficult operation when it is a case of laying the foundations of a *state of things*. Men respond easily enough to a suggestion to do something which is in line with their own inclinations. But, when the object in the promoter's mind is the establishment of something lasting, their imaginations are apt to be touched but feebly and the thing itself to make but a dull impression; even when it is something strongly desired and clearly envisaged, some of the links in the chain of actions necessary to its realization will be weak ones, for some of the actions will be intrinsically unpopular.

But, more than anything else, it is the keeping in being of an assemblage of human beings which will present difficulties. We are thinking now of a lasting composition of behaviors, of a durable running in common harness, of a dovetailing which should prove as durable as a building. Wills are inconstant things, and anything built by them will for that reason show an innate tendency to come apart. And with enlargement of the thing built the forces making for disruption and incoherence will themselves multiply. Therefore the maintenance of the structure must proceed day in, day out: conservation is a harder task than construction. The problems thus presented are political problems in the true sense, and the labors required are political labors.

It will be convenient to distinguish by words action directed to a rallying of wills for some once and for all purpose and action directed to forming a lasting concourse of wills: the former we will call "additive," the latter "aggregative." The one, of course, shades gradually off into the other, and the two words signify no more than the upper and lower zones of a single form of action—a form of action which is everywhere present in all human formations: the activity of a boy organizing a game is "additive," that of a man organizing a team is "aggregative."

So far we have regarded action of a political kind as instrumental in relation to some purpose or other. Every purpose, we have seen, whatever its nature, provided only that it requires the active participation of other men, demands of its promoter some political action, and sets in motion a technique for rallying assents—a technique denoting the art of politics.

Let us now suppose that the bringing together is no longer a means employed to achieve a given end but is looked on as an end in itself, that the promoter of the particular grouping is no longer concerned with a certain task for which he requires the energies of the group but has for his aim the existence of the group—and nothing more. His aim in that case is the construction of a group in and for itself.

Whenever action of a political nature has no other purpose in view than the construction of a group of men, it enters the category of pure politics. *The substance of action is then as much political as is its form.* And let us note at once that action of this kind can never be merely additive. For it would be a self-contradiction to·aim at an assemblage as an end in itself and to want it only as a thing of the moment. The virtue demanded of it is its mere *existence:* this necessarily implies that it be durable. Action in the sphere of pure politics is inevitably aggregative.

We may say, to sum up, that the action of grouping men together is political in form but that its end may or may not be political. When both the form and the end are political, when the action of grouping men together has no other ultimate purpose than the existence of the group, then there is pure politics.

Even if reality showed us no concrete instance of pure politics— an analogous case would be that of a chemical element which cannot be isolated—the idea would still be not without its value. But instances in fact there are. Indeed it is true to say that those only receive the title of *grands politiques,* who have founded, extended, and consolidated aggregates of men; more characteristically still, those only receive the title of *les politiques,* who, in times of trouble, have made it their essential preoccupation to maintain an aggregate in being.

The characteristic activity of pure politics may, therefore, be defined as an activity that builds, consolidates, and keeps in being aggregates of men.

With this definition, I have shot my bolt. This is really what I mean to put before you. And this concept is a main stem from which further considerations branch out.

This definition carries, we think, many advantages. It shows us at once the nature of a political achievement—it is a closely knit aggregate. It shows us at once the nature of a political operation— it is the formation and unending rehabilitation of an aggregate of this kind. Also we see at once that there is as well such a thing as political action of a negative kind—the kind that makes for disaggregation. We realize too the nature of a political force—it is one which conducts a political action; and it dawns on us that differing political forces, even when each is positive in isolation and all alike are constructive in tendency may have as regards one another a negative effect, with one tending to dissociate a whole which another tends to build or keep in being; the former, however destructive, *because* it seeks to build another whole.

Knowing as we do that a strong internal cohesion is what gives to a political achievement its essential durability, we can now understand that an effort directed to some merely additive end, however great its immediate effectiveness, may yet prove a political action of a negative kind, destroying the aggregates in being and unable to replace them with its own aggregate.

Now we appreciate the political battle as it really is—creators of aggregates disputing the allegiance of the wills that go to form them. We realize too what is sovereignty—the reification of an inner conviction held by the members of an aggregate that their aggregate has an absolute value. So too *raison d'état* (and every organized body has its *raison d'état* or *de corps*) is seen to be what seems rationally needful to the preservation of an aggregate, and therefore legitimate to those who treasure that aggregate and understand the action's relation to such preservation; and coincidentally illegitimate to others, who do not treasure the aggregate or do not see the relation.

Our mode of presentation focuses attention on two points; the capacity to initiate aggregates and the conditions making for their stability. The capacity to initiate aggregates should be called *authority*. Unfortunately, we cannot use this word, which has been twisted away from its true meaning. It should still mean what we propose to indicate, the ability to give rise to action of others. We should be able to say: Good men are under the authority of Jesus.

An *auctor* is properly speaking a source, an instigator, an architect. Significantly enough, the Latin word included the idea of that which causes increase. And in truth the creator of an aggregate causes an increase: for the aggregate is something more than its parts, just as the men who make it up are themselves something more than they were, materially and in most cases morally.

This power to initiate is the *vis politica,* the causing force of every social formation or company of men or *universitas.* Not for a moment must we be understood to think of this *vis politica* only in states: it is at work in every cooperative aggregate.[1]

The study of this *vis politica* must form an essential part of a real political science. We call it simply a force, imitating science which assumes a force where a displacement is caused, a work done. There are really two distinct works to be done, the addition of forces at this moment and the fostering of dispositions such that addition of forces for specific tasks can be made from time to time. The force which causes addition we can call *dux,* it leads, drives; the other we can call *rex,* it harmonizes, keeps together. Roman "affabulation" of social needs, strikingly analyzed by Georges Dumézil, had personalized these two forces in the mythical kings Romulus and Numa, and Rousseau had the intuition of understanding what this stood for: ardent initiator and wise regulator.

Let us here throw in some remarks on the parasitic talents needed by a professional politician for personal success. Two are enough, but those he must have: a flair for recognizing whatever currents of wills are astir in society, that he may use them to advance him, and, at its lowest level, the additive talent, which enables him to dispose men favorably to his person (his one aim), so that he acquires a sort of primacy among, as it were, grains swept along by a flood. The element of *auctoritas* (in the true sense) is here entirely lacking, for what these professionals do is substantially nothing at all, not even evil. The part played by them in the body social is that of colored particles which make it possible to follow the directions taken by the various eddies.

Let me now dwell upon the point that human aggregates are very different in extent and kind. A capital distinction seems to me to be that between a group gathered for a clearly defined purpose and a group whose mere existence confers a variety of benefits.

---

1. An example would be the formation by Ernest Bevin of the British Transport and General Workers' Union (1922).

The former type group for a given action or team can be pictured as the projection on an oriented axis-of-action of as much of the component individuals' energies as you can induce them to turn in the direction of action. *The vector* is the chief thing in such a group.

A group for *being* is different in kind from a group for *action*. In a group for action the *driving* force is the important thing, in a group for being the *binding* force is the important thing.

Groups for being are essentially the family and civil society, and groups for action are all those which pursue a purpose, their reason of existence. It is to be noted that men derive very different emotions from participation in the one or the other.

It is a fact of experience that men derive a sort of wild joy from participation in a small group of action, such as a football team and in the highest degree a group of infantry. The nostalgia which so many men feel for war, is due essentially to the mode of relation which arises in a small group of action.

This very excitement is a factor favorable to the transformation of a group of action into a group of being in which men enjoy different satisfactions and from which they reap different advantages. No group of action can last if it does not take on certain qualities of the group of being. And a group of being will fester and shrink if it is not the seat of actions, if indeed it is not from time to time transfigured into a group of action by the inspiration of some common purpose.

I find it convenient to think of the driving force as *dux,* of the binding force as *rex.* The binding is all important. This explains the fundamental affinity between the political authority and the keeping of contracts. The continued existence of the group of being rests upon the same unformulated will to preserve relation as the keeping of promises laterally. That is why Dius Fidius, the warranter of private contract, is also the Keeper of the City.

The conditions making for the solidity and stability of an aggregate are, naturally, a chapter of major importance in political science. One thing is certain, that no aggregate can hold together if the ties which bind it are *downward* only; I mean from *auctor* to each participant. Let us picture each element of an aggregate as fastened to its *auctor* (founder) by a force of attraction exercised by the latter. The strength of this tie will, by hypothesis, be in proportion to the power of attraction of the *dux,* though it will be weakened by any forces of repulsion at work, if they are too powerful, between the members of the whole.[2]

As forces of repulsion, liable to violent accretions according to circumstances, will never be wanting, the tie can only hold if the forces of attraction are both extremely strong and continually operative. The study of these forces of attraction is vital to our subject. They may roughly be divided into the centripetal and the lateral. Centripetal attraction is exerted by a nodal center as a dynasty, which is always visible and always operative. Lateral attraction is ensured by the links which come to exist between members of the group: that *auctor* has laid weak foundations who has not intermarried the associates. The intimacy established between them must satisfy needs material, needs sentimental, and needs moral. It is a condition of long duration for the structure that adhesions occur between its human elements. This is sufficiently shown by the advantages which flow from a mutual adaptability of behaviors and from the warmth of friendship arising from a well-conducted neighborliness. But the blessings of a good social feeling would not by themselves be adequate: also required is reception by each of the members of symbols common to all, which have become incorporated in the spirit of each and constitute for him the real tie binding him to the rest. The biologists tell us that in each cell of a living person the chromosomes are the same: in other words, a single operative principle brings it about that the cell is peculiar to this body and this only. Similarly, a complex of symbols brings it about that each member of a very advanced aggregate, such as an old nation, is the carrier of a complex of symbols which belongs specifically to a single nation.

A scientific study of the process of linkage has still to be made: here we can only give the merest outline of it. Suffice it to say that every aggregate that has in i.s nascent state come under our observation—a trade union, for instance—presents certain characteristic features: continuity of action on the part of the founders, a network of symbols, cooperation that has become institutionalized (organized provident benefits and recreation), formation of personal ties.

Let us note also that the less the particular aggregate lends itself

---

2. An instance of this is General Georges Boulanger (1831–91), whose support was drawn from very varied quarters and fell away with great suddenness.

by its nature to the formation of affective ties, the more successful it must be in conferring at all times on each of its members benefits of a material and tangible kind. So it is with enterprises of a commercial kind, which are for that reason most unstable aggregates.

Cooperation is the means by which a man procures himself material and intellectual goods beyond the reach of a solitary individual. Also, it is the occasion for his morality.[3] For this reason aggregates must be regarded as blessings and this *vis politica*— their source—as essentially beneficent. Naturally, therefore, a great respect is felt for builders of aggregates, and sometimes this respect becomes a cult.

What we have said earlier points the distinction between aggregates with one particular object and aggregates with no such object. Certain it is that cooperation for one particular object is a graft on cooperation of a general kind which never ceases—in short, that without life in society and a general association there can be no particular associations. Hence the politically pure formation, such as the state or the city, enjoys an acknowledged preeminence. It is in the nature of things that aggregates formed for specific ends should always have been subjected to the condition that they have no disruptive consequences for the political aggregate.

Always and everywhere the greatest social crime has been held to be that of working against the aggregate—*perduellio* or treason; and for the horror felt for an act of treason—for, that is to say, an act tending to dissolve the aggregate, there are the best of grounds.

In every highly developed society a man forms part of several aggregates, but these allegiances of his are arranged, naturally, in a hierarchy. And serious trouble has never failed to result when there is a conflict of loyalties to various aggregates, as when a party or an empire is preferred to the state itself—two forms of solvent of a state which are often seen in conjunction.

Every aggregate, whatever it is, is kept alive by the loyalty of its members, without which it dies; in the last resort the executive power rests in the hands of individual men and women. An aggregate without adherences is a contradiction in terms. It takes an

---

3. The material cause in the language of the School, it is something to be moral about. I would deny that it is the source of his morality.

unreflecting man to suppose that there can ever be a government of pure force, for this force must come from somewhere.

Allegiance, that necessary counterpart of this *vis politica,* calls for a profound study. The best approach to it, no doubt, is by way of the extreme case, when a subject still acknowledges the ways of an authority which does him injury. Force of habit could not by itself keep him in obedience, were he not restrained as well by strong lateral ties, by means of which the respect given to the authority by fellows of his whom it does not injure reaches him too by power of contagion. The weight of the motivated adherences carries along with it one which is unmotivated.

The capacity of an authority to work injury to some of its lieges rests wholly and exclusively on the essential advantages conferred by an aggregate. But for these advantages the authority could not continue at all. From this may be deduced a natural political ethic.

When the one aim set himself by the *auctor* (the founding father) is that of making an aggregate endure—the end of pure politics in fact—he must, inevitably, take care that the aggregate conduces in general to the well-being of its members. Let that condition stay unfulfilled and the aggregate is no more than a Tower of Babel which in the end collapses under its own weight, as the disruptive forces grow with every addition made to it.

It is, then, a condition of pure politics being successful that an ethic finds a place in them. This ethic, it must be noted, appropriate to a particular objective, does not necessarily comprehend all the moral ideas which are capable of attracting the mind of man. In our own time it is generally supposed that the aggregates of men which we see are given facts which are necessarily stable; they are looked on as capable of enduring whatever rearrangement of their internal configuration is attempted.

The role played by these conceptions of what should be is an "authoritarian" one, in the sense that they tend to create aggregates conforming to an ideal structure. But it is by no means certain that aggregates whose internal structure has been revised to order will prove durable. The study of the structure of aggregates suggests that the forms making for stability partake of necessity, not will. If this is so, though without a profound study we cannot be certain on the point, those aggregates which it has been sought to make conform to chosen shapes cannot survive for long; in that case these shapings themselves will be no more than "myths," useful for demolishing aggregates in being and building others—these last, however, conforming not at all to the myth that built them.

A useful definition of the subject matter of political science properly so-called would be, we think, the study of the way in which aggregates are formed and of the conditions necessary to their stability. In this way, in our view, the object of our search is clearly outlined, and it becomes possible to make observation of phenomena which are the same in their essential natures, though differing widely in degree of complexity and in expectation of life. One of the obstructions which has hitherto hindered the development of political science was its limitation to the aggregates called states, which are too long-lived for any summary comprehension of them to be possible. Just as genetics has greatly gained by the study of heredity as it operates over many generations of short-lived insects, so political science will gain greatly from an ability to work on aggregates that mature quickly; of these life in society presents instances all round us.

I would therefore want to begin the positive study of politics with a study of groups: how built, how maintained, how enlarged. As soon as we attempt this, we must clash with the idea of the group which is held by the Occidental mind. The human understanding works with a small number of patterns which it applies to reality. One of the most influential patterns we use is that of association. This conjures the image of a meeting which turns into an assembly and results in a covenant, which constitutes a group as such, which crystallizes the community of purpose out of which the meeting arose. Before the convention there was a diversity of individuals who were brought together by some urge individual to each and the same in all; now there is a body, with a common will to satisfy this urge, to achieve the purpose implied. Representatives are chosen *ad rem*. It is assumed that this is a mere convenience, that the labors of some are assigned to the common purpose, while the purpose is felt with equal force by all, and the common will is equally present in each.

This conception of association can be illustrated by the scheme of a circumference. All founders are attracted with equal force to a point of reunion, the center, where they meet and plant a tree. This is the visible outcome of association, but the participants, returned to their original positions, are not only covered by the

leaves of the tree, they also nourish at every moment its roots. The
trunk, the representative body, is only the most striking part of the
tree.

This concept of association has informed all the institutions of
the West. It rules over the law of associations, commercial law,
trade union law, and public law. It assumes that the efficient cause
of the group is an original and continuing disposition of the individual participant. Therefore the governors of the group have no
specific role, they are not creators; neither have they specific responsibilities, they are not rulers.

Any factual examination of the workings of any association be-
lies this view of things. No group arises because a similar and
simultaneous impulse has brought the founders together. But all
groups arise out of a process of call-and-response. There are initiators of association, whose mind is invaded by the image of a thing
to be done, a goal to be pursued, a project, in short, which needs
for its fulfilment more forces than they command. They invite
support, they seek seconds. Think of the word *prospectus,* common in the case of commercial ventures for which capital is to be
raised. Is it not telling? A prospect is unrolled, a vision of things to
be: there is also a prospectus for revolutions, indeed, for any
human enterprise. The initiators are then awakeners of intentions
which did not preexist in the minds of all the participants. Note
that in every enterprise some assenters will drop out while new
assenters will be brought in. At the outset there is an immense
difference between the kindlers and the kindled. The association is
therefore not to be pictured as a march of individuals from the
circumference to a center, but rather as the unfolding of a spiral
starting with the vital nucleus of initiators.

Now the group is functioning. Do we find it truly depicted by
the image of representatives *res gerentes* according to the common will of members? Is it not a more accurate description to
think of the group as an irregular pyramid, with a tiny fraction of
the associates in charge not only of execution, but of inventive
action? This spearpoint of the association is a smaller fraction of
the association as the association gets wider, as Rousseau remarked. Pressing upon this A grouplet, there is a circle, B, which
urges, criticizes, pushes forward to the leading positions, and
signals backwards to the greater number for their support. Then
there is a C layer, which does not influence the leadership of the

group, but is conscious of the purpose pursued. And finally the rest, D, which has only a confused and fitful perception of what it is all about. It is of course possible to classify participants of an association in a lesser or greater number of categories, and the dividing lines are by no means sharp, but there is little doubt that the pattern sketched here is nearer to reality than the ideal pattern of association. The great trouble with the ideal pattern is that it cannot serve at all for the discussion of political problems. If representatives execute a preexisting will of the associates, no problem can arise except that of their unfaithfulness. But problems do arise in every group, and I would like to express appreciation of Homans' pioneering work.[4]

Take the problem of civic spirit, *lato sensu*. This can in our terminology be called the enlargement of group C at the expense of group D, the reduction of the proportion of the dragged as against the walkers. Take the problem of efficient leadership. This can be divided in two; the best recruitment of A, the closest relation of A to C and even D. Take the problem of democratic control: this is really a problem of the best relation of B to A: enough criticism, enough opposition, not too much interference with government, and also of the attitude of B: this "upper class" in the sense of the politics of the group must be moved in its criticisms of A, the "ruling class," by its concern for the general purpose more than by its ambition. And so on.

It seems to me quite the major problem for the science of politics to debate whether the inner structure of groups is arbitrary, whether their constitution results from a decision, or whether it results from the very existence of a group. If the latter, there may be some traits inherent in any group, some others specific to the kind of group considered. But let this pass. Having decided whether the structure of groups is arbitrary or not, if the question is decided in the negative, the question arises whether the natural form of groups is on the lines of ideal association, or on different lines, such as those I have very roughly sketched. If the second holds true, then we can come to a positive study of political tensions and sort out those tensions which are natural, inherent in the existence of a body politic, and those tensions which are due to a disorder, a disarrangement of the body politic. It is implied in this

4. George C. Homans. *The Human Group* (New York: Harcourt, Brace, 1950).

latter point of view, which I admit to be mine, that in seeking to do away with tensions inherent to the body politic, we may create disorders, and the more dangerous tensions arising from disorganization. An illustration of Pascal's dictum: "Qui veut faire l'ange, fait la bête."

One of the inherent tensions of any group occurs between the master builder who is obsessed by the project which he has made his own and to which he has thereby *subordinated* himself in every respect, and those who are enrolled in the group serving this project and have only a faint and flickering view of the goal; the teamster who serves the project will tend to drive the workers, the soldiers, the seconds, very hard, in the pursuit of the goal. And they in turn will accuse him rightly of being inattentive to them. This conflict is ever recurring. Strange indeed that it should have been attributed to the duality of nobleman–plebian, master–man, capitalist–proletarian, for it is due to the difference in attitude which must for ever exist between the driver and the followers.

The man who pursues a project is really possessed by it. The humblest man, who has once formed a project, however unimportant—say that of taking his family on a definite trip next Sunday—will deploy all the qualities of a statesman and a ship commander to carry it through regardless of the importance he formerly attached to it. This capacity of man to wed himself to a project really defines man. He is the animal which acts not *quia* but *ut*, not pushed by causes but fascinated by a goal.

The foregoing exposition may possibly cast some light on the problem of liberty, or rather bring out an important and little noticed aspect of this problem.

Think of society as a vast group of being. This is normally the seat of many ventures of entrepreneurs of all kinds, master builders who comb society for followers to make up groups of action for this or that project which haunts their mind.

It is obvious that our society will present very different features according to the degree of liberty in recruiting afforded to the diverse would-be master builders. Suppose that only a certain closed set of people are allowed to do this recruiting. People lying outside this set who feel the capacity and urge to build groups will be exasperated by their exclusion: you will have a conflict.

This occurs if the building of groups is, so to speak, a privilege.

But more important is the discussion of the degree of liberty afforded in the building of groups. A society in which all those who have vision and energy are allowed to build groups in the service of their project must be a very different one from that in which the independent building of groups is not permitted. The freedom to form associations, to initiate groups, then appears as a means of classification of societies.

The group-builder is feared equally by stand patters* and tyrants. His freedom (entrepreneurial freedom) is a dynamic factor in society.

I have spoken of a number of different things which stem out of the key conception of politics as the building of aggregates. I might range even further afield and ask you whether you would not agree to regard the task of foreign policy as the rallying of foreign assents to some aim of "our" state, a rallying by means of which "our" state can be brought into the position of enjoying a majority of force over the threat to our state or the resistance to its interests.

Replace the word *state* by the word *group,* foreign policy and lobbying are brought into the same pattern of action. There is no difference in kind between the campaign for allies conducted by a group's lobby or a state's diplomats. Indeed the stifling of an inconvenient debate in the United Nations or of an inconvenient debate in a parliament follow the same model. Also, foreign policy can change from the additive to the aggregative; it can seek mergers. It is intentionally that I liken things which seem to stand wide apart. It seems to the credit of the definition of politics here suggested that I can bring under a same view those different things. Political action is a category.

*That is, conservatives.—EDS.

Authority: The Efficient Imperative

The polyvalence of individual words is a boon to the literary writer, but not to the scientific one. Our claim to be political "scientists" is currently denied by other scientists, and not without reason. We lack the first requisite of a science—a vocabulary of uniquely defined terms. The difficulty of endowing our political words with unambiguous meanings is of course great, because we share our vocabulary with political operators, who have a vested interest in ambiguity. Nobody can gain by twisting the meaning of the word *cycloid:* it is not so in the case of the word *democracy*. As the audience of political operators is very much larger than that of political scientists, the words we wish to use neatly come back to us glittering with many facets. Against this we have two means of defense: one is to mint completely new coins, but these will also circulate on the hustings, and be debased; the other is to bind ourselves to use words only in acceptations agreed among ourselves. The scope of the present paper is quite modest: it is merely to propose a definition of the term *authority*.

THE EFFICIENT IMPERATIVE

Let us start with a social phenomenon open to our observation at all times and everywhere. An agent A formulates an imperative statement; thereupon the action indicated in the statement is performed by an agent B or a set of Bs. Compliance of the Bs estab-

"Authority: The Efficient Imperative" is reprinted from *Nomos I: Authority*, ed. Carl J. Friedrich (New York: New York University Press, 1959). Used by permission of The American Society for Political and Legal Philosophy.

lishes for the observer an empirical relation, namely, that for the complying Bs, A's statement has proved an *efficient imperative*. If we find this process regularly repeated between the same agents, we shall feel inclined to say that A has a certain power to move the Bs, or again that he enjoys a certain authority over them: at this stage we need not pick our terms.

This power or authority has three dimensions: it is *extensive* if the complying Bs are many; it is *comprehensive* if the variety of actions to which A can move the Bs is considerable; finally it is *intensive* if the bidding of A can be pushed far without loss of compliance. It seems important to introduce this notion of intensity at an early stage. No power relationship is of unlimited intensity; there is always a point at which compliance breaks down, and it is at different stages for the different Bs.

Bidding and complying fall within the general pattern of human relationships, that is, suggestion and response. But bidding and complying differ from bargaining. In bargaining, A offers to perform a certain action *a*. This is a proposition which is either taken up or left alone or over which haggling may occur. However B responds, his response is prepared by a process of weighing in his mind whether the benefit to him of *a*, the action promised by A, is greater than the inconvenience to him of performing the action *b*. Therefore in the bargaining relationship, the response of B is mediated through a rational process.

This process is completely different in kind from the immediate response to A's imperative. All too many political authors, and indeed some of the greatest, have sought to make the relation of bidding and complying a special case of the bargaining relationship. Since in the case of the efficient imperative, no quid pro quo is mentioned, these authors have pulled in an imaginary quid: the "social contract" writers, for instance, will have it that B weighs against the inconvenience of complying the advantage to him of the social bond or his once-for-all "contracting-in." This is purely imaginary. Others will have it that B weighs against the inconvenience of the performance demanded of him the retaliation which A can mete out to him in case of refusal. The cases in which this fear, *metus,* intervenes cover but a very small area of the manifestations of the efficient imperative. We shall deal with them. The point to be made now is that bidding and compliance are a phenomenon sui generis.

NAKED AUTHORITY

Political authors have concerned themselves almost exclusively with the relations between the sovereign and the subjects in an established commonwealth. Then of course A is in a position to reward compliance and to punish noncompliance. Even though no inducement or threat is contained in A's imperative statement, all Bs know that A has means of rewarding or punishing, and there is no doubt that this "aura" of possibilities inherent in the sovereign contributes to his being obeyed. It is, however, a major error to regard the phenomenon of compliance as basically rooted in the feeling of fear. This would fail to explain a great many phenomena of compliance and, further, would fail to explain whence the means to threaten originated at the outset of political relations.

Let us now consider the great many cases in which we find compliance while A, the formulator of the imperative, has no means to reward or punish. He may, however, bear some outward signs which impress the Bs. For instance, A sits in a certain place, or bears certain stripes, or wears a certain hat, and the Bs are used to executing imperatives formulated by people thus sitting or thus adorned. Insofar as we shall find that B's compliance is due to association with these trappings, we shall say that the authority exercised by A is *derived authority*.

Finally we divest A of these trappings. Not only has he no means of bribing or threatening, but further, his prestige is not built up by any accessories. If then he obtains B's compliance, we find a *pure relation of authority*. Such a relation exists by our definition whenever B does A's bidding without A's enjoyment of any endowment whereby he may bribe or threaten B or any super-added prestige.

Is it important to focus attention upon such a relation? I believe that nothing is more important to our science, that here we come to the fundamental element upon which the whole complex fabric of society is reared.

THE GENEALOGY OF ESTABLISHED AUTHORITY

Political science has all too long dwelt upon a massive and ancient construction, the state. Why do subjects do the bidding of men whom as individuals they quite often admire or respect? Because civil obedience is second nature? Granted. How did it so become? Because initially subjects feared the punishment meted out by their ruler? Question: whence did the ruler secure the means of punishing insubordination? The Austinian genealogy of civil obedience resting upon acquired respect sired by initial fear of punishment will not do. The formation of the power to punish remains unexplained. Hobbes, who fostered this view, perceived that the first stage in the process was lacking, and filled in the void by the supposition of an initial agreement to endow the ruler with the means to punish. But such an agreement is a fiction. The reasoning which might lead men to make such a covenant postulates a vision of their long-range interest, which is not a universal feature even of our most advanced commonwealths, as Hume pointed out.

An enormous amount of intellectual effort, and of the highest quality, has been wasted on imagining the prehistory of the state while it is easy to watch the emergence of power relationships in our day and age. The birth of any association displays the building power of pure authority as we defined it.

It is a legal fiction that an association arises out of an encounter of wills. The founding members are assumed to have had the same notion at the same time and to have thus met upon common ground and coalesced naturally. But things do not happen that way. There must be an individual who takes the initiative, who calls others together, and prevails upon them (or some of them) to join with him. Thus, at the inception of a body politic of any kind, there is a relationship of pure authority.

The duration, growth, and success of the body generates in its members a loyalty toward *it,* and whenever the inceptor drops out, the historical loyalty lends prestige to the inheritor of his position who thus enjoys derived authority. Finally the means which are placed at the disposal of the body's ruler allow him to reward or punish the performance of members. Logically, this comes last and not first.

A CONFLICT OF AUTHORITIES

If we picture things this way, we must immediately recognize that conflict is a necessary feature of human society and that it is in essence a conflict of authorities. It is a vital necessity of civilization that bodies politic should endure. If companies of men had always fallen apart at the death of their convener, mankind would never have risen above predatory roaming. Securing a long lease of life to corporate entities has been one of the major achievements of our species and has been a fundamental condition of our other achievements.

But the relative endurance of bodies breeds problems. Consider the organized bodies in existence at a given moment with their appointed leaders. These leaders enjoy what we may call composite authority, an authority into which enters their own raw capacity of obtaining compliance, the prestige they derive from their status in the organization, and the powers with which their control of the organization provides them. At the same time, there are, foot-loose as it were within society, a number of people who have the naked capacity of mustering assent, of causing others to follow their suggestions. These people have an inherent tendency to pull down existing fabrics in order to build up new aggregates.

Is this a restatement of Pareto's well-known theme, "the circulation of elites"? No: Pareto's argument is that unless social ladders are provided whereby the gifted may rise to the top, they will wreck the existing structures. If this were the only problem, then the solution would be simple at least in principle; it would be enough to provide free competition for the leading positions. But it is not the case that the "new men" only want to run the existing bodies, nor are they necessarily the best qualified to do so. They may call upon men to do other things than those which are being done, and their appeal may cut right across the existing bodies. There is very little reason to believe that either Lenin or Hitler would have been quite happy and competent as the president of a big corporation in his particular country.

Such notorious examples are cited only for the sake of clarity, but the very same problem arises in the workroom of a plant, where men are subject to the formal authority of a supervisor but come under the informal spell of one of their number, who may not necessarily wish to take the place and perform the functions of the supervisor. Formal and informal authority are potentially at war at all levels of society, a fact amply recognized by American sociology. I wonder if political science does not blur it by reason of its vocabulary.

AUTHORITY AND THE INDIVIDUAL:
A FALSE PROBLEM

During the last few years we have had an enormous volume of discussion on the theme "Authority and the Individual," sometimes stated as "Authority and Freedom." I submit that the problem is wrongly stated. I have yet to meet the individual who moves freely on a field where the only prohibited areas and mandatory paths are those traced by the state—the individual who, but for these public restrictions, runs his life entirely by a continual process of bilateral bargaining with his fellows. The individual whom I can see is institution-ridden and institution-supported. The whole social field is built over with structures of various natures, offering goods, services, positions, and posting up the conditions on which they will deliver these goods or confer these positions; and with no one of these structures can the individual haggle: it is not for him to discuss the conditions of his joining either the staff of General Motors or the United Automobile Workers. This is a universe of posted prices, in the most general meaning of the word *price.* And it is highly doubtful whether any other kind of social universe can exist.

Understanding of this is widespread, as such terms as *adjusting, fitting-in* testify. The individual per se moves within this organized world, reaching the goal he has chosen insofar as he has taken the paths provided and satisfied the conditions. The individual cannot fight an organization unless he happens to be at the head of another organization (say Walter Reuther), or unless he initiates a move among his fellows (say John Hampden).

It is therefore clear that social conflict is in essence a conflict of authorities. We may find an established authority clashing with another established authority: the classic example is the fight between emperor and pope in the Middle Ages. Or we may find an unrecognized authority raising a powerful wind against an established authority: the classic example is provided by Luther.

Far be it from me to argue that everything which occurs is the work of strong personalities, though I think it is much greater than we like to admit. It is irrelevant to my purpose to discuss whether the genesis of a drive is due in greater measure to the dispositions of the Bs, the *causa materialis,* or to the call of A, the *causa efficiens.* It might be quite interesting to show by the confrontation of different instances, that the relative importance of the *causa materialis* and of the *causa efficiens* varies considerably from case to case, and one might be tempted to comparisons with chemical reactions, some of which set in only under the influence of a very specific catalytic agent while others develop under the impact of almost any shock. Such fancies may be suggestive and may be also misleading.

All that matters for my purpose is to stress the role of the efficient imperative. For purposes of illustration it has been necessary to cite instances of imperatives which have had gigantic results, which have gone down in history. This choice of illustrations should not obscure the fact that the efficient imperative is manifested every day in the most minute phenomena of social life.

CONSERVATISM AND LIBERALISM

This view leads us to a classification of human societies. Commanding suggestions may arise anywhere in a society, and we can regard them under two aspects: their origin and their character.

The extreme conservative feels that commanding suggestions should arise only from properly appointed sources, and that the character of each should be ever the same. Without question this provides maximum regularity. It should be stressed that nothing is further from totalitarianism: first, the appointed sources in such a system will be very diverse, and each will have its proper scope; second, the intensity of command will be experienced as very slight since the performances demanded are customary. Once more, to avoid any ambiguity, extreme conservatism is characterized by a dual constancy of imperative statements; constancy of sources and constancy of contents. In other words again, the members of such a society are told what to do (and what to avoid) by voices ever originating from the same places and saying the same things. It is obvious that under such circumstances, these voices, unaffected by the passage of time, must come to be regarded as starting timeless obligations. In other words, the voice of authorities is the very voice of social conscience. (For me social conscience is a shape which custom gives to the sense of obligation, innate in man.)

The extreme conservative arrangement has been described in positive terms. But it is just as valid, and more convenient, to describe it in negative terms: stating that commanding suggestions should not arise from unacknowledged sources or be of a novel character. Let the first exclusion be rule one and the other, rule two. When the proposition is so stated, it appears that an extreme conservative arrangement is practically impossible. For it must happen at some moment that a person invested with authority makes a commanding suggestion which is not hallowed by custom: he is thus breaking rule two. Rule two remains broken unless this innovating leader finds himself contradicted by someone who moves his fellows to disobey the imperative issuing from a seat of authority; and this contradictor may himself not be seated in a place of authority: therefore he is breaking rule one. This situation is by no means imaginary: the Bible offers instances of the bold king commanding something out of the ordinary, and of a prophet arising to condemn him. Therefore a system of extreme conservatism, such as we defined it, is not self-conservative. It is a pure concept of the mind.

The extreme liberal view is the exact converse of the extreme conservative view. Anyone may formulate an imperative statement, whatever his place is in society, and this statement may have any content. Such is the theoretical basis of our society. Without any title or office, I have the right to formulate a commanding suggestion and this suggestion may be anything. Further, with very few exceptions (and this is a legal point of considerable interest), I shall never be guilty by virtue of my commanding suggestion, while those who shall do my bidding may be guilty for having performed at my suggestion actions which are formally illegal.[1]

This throws considerable light upon what we so clumsily call "a free society."[2] It is in fact a society where members are equally

---

1. In French law, it is a general rule that suggestions are per se innocent. This rule has been impaired only by special statutes adopted at the time of anarchist bomb-throwing at the turn of the last century, which are practically never invoked. On the other hand, if criminal actions can be unquestionably traced back to one who has counseled this particular action to that particular person, then and then only is the adviser accounted an accomplice. The foregoing statement is all too simple, and a competent jurist may criticize it. The point is raised only to stress that it would be of the utmost interest to have a study of comparative law on guilt by suggestion, a study which does not, to my limited knowledge, exist.

2. The term *a free society* is blatantly improper. Literally it can mean only a society independent from any authority lying outside itself; that is, as Hobbes put it, "not the liberty of particular men, but the liberty of the Commonwealth" (*Leviathan,* Part 2, chapter 21). The term is, however, taken above in its common meaning; that is, a society where particular men enjoy individual freedom.

entitled to utter commanding suggestions, and where they are free to utter any such suggestions. The inherent possibilities of such a system are softened by the unequal readiness of individuals to adopt suggestions by reason of the latter's origin or nature. A commanding suggestion originated by a recognized authority has an advantage over the suggestion originated by a mere individual, and a suggestion which by its nature runs counter to custom or belief has a slender chance of acceptance. Nonetheless, every man is allowed to issue the imperative. Every man is entitled to be the generator of other men's actions.

THE SELECTIONS OF IMPERATIVES

From the foregoing statement it follows that a liberal society is one in which the selection of imperatives is achieved by those to whom the imperative statements are addressed. Every one of us is a potential A, capable of uttering commanding suggestions. And every one of us is a B, who chooses between a number of such suggestions. These suggestions may be materially incompatible, or worse, they may be morally conflicting.

It is therefore of immense importance to study the conditions of response to imperative statements. When and why does a call to action "ring a bell" and give rise to the action demanded? In other terms what makes the imperative an efficient one for me, an individual? Let us think of the suggestions actually compelling as a message duly received. What are the factors which ensure its reception?

This is presumably a problem for politically minded psychologists. But here is another which is truly a problem for political philosophers: is there, within the process of reception, a "natural selection" such that those messages which are most conducive to the preservation and development of human cooperation are more readily and widely received than others?

The mere statement of the question opens up, or so I believe, enormous vistas. Just to trace one of the perspectives, let us think of those enjoying vested authority as being in a position to broadcast their message far more widely than those who stand in the crowd at the foot of an established structure. Is this inequality a means for biasing men in favor of the most innocuous messages on the assumption that the men who have risen to the top of the pile have been tested on the way for common sense and prudence? A comparison immediately springs to mind. In our society anyone may speak freely, but not everyone is invited to broadcast, and while the sayings of broadcasters are indeed diverse, they are less so than the sayings of individuals. We find here an undevised but nonetheless operative selection of utterances a priori, which tends to bias the ex post facto choice of opinions of hearers.

One may attack this state of affairs on the grounds that all views do not get an equal chance. It is permissible, however, to think that any society needs a narrowing down of the range of opinions propounded and imperatives suggested. Not that these should be ever the same through time but that they must not be too far dispersed at any given moment. This is achieved in a liberal society, not by the suppression of extreme opinions or out-of-the-way imperatives but by weighting the near-to-median opinions or imperatives, which alone can be propounded from dominant and privileged positions.

The emphasis has been put here upon the elementary phenomenon of prompting, which I take as the common "root" of all manifestations of authority. Elsewhere[3] I have sought to work up from this first step toward elaborate relations; to show how this phenomenon permits the erecting of human aggregates and constructions, ensures their conservation, and thereby constitutes "fields" wherein the members of the "set" are susceptible to mutual promptings. Also I have stressed that it is the essential function of established authorities to preserve the "field," standing surety to individuals for the continuation of the cooperative condition established. In other words, I have attempted to study the "domestication" of this natural phenomenon, the efficient imperative, for the purpose of ever more confident and fruitful intercourse between men. But in this paper, no more could be attempted than to delineate a "root" which intervenes in every social complex. I shall account myself lucky if this is accepted as a useful tool of analysis, and used more efficiently by other hands.

3. *Sovereignty: An Inquiry into the Political Good* (1957).

On the Nature of Political Science

Political activity is dangerous. Arising inevitably out of men's ability to influence each other, conferring upon them the benefits of joint endeavor, an indispensable source of social boons, it is also capable of doing great harm. Men can be moved to injure others or to ruin themselves. The very process of moving implies a risk of debasement for the moved and for the mover.[1] Even the fairest vision of a good to be sought offers no moral guarantee, since it may poison hearts with hatred against those who are deemed an obstacle to its achievement.[2]

No apology is required for stressing a subjective dread of political activity: the chemist is not disqualified as a scientist because he is aware that explosives are dangerous: indeed that chemist is dangerous who lacks such awareness.

This feeling of danger is widespread in human society[3] and has ever haunted all but the more superficial authors. Although, to be

"On the Nature of Political Science" is reprinted from the *American Political Science Review,* volume 55, no. 4 (December 1961). Used by permission of the publisher.

1. "Tel se croit le maltre des autres qui ne laisse pas d'être plus esclave qu'eux," says Rousseau in the first lines of *The Social Contract*. He elucidates in *Emile:* "Domination itself is servile when beholden to opinion: for you depend upon the prejudices of those you govern by means of their prejudices."
2. It is a sobering exercise to count the expressions of anger (as against those of good will) which occur in the speeches or writings of political champions of this or that moral cause.
3. Different voices denounce the encroaching State, overbearing Lords, an established Church, or tentacular unions, or the dominant party: yet such voices, however discordant, all express distrust of some form of established power. In the same manner, emergent power is deemed frightening by some when an agitator musters a mob, by others in the case of a rising dictator—though one may turn into the other. The same feeling crystallizes on different stems.

sure, few have, like Hobbes, brought it out into the open, it has hovered in the background, exerting an invisible but effective influence upon their treatment of the subject; it may be, to a significant degree, responsible for the strange and unique texture of political science.

I

There are no objects to which our attention is so naturally drawn as to our own fellows. It takes a conscious purpose to watch birds or ants, but we cannot fail to watch other men, with whom we are inevitably associated, whose behavior is so important to us that we need to foresee it, and who are sufficiently like us to facilitate our understanding of their actions. Being a man, which involves living with men, therefore involves observing men. And the knowledge of men could be called the most fairly distributed of all kinds of knowledge since each one of us may acquire it according to his willingness and capacity.

As politics consists of nothing other than human behavior it seems that, over time, the study of it should have made great progress through accumulation, comparison and systematization of observations. If politics is understood restrictively as the conduct of men in offices of authority and the consequent march of public affairs, then all those who have over time found themselves in office have found out something about political behavior. I hold the view that we should regard as "political" every systematic effort performed at any place in the social field to move other men in pursuit of some design cherished by the mover. According to this view, we all have the required material: anyone of us has acted with others, been moved by others, and has sought to move others.

It is clear of course that mere "facts" can never compose a knowledge unless they be marshaled, and their marshaling always calls for a "theory" which seizes upon certain similar appearances, assigns to them common names, and supposes processes which bring them about. The processes we assume constitute a sort of model in the mind of what occurs in observable reality; a necessary attempt to reduce phenomenal diversity to intellectual simplicity. Such "theory" has a "representative" purpose; it guides us in the collection of facts. These in turn call for amendments to our theory insofar as it cannot account for them. We move from initial simplicity to increasing complexity of our theory until a possibly quite different one is offered which achieves the representative function with greater elegance and accuracy. Theory of this kind progresses over time, accounting for an ever-increasing store of observations. All this is trite: but it then comes as a surprise that political science should offer so little of such "theory": what is commonly called "political theory"[4] is an altogether different thing. In the theory of astronomy there is no place for Ptolemaeus, in the theory of chemistry no place for Paracelsus: not so in political theory. The theory of any science is an integrated whole from which past theories have been discarded. Political theory is a collection of individual theories which stand side by side, each one more or less impervious to the impact of new observations and to the advent of new theories. This can be the case only because political theories are normative (i.e., are doctrines), and are not meant to perform the representative function which the word *theory* evokes in the case of factual sciences.

Why is political science rich in normative theories, deficient in "representative" theory? Only a fool would opine that the masters of the past were incapable of establishing the latter: they must have been unwilling. And why? The reason may lie in the sense of danger which I noted at the beginning.

II

Libido sciendi is a noble passion: it is inherently incapable of debasing the man it possesses, and the delights it affords do not wait upon the possession of the object pursued but attend its very pursuit. This libido is indispensable to the making of a scientist,[5] and its seems also sufficient. Yet if one studies the personalities of the great scientists, one finds that their libido was habitually associated with one or both of the motives expressed in Bacon's timeless sentence: "for the glory of God and the relief of man's estate." The word *understanding* denotes the grasping of a pattern which

4. Discussed in Arnold Brecht, *Political Theory* (Princeton, NJ: Princeton University Press, 1959), and in Eric Weil, "Philosophie politique, Théorie politique," *Revue française de Science politique*, vol. 11, no. 2 (1960), pp. 267–294.
5. *Cf.* Michael Polanyi. *Science, Faith and Society* (London: Oxford University Press, 1946).

underlies the waywardness of phenomena: the scientist finds beauty in such a pattern and loves it the more the higher its aesthetic quality. The word *discovery* signifies the unveiling of what was both present and hidden. Such terms reveal that ancient inquirers into "the secrets of Nature" (another telling expression) assumed the existence of an "order": and what better warrant for it than the belief in Creation? If everything that is comes from the divine planning of a supreme intelligence—"Dieu est géomètre"—then the design which stands at the source guarantees that far lesser intelligences, partaking of the same reason, can grasp some parts of the design.

Such was the language of scientists in the Deist age of the seventeenth and eighteenth centuries, who felt that the displaying of some lineaments of the universal order was a new publication of God's wisdom. Few scientists would today speak in this manner:[6] they now state that their patterns are "made up" and disclaim that they "make out" the "true" structure of things. Deep down, however, they hardly doubt that their "made up" patterns are in some way representative of a true structure. Nor do they hesitate to choose between two equally "serviceable" models that which is the more beautiful; and, though careful to explain that this is a mere preference, in fact they act no differently from their predecessors who would have said that the more elegant model was the truer, as the worthier of God's sapience; indeed every day scientists resort to metaphysical convictions such as the Malebranche–Maupertuis principle of least action.

Turning to the second member of Bacon's sentence, it is true that scientists have ever taken pride in the practical results afforded to their fellows by their findings. Just as there has been a high tide of the first Baconian theme (Newton), more recently there has been a high tide of the second, arising from the very advance of technology. Science and technology have not always been wedded. For a long time practical advances were achieved more often by practical men[7] than by scientists whose minds moved on a different plane. But the social impact of technology

6. Nor was this language so natural to a more theological age: it sits specially well with Deism.

7. *Cf.* Singer, Holmyard, and Hall, *A History of Technology* (Oxford: Clarendon Press, 1954 et seq.).

affected science which rapidly became what it is today, the great source of material innovations.[8] Even when scientists are furthest away from any specific concern for practical applications, they cannot be unaware that the high esteem in which they are presently held is derived from the general opinion that the increase of knowledge promises an increase of power:[9] so much so that the sciences which hold out no promise of practical applications are put on a starvation diet.

The sole purpose of the foregoing rough notes for an argument is to stress that two powerful motives in general reinforce the zeal of the scientist for systematization of observable facts: these same motives, however, assume negative values for the student of political phenomena. He has no occasion to delight in the discovery of a seemly pattern, and every reason to distrust practical applications of his findings.

III

While the student of nature can rejoice in the fundamental harmony he discovers beneath disorderly appearances, such aesthetic enjoyment is denied to the student of politics. Never was there any such thoroughgoing apologetic of universal order as that of Leibniz: and never was a sharper blow dealt it than Voltaire's *Candide*. Trust this prince of controversialists to seek the weak point of the system he attacks: and where does he find it? Voltaire carries the discussion away from the harmonies of nature to the distempers of human affairs.[10] There is nothing here to evoke a reverent appre-

---

8. Science now "changes the world": not so in Chinese civilization. *Cf.* Joseph Needham, *Science and Civilization in China* (Cambridge, Eng.: Cambridge University Press, 1954 et seq.). Question: if science does so, is it not because of an urge which arose outside the scientific community and challenged it?

9. Hobbes's view: "The end of knowledge is power . . . the scope of all speculation is the performing of some action, or thing to be done." Opening of *De Corpore*.

10. This choice of ground is the more remarkable in that Voltaire, who originally subscribed to Leibnizian optimism, was shaken out of it, so the scholars tell us, by a natural event, the disaster of Lisbon. Yet he chose the ground of human affairs for his attack. Note that even on this ground, Voltaire had previously illustrated Leibnizianism (in *Zadig*, as stressed by Paul Hazard in *La penseé européenne au xviiième siècle* [Paris: Boivin, 1946]). But in so doing he must have felt the difficulty and thus when he declared war upon the system this was the battlefield he elected.

ciation of the course of things, there is no pattern to be found ("a tale told by an idiot . . . signifying nothing"). And whenever our mind can rest in the recognition and acknowledgment of "sufficient reason," this is but an uneasy repose: what is explained is not justified. *Causa efficiens* is neither *justa causa* nor visibly at the service of a plausible *causa finalis*.

We are inevitably more exacting when investigating human affairs than in the case of natural phenomena. Regarding the latter we may be content to find an order, whatever it may be; in human society, however, we are not content to find some pattern, we want it to fit our idea of justice.

The Deist Apologetic of Universal Order has exerted upon the social sciences a most powerful influence, displayed to the full in economics: each man's striving for his own advantage results in a social optimum. This has been taken as axiomatic, and whatever went wrong was attributed to "artificial" obstacles. Restraints upon trade and competition were first named; much later, "property" itself came to be questioned as an artificial restraint.[11]

However questionable the philosophic foundations of economic science[12] they had one great empirical virtue: economists could accept unquestioningly the motives of economic actors, since a good outcome was expected from the vigor of desires. Economists may take exception to my statement, but I feel that the "ethical neutrality" which has served them well has been made possible by a teleological optimism.[13] It is thanks to this promise of a good outcome that intellectual doctors could move to the business of understanding economic activity and away from a centuries-old attitude of upbraiding acquisitiveness.

Such a descent from a moral pulpit has occurred only quite

11. This theme appears in John Stuart Mill and in our day has been fully developed by Maurice Allais.
12. These have been less discussed than one would wish. See, however, W. Stark, *The Ideal Foundations of Economic Thought* (London: Paul, Trench, Trubbner and Co., Ltd., 1943); G. Myrdal, *The Political Element in the Development of Economic Theory* (London: Routledge and Paul, 1953); Lindely M. Fraser, *Economic Thought and Language* (London: A. and C. Black, 1947); and J. A. Schumpeter, *History of Economic Analysis* (London: Oxford University Press, 1954); but above all, Vilfredo Pareto, *Manuel d'Economie Politique* (Paris: Giard and Brière, 1909).
13. Openly stated by Adam Smith, and underlying Pareto's great work.

recently in political science,[14] arousing ardent controversy.[15] There are strong intellectual reasons to applaud this descent and call it belated; there are strong prudential reasons to deplore it and call it treason. Light can be cast on the matter only if we reject the fiction that the scientist can and should be soulless. It is not because the economist is an ethical eunuch that he can envisage phenomena with ethical indifference. Rather it is because he expects a desirable ethical outcome regardless of the ethical concern and enlightenment of the actors; his short-term or atomistic ethical indifference is warranted by his long-range or overall optimism. The proof thereof lies in the revival of moral passion regarding economic behavior in the most scholarly economists as soon as they find reason or occasion to question the assumption of overall maximization. Now in politics such an assumption seems untenable.

The postulate that economic activity is not to be feared and that the more of it the better is allegorized in Dupont de Nemours' picture of a giant in chains, with the caption: "Otez-lui ses chaînes et le laissez aller."[16] But in those countries where political freedom has been most prized and practiced, see what attention has been devoted to the formalization of political activity, and to imbuing political actors with a public philosophy.[17] We may hold the view that economic activities tend to combine harmoniously: we cannot hold it in the case of political activities. Indeed Hobbes devised a model displaying the chaotic outcome of political activities running wild. Rousseau subscribed to the Hobbesian picture in his very refutation, since he found it necessary to base his opposite picture upon the supposition of a tiny, closed, and static society.

14. This is most clearly recounted in Robert A. Dahl, "The Behavioral Approach in Political Science," *American Political Science Review*, vol. 55, no. 4 (December 1961): 763–772.
15. The most authoritative attack is that of Leo Strauss: "What Is Political Philosophy?" *Journal of Politics* (August 1957); see also Irving Kristol, "The Profanation of Politics," in *The Logic of Personal Knowledge, Essays presented to Michael Polanyi* (London: L. Routledge, 1961).
16. I allude to the frontispiece of Dupont de Nemours' pamphlet of 1788: *Réponse aux Observations de la Chambre de Commerce de Normandie.*
17. It takes an observer foreign to Britain and the United States to note the extreme formality attending the least political move (e.g., the decorous conduct of even the most insignificant meetings) and to notice the fundamental orthodoxy which underlies all political differences.

IV

The barbarians are coming, big men with a cruel laughter, who use the conquered as playthings, dishonored and tossed about. Our knees shake at the very thought of them. Our bishop, however, goes out in state and, bearing the Cross, he stands in the path of the fierce captain. Our town then shall be spared. The strange chief with the awesome mien shall indeed become our sovereign; but, guided by the man of God, he shall be a just master, and his son will, at an early age, learn from the bishop the finest examples of wise kingship.

The bishop, in my apologue, is political philosophy: its function is to civilize power, to impress the brute, improve its manners, and harness it to salutary tasks. In dealing with our wild chieftain the bishop will often say bluntly: "You cannot do this." That is not a factual statement; the very motive for the utterance is that the power-bearer can in fact do this thing. What lies in the bishop's mind, behind the simple statement, is far more complex: "He wants to do this and has the means thereof; I cannot convince him—nor am I certain—that from this bad action some harm shall come to him that he can recognize as a harm. He must be prevented from doing this; the moral prohibition, therefore, has to be made in his imagination a hard, concrete obstacle. Hence: 'You cannot. . . .' " This manner of speech is required for preceptive efficiency.

Similarly, when teaching the ruler's turbulent child, the bishop accumulates examples of princely virtue: "That," says he, "is what is done." He means, of course: "what is to be done." Not all that has been done by past rulers is relevant to his purpose but only those praiseworthy attitudes and actions which can contribute to the forming of a noble image, which, being firmly implanted in the youth, will exert its pull upon the conduct of the grown man. Deplorable instances are adduced only if they can be joined with a tale of ensuing disaster. Not until the love of virtue has been firmly established shall the pupil be faced with the hard saying: "there be just rulers to whom it happeneth according to the work of the wicked; again there be wicked rulers, to whom it happeneth according to the work of the righteous."[18] It is the test of virtue that

18. *Ecclesiastes*, 8, 14.

this bleak truth be accepted by the mind, yet serenely spurned by the soul.

The political learning which I sought to describe by means of an apologue turns upon two sentences: "You cannot . . ." (ideal of law) and "This is what is done" (right example). Such lessons are designed to *edify*: strange indeed that this word should have fallen into disrepute, since it means "to build up"; and surely it is important to build up the virtue of the men who rule, whether it be one, few, or many.

And here we come to the difficulty attending a factual science of politics: by its very nature it pulls down what the preceptive science has endeavored to build up. Where the preceptive science stressed "You cannot," factual science is bound to observe that "You can"; and what the preceptive science indicated as "What is done" is denied by the findings of factual science: actual doings are very different. A factual science in this realm is therefore dangerous medicine for weak moral constitutions.

Imagination, properly cultivated and addressed, imparts a magic prestige, the loss of which may be a public disaster.[19] Madame de Staël helps us here with two pictures:

> The Constituent Assembly ever believed, erroneously, that there was some magic in its decrees, and that all would stop in every way at the line it traced. But its pronouncements can be compared to the ribbon which had been drawn through the garden of the Tuileries to keep the people at some distance from the palace; while opinion remained favorable to those who had drawn the ribbon, no one dreamed of trespassing; but as soon as the people wanted no more of this barrier, it became meaningless.[20]

---

19. This seems to be the main lesson which Necker has drawn from the great events he was so well placed to witness. It impregnates the two main works he wrote in his years of retreat: *Du Pouvoir Exécutif dans les Grands Etats,* 2 vols. (1792, no place of publication); and *De la Revolution Française,* 4 vols. (1797). Strangely enough, in view of the very important political role their author played, these works enjoy a very limited reputation. But a preoccupation which imbues the whole work of Necker is sharply brought into view in these two vivid paragraphs written by his famous daughter, which are here quoted.

20. Baronne de Staël, *Considérations sur les Principaux Evénements de la Révolution Française,* 3 vols. (Paris, 1818), vol. 1, 416. [Translated by de Jouvenel—Eds.]

The grenadiers marched into the hall where the representatives were assembled, and hustled them forward by simply advancing in solid formation from one end of the room to the other. The representatives found themselves pressed against the wall and had to flee through the window into the gardens of St. Cloud in their senatorial gowns. Representatives of the people had already suffered proscription; but this was the first time that political magistrates were ridiculed by the military; and Bonaparte, who wished to establish his power on the degradation of corporate bodies as well as of individuals, delighted that he had been able, in this first moment, to destroy the reputation of the people's representatives. As soon as the moral power of national representation was destroyed, a legislative body, whatever it might be, meant no more to the military than a crowd of five hundred men, less vigorous and disciplined than a battalion of the same number.[21]

Indeed, the law is a mere ribbon, but traditional political science has been at great pains to make it seem an impenetrable wall; indeed, the body of representatives is incapable of standing its ground against a battalion, but traditional political science has been at great pains to so raise its prestige that battalions may never challenge it but ever obey it. The danger of the factual approach is that it should deflate these salutary prestiges.

The dangers of the factual approach are not yet fully manifest because studies of this kind have mostly been addressed to "weak" political behavior, such as voting. I speak of weak political behavior since it is precisely a finding of such studies that voters do not care very much. Strong political behaviors are those inspired by strong passions,[22] and into which men throw themselves wholeheartedly. The picture of politics which is apt to emerge from the factual analysis of strong political behaviors may be nefariously suggestive.

V

However little the scientist thinks of practical applications, whenever it comes to his mind it is with a favorable connotation: the

21. Op. cit., vol. 2, 240–41.
22. For example, militantism in its moderate and extreme forms (conspiracy, terrorism).

gain in efficiency to be expected from the increase in knowledge is a good thing. No such optimism is allowed in the case of the "technology" which may be derived from increased factual understanding of politics: political efficiency may be a bad thing. Knowing how men are won over and induced to lend their energies is a knowledge that can be used for good or evil. Indeed, it is more apt to be used for evil. A good man is humble and therefore advances his views with some diffidence; he respects his fellows and therefore is not apt to be an aggressive salesman. The presumptuous, overbearing man is most prone to exploit the technology of moving men for his purpose.

This thought is very disquieting. And it might suffice to turn the scholar away from a search for knowledge which may be ill-used, if the technology of politics waited upon his discoveries. But such is not the case: the technology has been mightily developed outside political science during the last half-century, and developed by the very men to whom the prudent scientist would like to deny it. Naturally enough those who are least sensitive to the aesthetic and ethical appeal of traditional theory have broken away from its restraints and guidance; while those with finer feelings are victims of processes which they cannot grasp. In such a situation all the harm which a factual science of politics can do is already loose, and it can come as a useful warning.

VI

It has been suggested here that recognition of the dangers inherent in political activity may have held up the progress of scientific inquiry in politics; but however important this factor, it can hardly serve as a full explanation. A useful complement is suggested by a comparison with medical science, a comparison current since the days of Plato.[23]

What is the purpose of medicine? The health of the body. What therefore is the knowledge required in a doctor? The knowledge of health. This seems a reasonable approach to medicine: it leads first

___

23. The two sciences are of equal antiquity. Hippocrates was born in 460 B.C., between Socrates (469) and Plato (427).

to the primacy of hygiene,[24] but second, to envisaging any disease as a derangement of a natural harmony.[25] Hence for instance Themison's classification of diseases: they arise from an undue constriction (*strictum*) or from an undue relaxation (*laxum*), or from a combination of both (*mixtum*).[26] In a case of *strictum*, antispasmodic, sedative medication is indicated; in a case of *laxum*, tonic, roborative remedies. This is very attractive, so much so that economic policies of our own day are "Themisonian": if there are inflationary areas in the economy, relieve the pressure of demand by the sedatives of deflation (including if necessary *saignare*, the removal of excess buying power); and if there is laxity in the market, administer stimulants.

However reasonable it seems to take the satisfactory state of affairs as the axial concept, it has not paid off well in medicine: the concept of health led neither to a close study of diseases attuned to their specificity, nor to a far-reaching physiology.[27] It is amazing that the emphasis laid upon the proper functioning of the body should have sparked so little curiosity about this very functioning. Physiology can hardly be said to have started before Harvey (b. 1578) when medical science was twenty centuries old, and it took wing only with Haller (b. 1708). I regard it as encouraging for my view of political science that the microscope proved so important an instrument of physiological knowledge, and led finally to the discovery that many illnesses are not mere derangements of natural harmony but arise from the intrusion of minute agents.[28]

When resorting to analogy, one should always stop to note contrasts between the systems compared. There is a most striking

24. "For the worshippers of Hygeia, health is the natural order of things, a positive attribute to which men are entitled if they govern their lives wisely. According to them, the most important function of medicine is to discover and teach the natural laws which will ensure a man a healthy mind in a healthy body." René Dubos, *Mirage of Health* (New York: Harper and Row, 1959), 113.

25. Galen said that the duty of the doctor is to conserve the natural condition, to reestablish it when perturbed, and to restore what is lacking as far as feasible. From F. J. V. Broussais, *Histoire des Doctrines Médicales et des Systèmes de Nosologie*, 4 vols. (Paris, 1829), vol. 1, 200.

26. Ibid., vol. 1, 107 ff.

27. Dubos stresses that the broad point of view of orthobiosis leads to "the danger of substituting meaningless generalities and weak philosophy for the concreteness of exact knowledge." Op. cit., p. 137.

28. The word *microbe*, now a popular term abandoned by scientists, was introduced by them as late as 1878.

contrast between the object studied by medical science, the body of man, and the object of political science, the body politic. In the former case, only the integrated whole has value in our eyes, while the component cells are expendable: not so in the case of the body politic, where the whole is justified by its components, real persons. But the contrast goes further. Human bodies are built on the same model; not so political bodies. The health of the human body is therefore a clearer and more distinct notion than a state of health in a body politic. The anatomy of the human body is a datum, while political anatomy changes. Therefore, if anatomy is already inadequate knowledge in the former case,[29] how much more inadequate it must be in the latter.

The "healthy body politic" is an attractive starting point but one that leads to little progress of knowledge. If the body politic wherein we find ourselves is accepted as presently healthy[30] we are inadequately provoked to look into the minute day-to-day processes which keep it so. If we regard it as presently distempered, we are apt to go back to some past moment of "health" with a strong chance of substituting our fancy for the true past, and only a slight chance of understanding what has changed, where, how, and why. Even worse is our picking upon some body politic distant in time and using it as our model of health. This leads, for instance, to the ludicrous mistake of the French Jacobins who wanted to build a Sparta, ignoring that it had rested upon extreme social inequality, its renowned "equals" forming but a minute fraction of the whole population.[31]

29. Claude Bernard wrote: "Descriptive anatomy is to physiology what geography is to history, and as it is not enough to know a country's topography for the understanding of its history, it is not enough to know the anatomy of organs for the understanding of their functions. An old surgeon, Méry, compared anatomists to those messengers who are to be found in great cities, and who know the layout of the streets, and the numbering of buildings but do not know what goes on inside. Indeed, in tissues, in organs, vital physicochemical phenomena occur which mere anatomy can not reveal." *Leçons sur les Phénomènes de la Vie Commune aux Animaux et aux Végétaux*, 2 vols. (Paris, 1878), vol. 1, 6–7.
30. This complacency is a most uncommon attitude.
31. Again, when one takes Athens as a model, one forgets that in its age of extreme democracy (which did not exclude slavery) the notion that "aliens" could not become part of the body politic was so fundamentally embedded that Pericles himself was the author of a law which struck from the registers a large fraction of the citizenry who could not prove that they were descended from both an Athenian father and an Athenian mother.

The notion of a healthy political body leads to pseudo-restorations of which the Germanic "Holy Roman Empire" is a striking instance.[32] It leads to transpositions which have never worked out very well.[33] It ceases altogether to be relevant if it is recognized that one has to meet new needs by means of new institutions, or if one cherishes the fancy of building up a body politic such as has never been seen before. In either case, one must form some idea of the probable working-out of new arrangements. And such an idea cannot even be formed unless one has acquired as much basic knowledge as possible about the elementary behaviors which are to be dovetailed in a new combination. Thus we always come back to factual inquiry into the elements of political behavior.

32. Though why the Roman Empire should have been looked back upon as a healthy political body is beyond my understanding.
33. For instance, the transposition of the U. S. Constitution in Latin America, or, for that matter, the transposition of the Westminster model in Continental Europe.

The Chairman's Problem

One of the major obstacles to the progress of political theory lies in the fact that people speak of rights without paying attention to the feasibility of their exercise. I propose to raise here some elementary problems relating to the right of speech. It is one of the basic tenets of our democratic political philosophy that all people (over a given age) have an equal right of speech. Making this right operational, however, gives rise to difficulties which have not been faced.

THE CHAIRMAN'S PROBLEM

I shall start out with a very simple problem, which moreover has the advantage of evoking familiar pictures: this is the chairman's problem. I find myself chairman of an assembly, and regard all participants as formally equal, which commits me to treating them equally. Feeling bound by this principle, I decide as follows: the duration of the meeting is m, the number of participants n: I shall give the floor to each participant for a time m/n; thus the equal right of speech will receive practical application. Assume that the meeting is to be crowned by a vote (the time of actual voting not figuring in m): before the participants cast their equal votes, they will have had equal opportunities to influence the voting; that is, they shall have had, insofar as depends upon me, equal voices.

Now if m the duration of the meeting (in speaking time) is three hours, and if n the number of participants is 12, my procedure is susceptible of being applied: it grants the floor to each participant for a quarter of an hour. This is not a long time but still it may be enough.

"The Chairman's Problem" is reprinted from the *American Political Science Review*, volume 55, no. 2 (June 1961). Used by permission of the publisher.

But, keeping *m* at three hours, let us set the value of *n* at 5,400. Then, adhering to the same rule for the allocation of time, I shall give the floor to each participant for 2 seconds, which is absurd.

Aware of this absurdity, I shall have to scrap my rule. On what principles shall I then exercise my chairmanship? Assuming that I cannot stretch the duration of the discussion (*m* is a datum), time is my scarce resource. How shall I divide it up? My ideal denominator, the number of participants, will not do. I shall then use as my denominator the minimum time (call it *k*) required to develop a meaningful argument. But the consequence thereof is immediately apparent: my number of speakers shall now be $s = m/k$; which means that it will be *indifferent to the number of participants* formally entitled to speak.

Let us leave *m* at three hours, and set *k* at a quarter of an hour: then I shall have a maximum of twelve speakers no matter how great the assembly. Which means that the greater the assembly, the greater the proportion of those who are denied in fact the right granted to them in principle. In an assembly of forty-eight, three out of four will be denied the effective exercise of their formal right. In an assembly of 5,400 no less than 449 out of 450 will be denied in practice their theoretical right.

I had a reason for using a figure in the five-thousand range. In that range, according to historians,[1] stood the number of the Athenian citizens, who, on the most important occasions, responded[2] to the calling of the popular assembly in the days when it was the sovereign decision-making body of the City. We are told that this body met from sunrise to sundown; call it twelve hours. But all the speeches which have come down to us suggest that the time taken by an individual orator was at least one hour. Thus, at the outside, there were twelve orators, probably less. We must conclude that in this direct democracy, the right to speak was in fact exercised only by a very small minority, and that there must have been some principle of selection of this small minority.

Looking to figures has yielded us three important results: (1) With an upper time limit for discussion *m* and a lower time limit for the formulation of a speech *k,* the feasible maximum number of people exercising the right of speech is determined. (2) There-

1. Gustave Glotz and Robert Cohen, *La Grèce au Ve siècle* (Paris: Les Presses Universitaires de France, 1931), 270.
2. The body of citizens was from five to eight times greater.

fore with an increasing number n, the formal right to speak is a delusion for an increasing proportion of those entitled to this formal right. (3) In any system which grants formal rights to more than can effectively be given the opportunity of exercising them, there must be some device whereby those who are allowed the actual right are singled out from those to whom it formally belongs.

These remarks lead us to consider a number of problems.

THE m LIMIT

Going back to my position as chairman, let us assume that I greatly take to heart the principle that each participant, entitled to the same right, should have an equal opportunity to expound his views. The one thing I cannot do is to share out the time into units so small that nobody can make sense. Therefore my first obligation is to set the value of k, of which more anon. Supposing I have set it at fifteen minutes, I now feel impelled to break the m limit. I shall thus tell the assembly that having made up my mind that fifteen minutes is the minimum time for an opinion, I propose that each member should have his fifteen minutes. Supposing that I have 5,400 participants, this means that we must sit for 1,350 hours in all, or, assuming 9 hours a day, a session of 150 working days.

I shall first make the wild hypothesis that this suggestion is adopted, and carried out, and I shall add the even wilder postulate that attendance and attention are consistently sustained throughout. Even giving myself such unattainable conditions, I shall fail in my attempt to afford each and every member an equal opportunity of influencing the vote occurring at the end of the 150th day, because the speeches made in the later days will obviously be more present to the memory of the voters than those made in the earlier and now distant days.

But obviously the suggestion is absurd. First, in some cases, a decision must be reached before this great space of time. Second, in all cases, the participants will prove unwilling to sit through this long succession of speeches. If they are a body of citizens, as in Athens, they have private affairs to attend to. If they are a professional decision-making body, as in the case of our parliaments, they have other issues to decide.

The m constraint is based upon there being a time limit to the attention which any one person will give to the discussion of any specific subject: this time limit varies with the individual's talent for concentration, with the importance in his eyes of the subject discussed, and especially in function of the other obligations or interests which compete for his attention.

To illustrate the existence of an individual m limit, let us consider the case of the democratic-minded radio producer.

The Case of the Democratic-minded Radio Producer

Let us picture a well-meaning radio producer, who decides to use his powerful network so as to give the public a full discussion of an important public issue. He is a principled man, who firmly believes in equal right of speech, and therefore he widely advertises that anyone, whoever he may be, who wishes to talk on this issue shall be granted say ten minutes. Let us suppose that he gets a great number of requests, and that, desiring his audience to judge each opinion on its merits, he decides that his speakers will follow each other in an order determined by chance, and that each will be announced by a numeral, not by name. He then begins to carry out his program up to the exhaustion of his number of speakers.

What can we expect to happen in terms of the audience? Eliminating influences due to more or less favorable hours or days, we can safely forecast that the audience will fall off very rapidly. Thus, even if our producer calls himself satisfied with the total number of ears-minutes afforded to the whole series, he will have utterly failed to ensure to all his speakers an equal hearing: the later they come the fewer listeners they get. Thus letting them exercise an equal right to speak will not have afforded them an equal hearing.

Maintaining the Congregation

Throughout we have been thinking of exercising the right to speak as equivalent to getting the opportunity of addressing a given congregation and we shall go on doing so now.

The opportunity of addressing the congregation lies in the hands of the chairman, given the congregation. But the congregation is not in fact given. It may melt away, as in the case of our radio audience. Much the same phenomenon can be observed in parliament, when a debate is long drawn: members wander off, and if they do not leave the room bodily, at least their minds wander off.

The chairman's problem, therefore, does not reduce, as would-be speakers are apt to think, to fairly distributing the congregation's time between speakers; it is also and indeed mainly a problem of upkeep, of keeping the congregation together and attentive. This obliges him on the one hand to limit the overall time of discussion; but it also forces him to look in his selection of speakers toward those who are most apt to command attention.

THE *k* CONSTRAINT

Let us now turn to the *k* constraint. This letter designates the time which I, as chairman, deem to be the minimum necessary to develop adequately an opinion on the subject under discussion. I offer no justification for my setting of *k* because I would find it difficult to explain the complicated computations which intervene in my mind and of which I am hardly aware. First I make some assessment of the difficulty of the subject. The more complex it seems to me, the more prone I am to raise *k*. Though my assessment of the difficulty of the subject is inevitably subjective, I am apt to take it as objective, and there is no practical harm in so calling it. But now I must take into account the qualification of the audience. It is to be hoped that I have not been chosen as chairman while having qualifications lower than the median qualification of the assembly. I shall assume that my qualification is quite a bit higher than median.

I must then take into account the fact that the expenditure of words required to convey an argument increases as the qualification of the listener decreases. An expert can convey his argument to a fellow expert in the same field with an economy of words or symbols, which makes his message incomprehensible to a layman. When speaking to the latter, the shorthand of jargon or conventional signs must be made explicit, and redundance must be introduced to increase the probability of understanding. Therefore, the lower the qualification of the audience, the more I must raise *k*.

We have now reached a conclusion which is capable of two alternative formulations. One: the more complex the subject and the less qualified the audience, the higher I must set *k*. Two: the greater the difficulty of the subject for the given audience, the more I must raise *k*. The two formulations are of course equivalent and the choice between them depends upon one's desire to include or exclude the notion of "intrinsic" difficulty.

But having come to such a conclusion, I have not exhausted the factors to be considered in the setting of k. We may not disregard what experience teaches us: that conveying the same argument to the same audience is a feat which some orators achieve in far less time than some others; for the given achievement, there is a considerable difference in speed. Obviously I cannot set k so that it suits only the fastest of potential speakers, in which case the allotted time would be inadequate for all others. But can I set k so that it suits the slowest of potential orators? Obviously not.

I am constrained by an inelastic m: total discussion time is fixed. Therefore the higher I set k, the fewer the speakers I can allow. Already, if the subject be one of some complexity and the audience of low qualification, I have to set k pretty high. I now want to set k so as to allow a maximum number of speakers. It is clear that I can maximize my number of speakers only by restricting my choice of speakers to those who require least time to develop their argument.

Let us set out the problem as one of simple arithmetic. Discussion time is three hours, and we shall make the assumption that sixteen potential orators require for their exposition times which from the first to the last rank from fifteen to thirty minutes, growing by one minute as we proceed from one person to another. The sixteenth potential orator would require thirty minutes: if that is the value at which I set k, equal sharing of time between the orators limits me to six speakers. If however I set k at twenty-two minutes, I can then afford eight orators, but they have to be the eight swiftest expounders.

CRITERIA FOR THE SELECTION OF SPEAKERS

Thus attention to k, with m held constant, gives me a recipe for choosing those who will be called upon to exercise the right of speech; that is, those who can formulate their argument, under given conditions, with maximum economy.[3]

But while we considered m, it became apparent that, apart from cases where the duration of the assembly is exogenously determined, which are many, m can be considered as somewhat elastic,

---

3. The conclusions are unaltered if one imagines that those who can develop their argument with maximum economy use up not their equal share of total time but only that which is necessary to them.

rising if the speakers be men who are capable of retaining attention. Here is another distinct criterion for the selection of speakers. It may occur that the two criteria coincide—a clear and concise speaker is apt to retain attention—but also the two criteria may not coincide because a "big name" is apt to attract attention even if its bearer be a diffuse speaker.

The two criteria which have been formulated arise logically from the problem examined. These criteria are in fact applied when for instance the BBC organizes a broadcast discussion: the name which appeals to the audience, and the ability to make points swiftly are both taken into consideration.

But another consideration also arises, and is of major importance. If a discussion is wanted, different opinions must be advanced. How is the chairman to choose bearers of different opinions, without making a prior selection of opinions on his own account? The procedure generally accepted is to choose bearers of opinions, different from each other, but of which every one is accepted by a notable portion of the body politic. The men's individual opinions are then severally representative of a body of opinion.

This completes our cursory examination of "the chairman's problem": he recognizes men whose names are apt to retain attention, who are representative of different bodies of opinion, and who are apt to present their argument with maximum economy.

THE CRITERIA SEEN FROM THE ANGLE OF *BONUM COMMUNE*

The criteria we have found for dealing with the chairman's problem are in no way surprising. They are those which any reasonably competent chairman applies in fact. They can however be assailed from two angles, from the *bonum commune* viewpoint and also from the individual rights viewpoint.

Beginning with the first, it may be said: (1) that a glamorous name, capable of retaining attention is not a guarantee of wisdom; (2) that the several opinions which are widely held may all be wrong, and that the best opinion may not be representative of a body of opinion; (3) that an argument may be presented tersely thanks to the neglect of important considerations, and that its economy of words may correspond to a poverty of substance.

To the first point, the answer must be brief. The chairman,

should he feel entitled to pick out the wisest, may well doubt his ability to discern them, and if he does not doubt it, the congregation may well call it into question. The second point will be dealt with as we come to discuss the criteria from the angle of individual rights. The third point is well taken.

We like our problems to be simple and our decisions to require little thought. Therefore if speaker A presents a problem as complicated and B as simple, we are apt to prefer B's argument. Rightly so, if B has taken the complexities into account and reduced them to simplicity, but wrongly if B has made the problem simple by overlooking important aspects, which is most frequently the case. There is a sure recipe for presenting any problem as simple: it is to disregard factual information and to reason discursively from general principles. The principles and the reasoning are easily grasped by listeners who are thus readily convinced, while many are apt to resent the effort required from them by speaker A who pours out and marshals a great deal of factual information.

We are prone to buy our opinions in the cheapest market: and that is the market where particular opinions are mass produced from general principles. This is a major danger which afflicts assemblies: it can be guarded against only by the chairman's closest attention to providing participants with the factual information relevant to the issue; and if the assembly cannot be asked to digest the adequate amount of factual information, then it is not the proper body for deciding the specific issue.

THE VIEWPOINT OF THE INDIVIDUAL RIGHTS

We started out, concerned not with the problem of reaching the right decision (a *bonum commune* problem) but with the gap which may occur between the right of speech and its exercise. Our examination of the chairman's problem has made it clear to us that the gap cannot fail to be considerable.

Our main point throughout this discussion has been that time is a scarce commodity; that is, the time during which a congregation can be held together attentive to speakers from a floor or pulpit, or the time during which an audience can be expected to remain attentive to a broadcast, is a limited quantity. The problem is not different in kind if we think, not of speakers competing for the opportunity of addressing a gathering, but of people addressing letters for the correspondence column of a newspaper: here it is the space which is limited. The editor who returns to the letter writer a printed note expressing regret that his communication could not be printed due to lack of space refers to a real concrete problem. There is a bottleneck of space in the correspondence column (or columns) as there is a bottleneck of time in an assembly. However the editor's answer by no means satisfies the letter writer who sees other letters printed while his has not been. Nor does lack of time pleaded by the chairman satisfy the would-be speaker who has not been recognized while others have had their say.

There is no place (as far as I know) in the political theory of democracy for the simple and glaring fact of bottlenecks. Individuals are told at every moment that they have an equal right of speech, and they find out in any concrete instance that the opportunity of expression is denied to them. This breeds the feeling that democratic principles are a lie. And indeed if the principle of right of speech is so formulated as to convey the impression "you shall have the opportunity of being heard by the congregation, equal to anyone else's" then it is a lie, because it is impossible to give such an opportunity. This comes back to the old idea so often forgotten that any right is meaningless which does not have as its counterpart an obligation in someone else toward whom the claim must be directed. Now, giving to everyone the right of being heard by the congregation would mean settling upon the congregation the obligation of listening to each and everyone; and that is not feasible.

People who are taught and told that they have an equal right of speech find out in fact that the avenues of expression are guarded by people who turn down their application. They do not realize that this is a necessity since here we are dealing with a scarce commodity which cannot be divided into less than given quantities. They are merely aware of being turned down, and are apt to believe that the guardians of the avenues of speech have turned them down personally: from there it is just one jump to thinking that the right to speech which rightly belongs to all (is this not tirelessly stated?) is in fact confiscated by a few, who form an Establishment. Whether or not the guardians of the many different avenues of expression do in some loose manner form one company, and can be called an Establishment, or whether in fact such guardians are in the several cases ad hoc and are linked in one body by our innate tendency to mythologize, is a sociological problem which does not concern us here. I personally lean to the second view. Different avenues are guarded by different people, and the only sameness which obtains is the sameness of the denial of the exercise of the right of speech.

Clearly this denial applies to a greater proportion of applicants, the greater the concentration of the avenues of expression. Say that every day one out of ten thousand readers of a newspaper feels moved to write to the paper. And say that there is room for ten readers' letters. A newspaper with a circulation of three hundred thousand will deny two out of three letter writers. A newspaper with a circulation of three million will deny two hundred and ninety out of three hundred.

Thus if you have ten of the smaller circulation newspaper instead of the one with the large circulation, you have less frustration. The same of course holds for assemblies. Thus every phenomenon of concentration in the media of expression or in the centers of discussion and decision making tends to decrease the percentage of received candidates among those who postulate for the exercise of the right of speech.

If one does not want people to feel that they are cheated it is important to explain to them this phenomenon of "scarcity" and also to make reasonably clear the criteria of selection used to choose among the many who have a formal right the few who are called to exercise it. It is better to stress the positive scarcity features of the system and the criteria used to allocate this scarce resource than to stress the formal right which can in so few cases be exercised. In fact *a system of expression is characterized by just these two things: its bottlenecks and the criteria for admission through the bottlenecks.*

THE RIGHT TO BUTTONHOLE

There is however a sense in which the right of speech can be exercised by each and everyone; it is the right to buttonhole, to address a fellow citizen, one to one, and convince him to hear you out (that is the speaker's business in which he may succeed or fail) and having done so to convince him of your opinion (that again is the speaker's business in which he may succeed or fail). By such "artisan" procedure, you may command successively the attention of n people, and in consequence you may collect these n people in a hall, and so fire them with your opinion that they shall go abroad and collect n^2 and then n^3 people, and so on. You may thus constitute a congregation of your own. That this should be allowed is essential to a free society; that, and not that *anyone* should be given the right to address *any* congregation.

Now consider the problem which arises in the case of Primus who has collected through toil and trouble a congregation of his own doing. An outsider, Secundus, comes in and claims the right to address this congregation on grounds of the right of free speech. Is Primus bound to give him the floor? I doubt it. He can reply to Secundus: "I have made up this congregation. Go thou and do likewise."[4]

CONCLUSION

It is essential to lay stress upon feasibility problems. Exclusive emphasis upon formal rights must inevitably breed in citizens the feeling that they are deceived, since the enunciation of such formal rights leads them to think that they should be enabled to exercise rights which in fact give rise to scarcity situations, frustrating the hopes aroused by the enunciation of formal rights.

With increasing centralization we move from the viewpoint of the right of speech to situations of increasing scarcity, which make the actual enjoyment of the formal right more and more subject to narrower bottlenecks. This is not generally understood and people feel mystified. This can be remedied only by speaking increasingly in terms of feasibility.

---

4. This would lead into another subject: the inequality of means for the building of a congregation and the increasing comparative disadvantage of the artisan process.

Thoughts on a Theory of Political Enterprise

The word *political* commonly occurs in four different associations: *political force, political problems, political conflict,* and *political organization.* I shall begin by setting some very tentative meanings upon these four terms. *Political force* will be taken to denote a number of people acting as a team, with the understanding that they vary greatly in their degree of involvement in the team. *Political problem* will denote the situation arising when a political force acts in such a manner, or presses for such a satisfaction, that it may inflict real or fancied injury upon others, offend them, or in any other manner cause them to be discontented and resentful. *Political conflict* will mean that the political force operating either gives rise to, or in any other way encounters, another political force opposing it. The term *political organization* does not lend itself to any simple definition, even for temporary purposes, and therefore I shall speak of *the political establishment,* meaning those people in whom the legal authorities of the Commonwealth are presently vested.

Let us consider the behavior of an individual in society. By the established standards of law, his behavior is either licit or illicit; if the latter he will, if found out, be prosecuted, and punished by ad hoc agencies. This individual addresses his actions to a certain satisfaction, the attainment of which, or the means of attainment of which, cause anxiety or anger in some other person. Here is a problem which turns into a conflict. But there is a solution to this problem which puts an end to this conflict. A judge, completely

"Thoughts on a Theory of Political Enterprise" is reprinted from the *University of Detroit Law Journal,* volume 36, no. 2 (December 1958). Used by permission of the publisher.

disinterested in this quarrel and quite independent from the contending parties, considers the facts in the light of the law and renders a sentence. If that is not final, at some stage in the judicial procedure there will be a final sentence, and there is nothing at all the losing party can do about it but submit. The law and the judiciary bodies are great instruments of social peace, and therefore are rightly honored. This inclines peace-loving thinkers to picture the political system as an enlarged version of the judicial system, operating in much the same manner. Unfortunately, such a point of view is unrealistic.

When we have a conflict between two political forces, can the political establishment, or some part of it, act as a tribunal passing a sentence? Practically every feature of the judge and of the relation of judge to party is lacking in the case of the political tribunal. The political adjudicator is neither indifferent to nor independent from the parties, when these are political forces: indeed, these are capable of changing the judge himself and the law itself. Furthermore, the political adjudicator cannot be content with uttering the "right" sentence. If the sentence gravely antagonizes a political force, it may be impossible to execute it, or its execution may inflict a great and festering wound upon the body politic. While the intensity of feeling of the litigants is not to be considered by the judge, it has to be a major consideration of the political adjudicator; and while the parties in a court of law must bow to the "right" decision found by the judge, the political adjudicator has to evolve a decision that will be found acceptable by both parties. In short, while the judge stands immovable above the individual parties, the political adjudicator finds himself within the field of contending forces, and even subject to them.

Faithful custodians of simple, coherent, and stable laws, farseeing guessers of future needs, efficient wardens of social harmony, such we may desire our political magistrates to be, and it is never idle to suggest such visions, since pictures contribute to form men's character, and their character helps them to withstand circumstances. However, the political observer must face the facts. Frequently men ride into positions of legal authority on the crest of a political force, and when thus installed they have to cope with the various stresses of political forces. Therefore, political forces stand out as the most obvious focus of inquiry of political science.

The investigation of political forces has been hampered by various reasons. One is the juristic bent of political science in many nations. For example, let us suppose that C is a magistrate who has, within his competence, the right to move certain people, the Bs, to certain actions. That is his *potestas,* and that is what the jurist, as such, is interested in. Now let us suppose that a considerable portion of the Bs (let us call them the Ba's), habitually follow A, that they habitually act in some respects as he instructs them. Now let us admit that C owes his present office and *potestas* to the action of the Ba's, so instructed by A. In that situation we have a formal relationship of authority of C over all Bs; but, moreover, we also have an informal relation of dependence of C upon the Ba's, an informal relation of authority of A toward the Ba's, and an informal relation of patronage between A and C. Now of these four relationships only the first—the competence and right of C to move the Bs—comes under the formal purview of the jurist. To the political scientist, the other relationships are of the utmost interest. The fact that the Ba's act in concert is characteristic of a political force.

Legal *potestates* are to a considerable degree controlled by political forces. However great the popularity of General Eisenhower, it is improbable, to say the least, that he could have been elected President in 1952 had he not been adopted by one of the two great parties. But again he would not have been nominated by the Republican Party if political operators had not coalesced some forces within the party to carry his nomination. And here we come upon another reason which impedes the investigation of political forces: they are not easily delimited; there are forces within forces.

For example, let me turn to the political conflict which reached an acute stage in Cyprus in the late 1950s. We are likely to describe it in the following simple terms. *The* Greek Cypriots demanded full independence from British rule and majority rule of the whole island; on the other hand, *the* Turkish Cypriots would not accept this and in case of cessation of the British administration, demanded partition of the island. This wording implies that "all the Greek Cypriots" on the one hand, and "all the Turkish Cypriots" on the other hand take up these incompatible attitudes. For all I know this may have been true, although I would be inclined to believe that many on both sides just felt they had to follow the movement. But even assuming that perfect polarization would be achieved, this is obviously not the mere outburst of preformed collective wills. Each great array is the outcome of a snowballing process, whereby an active kernel has drawn to itself layer upon layer of followers. Political forces, when they make headlines, are the accumulated product of political drives, accomplished by political teams, which are the elementary political forces. All of these are of major interest to the political scientist.

The building of a basic coherent team I call political entrepreneurship. A political enterprise, once launched, may peter out or prosper. If the latter, it competes with others for followers and clashes with others by reason of contradictory goals. The best analysis known to me of political enterprise is Shakespeare's *Julius Caesar,* where Cassius is the entrepreneur. He recruits fellow conspirators, inflames them with his purpose, welds them into a team, invigorates them by setting up Brutus as a figurehead, and finally the "We" he has constructed moves to successful action: Caesar is murdered. However, the political enterprise, triumphant thus far, fails to rally the Roman people, because of the adverse intervention of a competing entrepreneur, Mark Antony.

Political enterprise is of major importance in political history. A political enterprise may run in lawful grooves, and again it may not. Take the case of the entrepreneur Poujade.* On the one hand he lawfully achieved the election of a few dozen deputies to the National Assembly of France. But on the other hand, by unlawful agitation against the enforcement of tax laws, he obtained an important alteration of the latter. It is of course eminently desirable that political enterprise should move within the law, but history testifies that quite often it does not. There is indeed some difficulty in teaching that political enterprise should restrict itself to legal paths, since there is hardly a political regime in existence which does not owe its origin to what was then an illegal subversion of the established institutions.

Political science has moved a long way in a generation from legality to reality, from the description of constitutions to the study of pressure groups. It seems easily predictable that it shall move toward a theory of political enterprise. It will investigate the succession of phenomena whereby the will of a few kindles an associate will in others and builds up an increasing "We," which then

---

*Pierre Poujade was the founder of the right-wing *Union démocratique des commerçants et artisans* (U.D.C.A.), which scored its first legislative victories in 1956. The party was disbanded in 1962—Eds.

by its sheer energy attracts others and adds them to its weight. Having thus grasped the nature of political enterprise, it will consider the impact of political enterprise upon the social field, and from there political scientists may conceivably move toward a discussion of the stresses and strains tolerable by the body politic, and the means, if any, of keeping such stresses and strains within the limits of tolerance.

However, emphasis upon political entrepreneurship is at the present time unwelcome to a great majority of our contemporaries. They are steeped in a mythology of social forces and political bodies, according to which every force or body now figuring in society has appeared by spontaneous generation and grown by an inevitable process, by a sort of ground swelling of which its successive leaders are merely representative excrescences. It would seem absurd to argue that the Ford Motor Company in some way preexisted Henry Ford, who was merely an aspect of its actualization. This, however, is the fashionable mode of thought in the social and political realms.

The common misconception is linked with the belief that historical events occur "when they are called for," a gross secular providentialism which deserves here only the briefest notice. Those who feel that the Roman Empire was "called for" should perhaps pay attention to the fact that an express letter addressed from Rome to Cicero, as Governor of Cilicia, took forty-seven days to reach its recipient. Surely, if the Roman Empire was "called for," then also faster means of transportation and communication were "called for" at the same time. But, as it happens, they were not then invented.

Another prejudice impeding the recognition of the role of the entrepreneur in politics is the fiction of the "collective will." There is no such thing; willing is an attribute of the person. It is of course no less an attribute of the backer than of the initiator; response is no less an activity than instigation, no less a manifestation of human freedom. I have elaborated this point elsewhere, making it clear that there is no inferiority inherent in being a "joiner." But the time sequence between starting and joining is unmistakable: it flies in the face of evidence to regard those now acting together as having begun to act simultaneously.

A current objection to spotlighting the political entrepreneur is the attendant possibility of "hero-worship." Political entrepreneurs are as important dramatis personae of the social scene as economic entrepreneurs: the former need not fire the imagination of the scholar any more than the latter. Indeed, while some political entrepreneurs of history do evoke our sympathy, and others very much the reverse, the inquiring mind, addressing itself to political entrepreneurship as such, finds some unpleasant occupational traits inherent in that activity. An economic entrepreneur regards some men as potential customers and stands to some men in the relation of employer, but for the political entrepreneur all men are potential recruits and auxiliaries. There is no form of activity more conducive to regarding men as means. And indeed it seems that the nobler the entrepreneur deems his political goal, the more he feels entitled to consider men as means. The interests and sentiments of others are essentially handles whereby these others can be drafted. And again there is no form of activity wherein the arousing of sympathy and respect is more a tool and trick of the trade. All this does not of course imply that a political entrepreneur cannot be an ethically pleasing person, but he certainly is not such by virtue of his occupation.

What is here called "political entrepreneurship" is the activity which tends to the banding and bunching of men in order to create a force capable of exerting pressure upon a social field, large or small. Suppose that I create a circle for the exchange of views on public affairs. However much our preoccupation relates to government, this is not a political enterprise in the sense here given, because it is not proposed to exert any pressure. But if some one of the members, possessed by some strong passion, proposes to take over the association in order to make it campaign for his views, his process of colonization of the association is itself a political operation, and its success turns the body into a political enterprise. In short, political enterprise is the process of mobilizing energies for the victory of a certain will. Thus, the political entrepreneur may be thought of as a warlord of the social scene. The form of political enterprise which immediately comes to mind is the constitution of a de facto power aimed at the capture and exploitation of a seat or stronghold of de jure authority. As such seats of de jure authority have existed as far back as human chronicles stretch, we of course regard them as preexisting the political forces built up for their conquest. However, we should remember that such seats are artifacts, while the propensity to enlist the energies of other men is natural. It is therefore obvious that political enterprise is more ancient than established authority, and has indeed been a source of the latter.

A political enterprise need not be addressed to the capture of political offices. For instance, the creation and development of labor unions fits our definition of political enterprise: here is a banding and bunching of men to exert pressure. Indeed, I regard the history of labor unions as offering perhaps the most promising material for the analysis of political enterprise. In the very beginning we find here and there a few men who feel that they and their fellows have no say-so, make up no weight. They dream of organization, but long working hours and lack of experience in handling men hamper them. Furthermore, they have no secure basis of operation, since their being recognized as agitators leads to their dismissal. Moreover, they are so much on the same footing as their fellows that they can count only upon their strength of character to give them some leverage. It is only slowly that small teams are built up, and these find it difficult to attract a stable following. At some moment the workers do rally around a kernel, but after suffering a defeat they desert it. Yet the force grows, makes itself felt. It is worthy of notice that this political force, which does not aim at the capture of any public strongholds, is at certain stages of its development driven into the latter course by reason of the obstacles which existing laws offer to its growth. Thus, in Britain, the *Taff Vale* decision of 1901,[1] which affirmed that union funds were liable to suits for damage (torts), oriented union leaders toward electioneering activities which resulted in the favorable Trade Disputes Act of 1906.[2] This goes to show that a political *enterprise* (in my sense of the word) formed for purposes which are nonpolitical (in the current restrictive acceptance of the word) may easily find itself induced to press upon or invade the political establishment in order to suit the laws and the uses of lawful authority to its purpose.

Political enterprise is a natural phenomenon. A man intent upon a certain purpose which he cannot achieve by his unaided force, gathers up the energies of other men insofar as he can find

1. Taff Vale Ry. Co. v. Amalgamated Society of Ry. Servants [1901] 1 K.B. 170.
2. 1901, 6 Edw. 1, c. 47, 5.

in them dispositions allowing him to do so. He thereby builds up a mass which by its very existence attracts other units. This weight produces effects, makes displacements, does work. The phenomenon is natural: this means that it occurs independently of any legal licensing, although its course can be affected by the latter. But further, this means that political enterprise is an object of inquiry in the spirit of the phenomenological sciences,[3] not of legal science. The relationships obtaining within the political enterprise evade the neat descriptions which legal science necessarily demands. There is no definite membership. Some people are deeply involved, some less, and there is an ample fringe of people with faint traces of involvement, either in the process of vanishing or of waxing. Even among those who are substantially involved, there is no contract. Those who are presently leading have no formal right and those who are presently following have no obligation. Also, the pressure which the political enterprise exercises upon the outlying social field is not a matter of right, but a matter of fact.

Just in order to show that political enterprise operates throughout the social field, let us take a minor and sordid example. A manages a large block of rented apartments, a few of which have been vacated, and we shall assume that the market for apartments is sagging. A black family offers to take an apartment, and the manager is ready to sign it up. But B, a tenant with violent racial prejudices, goes around to the other tenants, stirs them up, and they go in a body to A, demanding that he should not admit a black tenant. Here we have an elementary case of pressure exercised without right by a body without legal existence. It may be asked why I pick upon such a nasty little operation as an illustration. It is to stress that political enterprise is not necessarily wide in its scope nor ethical in its purpose. I find it present wherever and whenever a person or group of persons succeed in causing others to "go along" with them and thereby can exert a pressure upon some point or points of the social field. The law, of course, may forbid and punish certain pressures, but the legislator cannot foresee everything, nor can the law enforcement agencies be present everywhere. Not only is complete coverage impossible, but its pursuit would lead to "overgovernment." Moreover, it is clear

3. This unwieldy term is used instead of the more obvious one, *natural sciences*, because the latter term designates sciences dealing with nonmoral agents. An acute realization that we are dealing with moral agents is essential to political science.

that political enterprise, operating in certain "strategic sectors," can paralyze the legal authorities, and also, in attaining a certain power, it can change the law itself.

Paying due attention to political enterprise may cause us to somewhat revise our views on majorities. Given a certain set of people and a decision to be taken ("H" or "non-H"), we are likely to assume that even before the H issue is brought up, there exists in that set two subsets, the H-ers and the non-H-ers, one of which is more numerous than the other (let us say it is the H subset), so that the mere raising of the H issue will actualize the two subsets and make manifest the H majority. But it can be observed that the majority in fact occurring in the set may be either H or non-H, according to whether a political enterprise has been started on an H or a non-H theme.[4]

This raises the important question of what I shall call "the expressionist postulate." Assume that within a given body of men, before the H issue is raised, there is an H preference inherent if dormant in a majority (i.e., a potential if unformulated H will). It follows that the mere raising of the H issue must cause the manifestation of this will, that therefore any non-H political enterprise is doomed, while indeed the H political enterprise is merely an occasional cause of the H majority, and by no means an efficient cause. It does not seem to me reasonable to deny that there are situations approximating this model; neither does it seem reasonable to assert that the expressionist postulate is valid in general. It should immediately be clear that if one accepts, however unconsciously, the expressionist postulate as of general validity, one's view of politics and of history must thereby be deeply affected. It would be of great interest to track down the expressionist postulate in the many arguments which it underlies; but this is no place to do so.

Far more misleading and mischievous than the expressionist postulate would be, of course, the idle fancy that a body of men offers a plastic availability to the designs of the political entrepreneur. Political enterprise has no forces other than those it recruits,

---

4. A minor but striking illustration of this point is afforded in Part 15, *Hearings of the Eighty-fifth United States Congress on Improper Activities in the Labor–Management Field.* Within a small plant, and at a year's distance, an antiunion majority and a prounion majority have been obtained, and to cap the irony, by two successive agents of the same labor-relations agency.

and it cannot recruit any except by close attention to the data of human dispositions. The fact that in the same body of men an H or a non-H majority may be obtained, by no means proves the weakness or gullibility of the men forming this body. Let me show this by a very obvious argument.

The H issue may be raised at a given moment by an H champion and an anti-H champion, each starting from a position of isolation, each addressing himself to all at once. But this will not be generally the case. An entrepreneur (let us say a pro-H entrepreneur) will have started discrete operations, addressing himself to individuals whom he thinks capable of adopting the H thesis and of campaigning for it ardently. He assembles and enlarges his team and drives forward: at some moment the issue bursts into the limelight and the forceful H team makes an impression. Its various members each attract some sympathies, and interpersonal links are brought into play; a number of arguments have been rehearsed, the team makes an impression, and this impression may be such as to attract enough consent to decide the issue before the anti-H group has had time to organize and counterattack. The decision may thus be H while it might have been non-H if the opposing party had been first in the field.

It is an advantage to be the first in the field, but it is a far greater advantage to dispose of a "standing army." What is meant here by a "standing army"? A body of men coherently organized to win social battles. In the Middle Ages the possession of a small body of armed men was a sign of social power. The time came, sooner or later in different countries, when such private armed forces were regarded as incompatible with state authority. But nonmilitary armies have arisen in the political field, and we regard them as entirely normal. We do feel uneasy about the behavior, within loose social bodies, of tightly knit and well-disciplined teams when these seem to us subversive, as for instance the Communist cells within labor unions. But we are rather at a loss in dealing with such cases since we do not only recognize man's obviously natural right to influence his fellows, but also the right of association, formal and informal. Indeed, the right of coalition is today regarded as essential to democracy.

Far different was Rousseau's scheme of pure democracy, which excluded fractional associations, the organization of particular bodies of men. He felt that any sectional combination tended to make men conscious of another interest than that of the Commonwealth, of another loyalty than that due to the Commonwealth, and made it possible for blocs inspired by these sectional feelings to weigh upon the decisions of the people, and indeed he dreaded the conflicts arising between such blocs. He conceived the assembly of the people to be composed of individuals unlinked in any other manner than as co-citizens. Within such an assembly a different majority, and therefore a different minority, would arise on each specific issue, giving no opportunity for the hardening of "sides." Finding myself on a given issue in a minority with some others, these would not be the same people with whom I had agreed on some previous vote on another day, or even on the same day. Therefore, I would find in my haphazard association with them no encouragement to balk at the decision reached. We may indulge in the fancy of likening Rousseau's forum to the perfect market of classical economists, where each atomistic agent contributes to the conditions over which none has the slightest degree of control. Pursuing this fancy we might say that our forum departs far more from this model than our market, that dominant firms, corporate and party associations, rings, and so forth, are characteristic of our forum.

There is a great similarity of preoccupations between Hobbes and Rousseau, in that the English philosopher also was an enemy of particular associations. He did not, however, trust to atomistic confrontation and looked to the sovereign to preclude their development. If he made the rights of the sovereign so large and those of the subject so slight, it was by no means because he had in mind anything like the totalitarian regimes of our century, where subjects march to the tune of state bugles. It was because Hobbes wished to preclude the appearance of political forces within the body politic; and this because of the pressures they may bring to bear upon the individual, and mainly because of the conflicts to which their drives may give rise and of the resulting insecurity. The theist Rousseau, yearning for social harmony, and the materialist Hobbes, concerned for individual safety, were at one in banishing fractional organizations from their imagined commonwealth. This identity stands revealed in a famous letter addressed by Rousseau to the father of the great Mirabeau: "In short I can see no tolerable solution in between the most austere democracy or the most perfect Hobbism: for the worst of political situations is that in which the commonwealth is agitated and divided by the strife of men and laws."[5]

The two great political philosophers just quoted were equally concerned that policy decisions should be made and received without political clashes. Let me make this formula more explicit. Within any body of men, policy decisions have to be made for that body. We can observe that people organize drives for this or that decision, and that such drives clash. The majority rule gives the right of way to the heaviest drive. It is like a traffic rule prescribing that a tourist automobile must give way to a truck; this is an expedient rule, but it is utterly unrealistic to assume that those who have gotten involved in the weaker drive automatically are reconciled to the decision once taken. What Rousseau and Hobbes were concerned about, either in the cause of harmony or of peace, was that members of the social body should not get so involved in drives as to give the decision-making process the character of a clash of forces, and to leave after the decision, a sense of victory in some and of resentment in others. The devices resorted to were different in the case of each philosopher. Rousseau wanted all to participate but each to come without previous concert and combination with some of his fellows. Such a condition may seem to us incapable of being fulfilled. It is noteworthy, however, that this condition is precisely that which we seek to fulfil when bringing together a body of jurymen to make a decision on which a man's life may depend. Any evidence of prior collusion between some persons called up for jury service would justify their rejection. The Hobbist solution to the same problem is to leave decision making in the hands of one man set high above any pressures. And this again is what we do when we leave a decision to a judge.

It is utterly unrealistic to assume that there will be no factions in a jury, that all will make the same decisions affecting everyone. In ancient Athens, which was ruled by a popular assembly, there were many factions. It is equally unrealistic to assume that conflicting interests and passions shall not form cabals, and occasionally revolt against a supreme ruler. Our great authors were not so naive as to ignore such facts. As any normative thinker must, they were seeking to define optimal conditions, from which reality differs more or less. What deserves our close attention is that their

5. Rousseau, Letter to the Marquis de Mirabeau, *Correspondence*, vol. 17, 157.

diametrically different formulas were equally meant to minimize political conflict, and therefore political forces and therefore political enterprise. This must be of the utmost interest to those who regard political enterprise as natural, political forces as legitimate, and political conflict as a necessary outcome.

However, we do regard some political conflicts as utterly disastrous, such as those which sharply polarize on grounds of race, religion, or national origin, populations physically jumbled on the same territory. We do regard some political forces as "subversive," such as communist or fascist parties or movements. Thus, we certainly cannot regard political enterprise as an unmitigated blessing. We may not agree with Hobbes and Rousseau that the less there is of it the better, but we dare not take the opposite point of view that the more of it there is the better, whatever its goals and tone.

Let me for a moment move away from the field of politics into that of economics. Several generations ago economics was in the stage of a priori general value judgments. The so-called "Economists" argued that the moneymakers automatically worked toward the social good and the "Socialists" took the diametrically opposite view. Gradually economics passed from an a priori era into the closer and closer study of business enterprise. Now in politics it seems to me that we stand very much at the a priori stage, with almost all of us as optimistic in relation to the "force-makers" as the economists were in relation to the moneymakers. It is time for us to pass into the stage of a close study of political enterprise. This seems all the more timely in that political entrepreneurship is developing away from a natural activity of gifted amateurs into a systematized technique.

The danger inherent in resorting to analogies is that one feels tempted to push them too far. Business enterprise can be subjected to political regulation, which forbids certain forms of enterprise (i.e., the trade in drugs), and provides for "trust busting." Similar political regulation of political enterprise is conceivable, but such regulation is itself subject to political enterprise. This, therefore, is a field wherein there exists a basic homogeneity between the forces to be controlled and the controlling forces, and where Juvenal's question is most apt: "*Sed quis custodiet ipsos Custodes?*" We would regard it as abnormal that the positions through which business enterprise is regulated should be taken

over by the predominant business entrepreneurs; but this is regarded as normal when applied to the effective regulation of political enterprise; the process, in short, is dialectic.

The foregoing remarks should not delude the reader into believing that I am trying to move toward normative prescriptions. Not
that I regard the latter as improper goals for the political scientist;
very much the reverse. But my present purpose is to draw attention to a certain order of phenomena, to stress their importance as
an object of intellectual observation and analysis.

Confucius emphasizes the importance of naming things. And
indeed any science relies for its progress and communication upon
the elaboration of unifying and discriminating terms. An example
of a unifying term is the word *catalyst,* which subsumes very different substances, causing in very different settings very different
effects, and yet seems to perform analogous functions, to have the
same modus operandi. This instance is certainly not adduced to
suggest any comparison between the catalyst and the political entrepreneur: the game of comparisons is to be deeply distrusted.
My example aims merely at underlining the value to science of
gathering up under the same name agents performing a similar
function.

Wherever I look around the social field, and whether I use a
telescope or a microscope (figuratively speaking of course), I find
the same process of generation of forces capable of exerting pressures, and within this process I find the will of some gathering up
the energies of others. This is not a phenomenon of which I am
especially enamored; in fact, my sympathies lie with the "peace
lords" who are concerned with relaxing strains and stresses. But
that is another story. The point is that political problems, political
conflicts, practically everything which attracts our eyes to the political scene, arises out of political forces. The generation of such
forces by political enterprise must therefore be a very important
subject of inquiry for political science. This can be called a theory
of political enterprise.

Political Configuration and Political Dynamics

I

Our mind strives for statements of configuration and statements of consequence. Where different things stand in relation to one another, that is configuration. How successive events arise from one another, that is consequence. We grasp far more easily disposition in space than process in time; further an incomplete "geographic" account can be valid as far as it goes while an incomplete "historic" account can be highly misleading. The difference in difficulty and reliability between "where" and "how" statements is at a maximum in politics. It is therefore not surprising that political science should have dealt mainly with configurations.

The baggage borne by a student of politics returning from a grand tour of many countries is apt to consist of "maps" exhibiting the "commanding heights" of the lands visited. Let us picture our student beginning with a pilgrimage to Athens. First, he ascends the Acropolis; here the gods were worshipped, but here also was the residence of the erstwhile monarchs; next he ascends the hill of Arès, where an aristocratic tribunal made its decisions, grown more important after the overthrow of the monarchy; finally, he ascends the Pnyx and evokes the Assembly of the People. These three hills respectively suggest the authority of one, the few, and the many, as depicted by Aristotle. They assist our imagination in conceiving the shift of authority from one eminence to another as well as in conceiving the mixed forms which combine the voices issuing from different hills. The same tangible assistance to imagination is afforded in Washington by L'Enfant's skill in posing the Capitol and the White House upon confronting hills. But even

"Political Configuration and Political Dynamics" is reprinted from *The Review of Politics*, volume 23, no. 4 (October 1961). Used by permission of the publisher.

where such physical aid is lacking, we are sharply aware of "commanding heights." Thus in London, our student visits Westminster and Downing Street, and casts an eye upon Buckingham Palace. In Paris he views the Palais-Bourbon, the Hotel Matignon, and the Elysée. So, he will carry away a series of raised maps of the seats of decision and authority. If he is at all shrewd, he will note what is written in stone beyond what is written in the constitutions. In Washington he will pay attention to the proliferation of buildings housing executive departments and agencies. Nor will he neglect the mansions erected by trade unions and other nongovernmental bodies.

There is ample material here for a comparative and critical geography of seats of authority or influence. For example, ground plans suffice to show that the dependencies of the legislative branch have nowhere kept pace with the dependencies of the executive branch, that indeed they have been developed only in the United States, hardly in Britain, not at all in France. Discrepancies may thus be brought out between relative attributions of authority and relative means of implementing attributions.

Mapping the configuration of authorities is a natural and necessary concern of political science. While theoretical writers have ever been interested in advocating this or that ideal map, derived from some principle, practical politicians have ever needed accurate and detailed knowledge of the actual map, as a guide to efficient action. The importance of configurations is great but fully recognized and they are dealt with more than adequately by other authors. Therefore it has seemed to me that a different approach to politics might be tried.

II

Let us fancy that we visit Athens in 415 B.C. just before the decision is made to send an expedition against Syracuse. As ignorant foreigners we ask our hosts three questions. First: to whom does it pertain to decide and eventually to lead such an expedition? Second: is it right and advantageous to undertake the expedition? Third: in fact, will it be decided and undertaken?

The first question is one of constitutional competence, which any Athenian can and must immediately answer in the same manner with complete certainty: the decision belongs to the Assembly of the People which shall also, if it makes an affirmative decision, elect the generals. This falls in the realm of configuration. The second question is one of political Prudence: I use the capital P to stress that I have in mind not the skimpy notion of prudence prevailing nowadays but the classical notion of Prudence as the virtue of giving the right answer in specific circumstance, a virtue which we may find in some of our hosts and not in others. The third question falls in a different realm. It calls for a statement of fact concerning a future event.

Let us then consider shortly our foreknowledge of future events. There are a great many future events which we take entirely for granted: if we did not, we could not conduct our daily lives. Upon examination it appears that most such *certa futura* are mere manifestations of configuration. That the sun will rise tomorrow is an event only from an extremely subjective point of view. Stable natural configurations allow us to expect, indeed to produce, "events" with no doubt as to their occurrence. Further, stable social configurations lead us to expect some events with hardly less assurance (for example, a Presidential election will be held in the United States on the second Tuesday of November in a particular year): while for the philosopher, there is a great difference in nature between these two assurances, for the practical man there is a very slight difference in degree. But the political event we are now considering, the decision of war or peace to be made by the Athenian Assembly, is one which by definition depends upon the free choice of men between alternatives. And here we know for certain that we can have no certain foreknowledge of the outcome. If we could have certain foreknowledge of the use which other men will make of their freedom to choose, we would be possessed of what theologians call *Scientia libera*.

However impossible it is for us to say for certain what other men will do when they manifestly have a choice and are visibly hovering between alternatives, nonetheless we are apt to say that a given alternative seems to us probable or even very probable. Indeed, supposing that we are envoys from Syracuse, our city expects us not only to argue with the Athenians for the purpose of persuading them that they should not send an expedition against Syracuse, but also to guess what the decision will in fact be. On our return to Syracuse, we shall be accused of a disservice to our city if we have failed to convey advance information that the Athenian decision is going to be war; it will then be an inadequate defense to argue that we could not know what the Athenians would decide as long as the decision was open: though it is rigorously true that we could not know of certain science, we should have formed a true opinion of the future event.

Surmising is essential to the conduct of human affairs; a mistaken surmise can be disastrous. Napoleon surmises that Grouchy would and Blücher would not intervene on the field of Waterloo. The tragedy of King Lear turns upon erroneous surmises: examples thereof are not hard to find in our time. Within one year Chamberlain made three major erroneous surmises: that Hitler would be satisfied with the Munich settlement, that he would be intimidated by the giving of a guarantee to Poland, and that Stalin would join hands with Britain and France.

Surely an interest in politics implies an interest in surmising. However important it is to describe a configuration deemed static, to recommend attitudes wholesome and virtuous, it is important also to foresee what men will do and what will happen.

III

Indeed when we discuss politics, not in the character of political scientists but as mere men, we are apt to speculate about some future event. Thus, in September 1960, a man may well have said: "I believe that Kennedy will be elected in November." The speaker, asked the reason for his statement, may answer: "I could not really say." But this is a natural reaction of defense against a challenge to considerable intellectual effort. It is difficult to state the reasons for a surmise, but introspection might bring them to light. It would then appear that the mind supposes certain dynamic relations; because of certain past events people of certain dispositions will prove responsive to a certain call and act in a certain way. The chain of conjectures may be very weak in itself and it may be perceived only faintly by the speaker, but nonetheless it exists in his mind.

While people are most unwilling to work out their chain of suppositions leading to their expectation of some future event over which they have no control, or only a very insignificant share of control, the same people do carefully work out their chain of suppositions when they propose to bring about something which they ardently desire and conceive as largely dependent upon their own actions. The Latin has a convenient duality of words for those two kinds of events: the masculine *eventus,* with its connotation of outcome, can be taken to designate the event which I propose to bring about, of which I am somehow the author, while the neutral *eventum* can be taken to denote the event which is utterly out of my hands. For the British Foreign Office or the Quai d'Orsay, the Kennedy election is *eventum,* for the campaign team *eventus.* However hazy we may usually be about the sequence or intermingling of sequences that will bring about an *eventum,* in the case of an *eventus* we bring our mind to bear far more sharply.

IV

The future is present to the mind of acting man. The great German jurist Rudolf von Jhering discriminated between human action and animal action in terms of *ut* and *quia. Quia* actions are those I perform under the pressure of outside causes, without choice or deliberation. *Ut* actions on the other hand are those I perform in view of a certain result I wish to bring about. They involve a certain vision of a future state of affairs I propose to obtain and of a "path" to that state.

There is nothing of which we are more aware, whatever philosophers may say, than of our ability to bring about certain situations by our choice served by our efforts. I can, if I want to, raise this glass to my lips. When I do raise it, I am aware that I am "causing" its new position. But, to speak more accurately, the very notion of "cause," common to all men, is a product of such experiences. From my earliest childhood, I have found that I can change something, however little, in my environment, by my action, and from this microcosmic experience of a relation between my effort and this change, arises the general idea of "cause and effect."

This is confirmed by elementary etymology. In law the word *causa* was mainly used when referring to the trying of causes at law. A *causa* was what one of the parties wanted, a meaning conserved in English when we speak of "espousing a cause," "fighting for a cause." The words Romans were prone to use when they meant the bringing about of a certain result was *efficere,* which contains the idea of *facere,* that is, doing, but which reinforces it, adds the idea of completion, achievement, a sense which has been reflected in the modern word *efficiency*. The well-known formula *causa efficiens* associates the two ideas that something is wanted, *causa*, and is achieved, *efficiens*, into the one idea of operational wanting.

In the case of my lifting this glass, there can be no doubt that if I want it lifted I can effect this change: it lies entirely within my power (the word *power*, let us incidentally note it, denoting the ability to do). Nobody but a madman, or a philosopher for different reasons, will give thought to an *eventus* which he can so readily bring about.

But as we well know, men do give thought to an *eventus* that they deem both desirable and difficult to achieve. Presumably it was quite a number of years before his eventual election that John F. Kennedy first had a brief vision of himself as President of the United States. Between imagining and achieving this position there was a vast difference to be spanned. The spanning of this difference required a long sequence of actions. This sequence had to be conceived and planned from the outset, even though many amendments were found necessary in the course of the operation. Clearly, devising a shift from the situation of Senator to that of President offers a great contrast with devising my transport from this to that room of my house. In both cases steps have to be taken; but in the latter case they are literal steps, and the outcome of each is assured: in the more important case, they are metaphoric "steps," that is, "moves" by the actor, and the outcome of each move is uncertain, dependent upon the reactions of other men. Well-calculated steps are those which elicit reactions helpful toward the attainment of the goal. The problem of achieving the wanted *eventus* then calls for correct surmising of responses. The actor's "steps" in fact advance him toward the goal only or mainly by virtue of the alien actions which they spark. Far the greater part of the energy expended in bringing about an important *eventus* is provided by others whom the designer sets into motion.

The practical politician is well aware that his means for the attainment of any political objective are the contributory actions of other men. Knowing in general how to obtain such actions, and specifically for what, when, and from whom he can hope to obtain them, this constitutes his familiar lore. The technology of politics is essentially concerned with dynamics while its science cleaves to statics.

Should political scientists address their attention to dynamics? A negative answer is plausible. It can be argued that standards of scholarly accuracy can be sustained only in description and classification of given states of affairs, and that standards of logical deduction can be sustained only in deriving prescriptive arrangements from clearly enunciated ethical principles. While it cannot be denied that we do in fact attempt to understand by what process certain events have come about and to guess what shall occur, it is easy to point out that our assessments of past causes are controversial and our conjectures of future events highly adventurous; and therefore it may be held that we should not be so bold as to seek an understanding of the political process over time. But such a negative answer would singularly restrict the scope and advisory capacity of political science. The statesman, nay the mere "boss," resorts daily to some empirical understanding of operational relationships: can we not elaborate such understanding? For that purpose, we may start with the observation of what politicians do.

V

The word *designing* has, in common English usage, an unfavorable connotation, when applied to a person. Used neutrally, the term conveniently designates the occupational trait of the politician. He seeks to bring about a certain *eventus* requiring actions of other persons, and therefore he seeks to elicit the adequate contributory actions, and for this purpose makes the moves apt to elicit these actions: all of this constitutes the *design* of the politician, which, on being carried out, constitutes a *political operation*. The political operation is analyzed in the following emphatic self-portrait of a politician:[1]

> Neither Montaigne in writing his essays nor Descartes in building new worlds, nor Burnet in framing an antediluvian earth, no nor Newton in discovering and establishing the true laws of nature on experiment and a sublimer geometry, felt more intellectual joys, than he feels who is a *real patriot*, who bands all the forces of his understanding and directs all his thoughts and actions to the good of his country. When such a man forms a political scheme and adjusts various and seem-

1. Bolingbroke: *Letters on the Spirit of Patriotism*, ed. A. Hassall (Oxford: Clarendon Press, 1926), 19–20. The italics are Bolingbroke's.

ingly independent parts into a great and good design, he is
transported by imagination, or absorbed in meditation, as
much and as agreeably as they: and the satisfaction that
arises from the different importance of these objects, in
every step of the work, is vastly in his favor. It is here that the
speculative philosopher's labour and pleasure end. But he,
who speculates in order to *act,* goes on, and carries his
scheme into execution. His labour continues, it varies, it
increases; but so does his pleasure too. The execution indeed
is often traversed, by unforeseen and untoward circumstances, by the perverseness or treachery of friends, and by
the power or malice of enemies: but the first and the last of
these animate, and the docility and fidelity of some men
make amends for the perverseness and treachery of others.
While a great event is in suspense, the action warms, and the
very suspense, made up of hope and fear, maintains no unpleasing agitation in the mind. If the event is decided successfully, such a man enjoys pleasure proportionable to the good
he has done: a pleasure like to that which is attributed to the
Supreme Being, on a survey of his works. If the event is
decided otherwise, and usurping courts, or overbearing
parties prevail, such a man still has the testimony of his conscience, and the sense of the honor he has acquired, to
soothe his mind, and support his courage.

Here Bolingbroke indicates that there is: (1) a patriotic objective; (2) a grand strategy designed to ensure the attainment of the
goal; (3) an active and flexible maneuvering to carry out this strategy; (4) an intense pleasure inherent in the whole performance.
One would like to think that such pleasure depends wholly upon
the excellence of the project, that the scheming and handling are
made enjoyable only by the merits of the goal. Observation regret-
tably suggests that the sport of moving men is enjoyed in itself
even when the operation is not inspired by a high purpose or
addressed to a salutary end.

The worthiest and wisest men engaging in politics are least apt
to experience the sporting enjoyment described by Bolingbroke.
The wielding of power or influence must, in a truly good man, be
attended by a constant fear of its misuse, by doubts regarding the
goal to be sought and scruples concerning the means to be used.
This has been expressed by Fénelon: "Indeed men are unfortunate

that they have to be ruled by a King who is like them a man, for it would take gods to set them right. But Kings are no less unfortunate, being mere men, weak and imperfect, to have the ruling of a great multitude of sinful and deceitful individuals."[2]

What a contrast between these two statements! Pride colors the one, humility marks the other. Surely we must prefer that which stresses the statesman's responsibility. But if our purpose is to understand the generation of events, then what is relevant is Bolingbroke's picture of the politician's activity.

VI

Our times are marked by a precipitate course of events and an attendant instability of configurations. Political maps and constitutions are highly perishable commodities.[3] On each New Year, there are countries where foreign diplomats have to shift their compliments from the authorities of yesterday, now outlawed, to the outlaws of yesterday, now in authority. Those parts of the world where only small events occur within an unchanged framework have shrunk relatively to those where major events shake and transform the framework. The character of the times therefore focuses our interest upon the event.

Some minds are so secure in their a priori understanding of future history that for them great events fall into place within a preordained scheme. Those of us who do not think so sweepingly regard each event as posing a problem, calling for analysis of the many factors which have entered its composition.

The smallest identifiable component of any political event, large or small, is the moving of man by man. That is elementary political action. The man who seeks to elicit a given deed from another I call "instigator"; "operator" insofar as he strives to obtain from different people different actions contributing to a given *eventus;* "entrepreneur" as he builds a following habitually responsive to the same voice or a voice proceeding from the same place.

2. François Fénelon: *Directions pour la Conscience d'un Roi,* published long after they were composed for the instruction of the Duc de Bourgogne (Paris, 1748), 140.

3. The average life span of a map of Europe since the beginning of the century has been fifteen years. Germans since 1914 have lived under four regimes. When I first wrote this the French had lived since 1938 under three regimes; now it is already four.

The spotlighting of the protagonist should not be taken to imply a "great man" view of history. First, it should be stressed that he does not, as such, exist by himself, but only in relation: the primary element is not the instigator, but the relation instigation-response. Second, every such relation is itself only a link in a complex chain. *Eventum* is an intricate structure arising out of many chains of which the elementary relation is a link. This link deserves scrutiny because it is the basic constituent of any course of political events; being present *semper et ubique* in the formation of any event it is of course incapable of explaining any singular event. In the same manner the great variety of chemical compounds cannot be deduced from the notion of chemical link. In every science other than that of politics, there is a determined endeavor to reach down to the simplest identifiable relations, breaking down the complexity of reality to well-defined elements, which can henceforth be used as intellectual tools. This is what is called "pure theory" in sciences other than the political, and that is what I propose to attempt, though fully aware that I shall not proceed very far.

VII

It is important to avoid any confusion between the elementary prompting and the large event, to place rightly the first in relation to the second. A fable may be helpful.

Macedonia wants political information about Megalopolis. We shall assume that no Macedonian understands or can learn the Megalopolitan language but that three observers can be made invisible, and endowed with the means of immediately reporting what they see. Observer A is set up in a balloon high above the city, observer B in another balloon much nearer to the ground, observer C roams in the streets. A's altitude is such that he discerns nothing but the buildings, the general layout of the city, in short configuration. This he maps out carefully, it may be a long task but when completed he has nothing more to report. Surely the analogy with the description of a constitution is obvious. B hovers at a height which allows him to study traffic; he notes streams, the density of which is variable; after some time he recognizes that density at given points fluctuates within the day according to a recurrent pattern; he also finds patterns of longer span: days of abnormally low density (for example, Sundays) immediately preceded and followed by some increase in density; seasonal variations and possibly a long-term trend to increase: indeed he may note growing pressure upon bottlenecks. Even if B—who calls to mind the sociologist—notes a building up of pressures over time, his observations offer, once he has mastered the patterns, but little variety. It is otherwise in the case of C who, moving on a level with the individual inhabitants, witnesses an inexhaustible variety of incidents. While A has ceased transmitting when he has conveyed the map, while B transmits only in the case of a departure from pattern, a scrupulous C transmits all the time a succession of minor scenes.

One day, however, A is shaken from his calm. He has seen a major building of Megalopolis, call it the Palace, going up in flames. This he hastens to transmit and receives from Macedonia the answer: "Thank you. This confirms our previous information." What previous information? Sometime earlier B has communicated that a great mass of people were moving toward the Palace and breaking up a thin line of guards. To this communication however he also has received the answer: "Thank you. This confirms our previous information."

Why? Because C was on the spot and saw how it all started. He witnessed the formation of the push, which was noticed by the student of movements only when it had gathered momentum, and by the student of the Constitution only when it had produced its effect. C is the earliest and most sensitive indicator. Also, however, he is the least reliable.

What exactly has the street observer seen? At the beginning, a man holding forth, gesticulating, attracting a crowd, and within this crowd an increasing agitation. This is the event at its birth, the small beginning from which by an increase in mass and acceleration the tidal wave shall arise. But let us remember that not every such beginning culminates in such achievement. Our man may well have formerly witnessed and conveyed scenes of this type out of which nothing has come. The decipherers at the receiving end are apt to remember that they have already received a number of descriptions of this kind; and while this nth instance may be momentous they are not prone to suppose it. Any man who has had occasions to convey warnings is aware of the incredulity which greets them; nothing indeed is more unwelcome to the routine of the staff man than the fever of the field worker.

It is only under the impact of successive information, pouring in more and more rapidly that increasing notice will be taken of a possible event, to which the receivers shall come to allow a growing degree of probability. Of course the event will not be held certain until it has been completed: only postdiction is assured; never prediction. The initial piece of news then presents over the description of the culminating havoc a great chronological superiority but a great inferiority of assurance. This touches upon a problem well known in the press. A reporter cannot forgive his editor for failing to publish the dispatch noticing "the first step" of a revolution; but this the editor acknowledges as effectively the first step only when the revolution has unmistakably occurred. And the reluctance of an editor is nothing to that of a foreign office: newspapermen are functionally prone to believe in events, diplomats are functionally prone to disbelieve them.

The fable used points out both that an elementary political action stands at the start of the large event, and that a large event may or may not follow from this elementary action. The important element of doubt in the second statement in no way impairs the affirmation of the first. Even if not all acorns turn into oaks, it is important to know that all oaks arise from acorns. If only oaks are worthy of our notice, and not acorns, then we shall not understand oaks.

VIII

In the foregoing tale, an *elementary action* has given rise to a major event, presumably because this action was part of a *design* the carrying out of which was favored by a *situation*. Why is the example chosen that of an upheaval? Possibly because upheavals are so common in our day. But beyond this reason of circumstance, there is another. Periods lacking in great and tumultuous events are not necessarily such for lack of primary pushes, the social field may be rife with instigations but these are then so evenly distributed and addressed to such various ends, that they do not build up to a grand dramatic impulse. Tragedy occurs when processes naturally diffuse throughout the body politic, acquire a concentration, an intensity, a polarization which affords them an explosive power. Nothing then is more important to the guardians of a body politic than to understand the nature of these processes, so that they may be guided to irrigate and precluded from flooding.

Political Science and Prevision

The political scientist is a teacher of public men in the making, and an adviser of public men in activity; "public men," that is, men who are taught, invited, or assumed to feel some responsibility for the exercise of political power; "political power," that is, concentrated means of affecting the future.

I

Obviously we cannot affect the past, or that present moment which is now passing away, but only what is not yet: the future alone is sensitive to our actions, voluntary if aimed at a pictured outcome, rational if apt to cause it, prudently conceived if we take into account circumstances outside our control (known to decision theorists as "states of nature"), and the conflicting moves of others (known in game theory as opponents' play). A result placed in the future, conditions intervening in the future, need we say more to stress that decisions are taken "with an eye to the future," in other terms, with foresight?

Thucydides puts this utterance in the mouth of Archidamos, addressing the Assembly of Lacedemonians on the eve of the Peloponnesian War: "For we that must be thought the causers of all events, good or bad, have reason also to take some leisure in part to foresee them."[1]

"Political Science and Prevision" is reprinted from the *American Political Science Review,* Volume 59, No. 1 (March 1965). Reprinted by permission of the publisher.

1. Thucydides, 1, 83. From Hobbes's version, republished by the University of Michigan Press (Ann Arbor, 1959), vol. 1, 48.

This can serve as our text: the greatest of historians warns us that we are the authors of our fate. It is levity in an individual to make a decision fraught with serious consequences to himself without forethought; but such levity turns to guilt in the case of the magistrate or citizen participating in a public decision the consequences of which will fall upon a great many. The political scientist then must recognize in foresight a moral obligation, to be felt and taught.

But saying that public decisions *ought* to be taken with foresight is a precept: how can we follow this precept unless we develop the corresponding *skill?* Knowing that foresight is required, the political scientist must therefore seek to develop that skill in himself, and in his pupils, and offer it to statesmen he has to advise. *Foresight is an expertise required in the political scientist:* that is my first point.[2]

Need I stress that expertise does not mean infallibility? A political scientist will often misread the course of events or miscalculate the consequences of a decision, but the frequency of his successful forecasts should be higher than that of the average politician or lay citizen; this is not a great deal to ask, and whoever denies that it can be achieved, thereby denies any practical value to political research. The moral philosopher who deems it his function to teach discrimination of what is best in an absolute sense, does not need to prove himself a good forecaster. But it is otherwise for one who presents himself as a student of behavior. Such a study must be called idle or unsuccessful unless it results in an increasing ability to state what is to be expected.

There is in every science a well-known relationship between factual investigation and marshaling hypotheses, meant to account for the facts and assumed to have some predictive worth. It is true that there can be no certain knowledge but of the past: indeed the past is the realm of the "true or false," with which the future contrasts as the realm of "possibles," which are neither true nor false. Therefore only probable statements can be uttered regarding the future, but it is solely through such utterances that the sciences are of practical utility. As I shall stress, it pertains to the nature of the object that such statements should be least reliable in matters political. But if they are not to be attempted, the term

---

2. For a more extended discussion of the general topic see my *L'Art de la Conjecture* (1964); eight of the SEDEIS studies in conjecture have been collected, in English, in *Futuribles* (1963).

science should be rejected: nor can we then think of the discipline as conferring positive boons upon the body politic.

II

Since probable statements concerning the future are an outcome of factual investigations, they can, of course, concern only the realm of those phenomena which the student investigates. It is a verbal convention of our time that of two once synonymous terms, one of Latin, the other of Greek origin, both designating originally the whole of human relations, the word *social* has been retained to mean the whole, while the usage of the word *political* has been narrowed down to a part of these relations. In the meantime, however, the functions of government have grown more embracing: therefrom a noncongruence between the field of studies of the political scientist, and the field of concerns of the political magistrate. It follows that the kind of foresight which the political scientist may provide refers to but part of the phenomena the political magistrate has to deal with. This immediately suggests that it falls to other departments of the social sciences to provide complementary varieties of foresight, arising from their specific investigations, and relevant to some kinds of public decisions. It is indeed the practice of governments to consult experts other than political scientists, for the preparation of decisions concerning what Cournot very aptly called "the social economy." When it is future "traffic in towns" which forms the subject matter of the decision, forecasts regarding the automobile population, the location of industry, the grouping of people, and so on, are required of specialists quite other than political scientists.

This need not be labored and forms my second point. *Public decisions require a variety of foresights other than that of the political scientist.* We may well think of these diverse foresights being brought into play as each occasion demands. But there is a problem here, of no mean importance.

III

I shall introduce this problem by means of a concrete instance: the quotations here are from the *Survey of International Affairs* for the year 1930.[3]

3. Royal Institute of International Affairs (London, 1931), 531–56.

Dr. Brüning became Chancellor of the German Reich in March 1930:

> [T]he Budget problem was by far the most untractable of all the problems with which Germany had to deal. . . . [U]p to the time of writing [the Summer of 1931] it was only under the Chancellorship of Dr. Brüning that measures were taken of such a character as to promise real improvement. . . . The cumulative deficit was . . . the prospective deficit was. . . . Action was therefore urgent. Dr. Brüning met his immediate necessities by an emergency decree promulgated in July 1930, and, as the situation was not righted by this measure, it was succeeded by two further emergency decrees issued respectively in December 1930 and in June 1931.

While drastically cutting down expenditure, these decrees also raised taxes. "Such were the draconian measures to which Dr. Brüning was obliged to resort. Their effectiveness in practice remained to be seen: their value as proof of the changed attitude of responsible German statesmen in the matter of public finance was beyond question or cavil."

Let me add that, on taking office, Dr. Brüning found three million unemployed: after two years of "draconian measures," he had six million; that he found twelve Nazis sitting in the Reichstag: after six months in office he saw their number raised to one hundred seven (September 30 elections), and soon after he left office (May 1932) the Nazis obtained two hundred thirty seats (July 31, 1932).

Now let us imagine a political scientist addressing Dr. Brüning in April 1930: "Ignorant as I am of public finance, I must assume that the measures which have been recommended to you by financial experts are the best for balancing the budget (which in fact they were not); ignorant as I am of economics, I cannot tell you what measures would effectively reduce unemployment: these are matters for different specialists. But it is my office to tell you that unemployment is a more serious evil than budgetary deficit, constitutes a more pressing problem, and that you should give it priority. Further it is my office to warn you that you will put the country in great political peril if you fail to address yourself to the major problem."

There is indeed a very heavy bill to be paid for the misinvestment of public attention, which is a very common fault of politicians. Consider the sad case of Dr. Brüning, an earnest and honorable man, who conscientiously and courageously addressed himself to what he deemed the major problem: but his ranking was quite mistaken, so that his virtuous efforts led to political disaster. This brings out the utility of properly ranking problems. Here I am not thinking of a lasting hierarchy in terms of values (however important that is) but of a here-and-now order of priorities, in terms of the costs of letting various problems fester and come to a crisis.

Politicians having proved remarkably poor judges of such priorities, a better judge is needed to redress their assessments: and this is a role for the political scientist, who to this end must operate as a "generalist," not only as a "specialist" among others. No matter that he is competent to deal only with certain problems, he must also be competent to appraise them all. And this role of "generalist" is logically linked with his role as specialist: because any social problem which is left inadequately attended will ultimately land in that court of passions and conflict which is his particular concern. He can be compared to a suzerain of the social field, who runs but a small part of the realm, but must oversee the whole, as any trouble arising in any other part must seep into his own. He is competent to request attention for a problem, and demand that experts competent therein be called. More than that, he is competent to state what questions they should answer, because he must be aware of interrelations between problems.

Another instance will serve to stress that aspect. Left alone after World War I to maintain the new map of Europe which Woodrow Wilson and Lloyd George had taken so large a part in drawing, France formed alliances with four Eastern Europe states, of which two, Poland and Czechoslovakia, were immediate neighbors of Germany. These alliances committed France to military intervention should Germany attack Poland or Czechoslovakia. Military intervention in what form? A mere glance at the map made it clear that effective intervention could occur in no other form than the invasion of Germany. Therefore these alliances required that the French army be shaped as an offensive instrument: exactly the reverse was explicitly decided, and a purely defensive apparatus was set up. So it was quite easy to foresee a good ten years in advance what happened in 1939: while practically the whole of the German forces was thrown against Poland, the French army sat uselessly on its defensive positions, having been designed for nothing else.[4] Not only was it easy to foresee but it was foretold behind closed doors by certain military leaders, and openly by some young civilians without authority. Now is this not again a clear case for the political scientist? Was it not proper for him to point out the discrepancy between the diplomatic policy and the military policy?[5]

I have chosen two instances of fatal mistakes, of which I can bear witness that they were perceptible at the time. Mistakes, one of which proceeded from a wrong priority of policies, the other from an incoherence of policies. Is it not the political scientist's role to take a view sufficiently panoramic to call attention to such blunders? That is my third point. *The political scientist is competent to appreciate priorities and consistency in policies the details of which he is incompetent to judge.*

IV

The foregoing statement means that the political scientist has to keep track of current and impending changes in nonpolitical fields, and for this purpose to achieve a continual exchange of forward looking views with experts in these other fields. To take a simple instance, suppose that the balance of payments specialist foresees the necessity of slowing up the rate of wage increases. Some economists feel that this cannot be achieved otherwise than by a "squeeze," diminishing, as they put it, the pressure on the labor market—in more common parlance, maintaining a certain percentage of unemployment. Others, shocked by this prospect, re-

4. And not well designed even for that, as commandant Lucien Souchon noted in 1929, uttering this prophecy: "Our future army will be dissociated, pushed around and cut to pieces before having struck the least blow." In *Feu l'Armée Française,* published without signature (Paris: Fayard, 1929).

5. One might elaborate upon the consequences of this inconsistency. First, the discovery of the impotence of the French army was a major cause of the French government's attitude at the time of Munich; but as they could not believe this impotence, the Soviet leaders quite understandably interpreted our shameful desertion of Czechoslovakia as inspired by a machiavellian desire to orient Germany toward an attack upon Russia, which was thought of by no responsible Frenchman. Second, as the Poles trusted the French army—as I found while attending them in the 1939 campaign—they thought it quite unnecessary to agree in the previous Anglo-Franco-Russian negotiations to the entry of Russian troops upon their soil, which the Soviets quite understandably made a condition of their military support. And this increased the Soviet suspicion of our good faith, which may have determined the Ribbentrop-Molotov pact.

ject that method and advocate an "incomes policy." Now the political scientist, informed of these views, foresees from the one procedure unpleasant political consequences; while the second poses a problem of political feasibility. Therefore such views are very germane to his concerns: indeed it may be the case that one policy seems to him inadvisable and the other impracticable, which may cause him to ask the economists for some other way: would a flexible exchange rate achieve the object?

As every change assumed to occur has repercussions in many fields, as every change devised has a variety of implications and calls for a variety of adjustments, it is clear that in a society characterized by rapid transformation, there is need for what I have called elsewhere a surmising forum where anticipations are confronted, and where incoherences discerned indicate measures to be taken, or alternatives to be considered. I do not propose to restate here the case for the surmising forum; all I need is to make the fourth point: *the political scientist must seek to coordinate anticipations.*

This attempt to overlook the whole field is useful for the long term, but it also meets a pressing need of the political scientist.

V

This overall watching allows him to detect sources of future political perturbances. *The political scientist should be a detector of trouble to come:* that is my fifth point.

Trouble is indeed his business. Who would deny that he is at his most useful if he warns of war or advises how to avoid it? That the foresight of the foreign policy expert revolves around the possibility of war, will be readily granted; but not so easily that the domestic equivalent of war must play the same central role in the speculations of the domestic expert. The contrast is understandable enough: the international system is thought of as a system of antagonism, the national system as one of cooperation. The very accent of words changes as we move from one system to the other. If we speak of a system of Powers (international), we use the capital letter to denote independent actors by their factual resources, their *means;* while if we speak of the system of powers (national), the powers we now refer to are *rights* to be exercised functionally in the service of the national whole.

"Home affairs," as the British tellingly put it, are supposed to be altogether quieter than foreign affairs. It is assumed that the institutions set up to take care of home affairs are and will remain adequate to cope with any problems arising: there is a political division whenever people strongly disagree as to what should be done, but this division is thought of as overcome when the matter has been settled by an established procedure of decision (such as a parliamentary "division").

The political scientist should be keenly aware that things are not so simple, but his function as teacher of institutions leads him to convey and therefore to adopt an optimistic vision. His first and foremost function is to address future citizens and potential magistrates, and fit them for participation in the management of public affairs, a management organized according to a certain system. This system must be described and explained to them, so that they shall feel "at home" in it, in the two senses of knowledge and acceptance; and it is surely of great importance to a republic that its citizens should have confidence in and respect for the form of its government. Political institutions, inherently precarious, are made solid and stable by belief, which must therefore be fostered; but, in the process of so doing, it is easy to become overconfident. It improves mores to think that what may not be done can not be done, but it deteriorates prudence. It is good that actions should run between the banks of established procedures, but it is dangerous that the imagination of the expert should be confined between these banks. To cite an admittedly extreme and caricatural instance of such confinement, it was apparently believed by those who called Hitler to the Chancellorship at the end of January 1933, that he would find himself quite paralyzed in this position by article 58 of the Weimar constitution, which stated that all government decisions should be taken by a majority of the members of the cabinet, wherein he was placed in a minority, having only two ministers of his own party! As I warned, this is an extreme and caricatural instance; it is not suggested that political scientists are prone to such mistakes. But it is true, surely, that, not only as teachers of good civic behavior, but also as law-abiding and reasonable men, they are not inclined to lend any great likelihood to strong departures from regular courses.

They are not prone to foresee dramatic events. Surely the United States is the country far the best endowed in political scientists—indeed possibly as many as nineteen out of twenty political scientists operating in the world today are Americans. It would be interesting to know what proportion of these political scientists foresaw—and how early—the sensational rise of McCarthy and his no less sensational collapse. Or again, what proportion foresaw the capture of the Republican Party by the Goldwater group in the 1960s.

This is not meant as a criticism: first, it is in any realm difficult to be a good forecaster; second, the difficulty is at its greatest in politics; last, and chiefly, political scientists have not, in general, deemed it their function to forecast, and when so doing they are apt to stress that they do so as citizens, not as scientists. The only purpose of my remark, therefore, is to note a psychological disposition, which I think would still be operative if political scientists were willing to adopt the view here advanced, that they should regard it as pertaining to their function to forecast, and should indeed regard such forecasting as a practical end-product of their science. Under such conditions, they would still, I think, be reluctant to foresee perturbation, disturbance, trouble. So, if this foresight of trouble is, as I think, the most important, a psychological effort will be required to overcome the tendency to project a relatively smooth course.[6]

That tendency is to be found also in other fields of social science: everywhere prevision resorts to projection of current trends and to reproduction of periodic changes. Economic prevision, to whatever degree of complexity it may be worked out, ultimately rests upon the assumption that certain structural relations are relatively invariant over time. It is natural enough that prevision should assume continuity and recurrence. Therefore it takes an effort to predict discontinuity, a break—in short, trouble.

VI

Political foresight requires study of political behavior: this sixth point is self-evident; every science studies the behavior of those

6. In his masterly treatment of economic forecasting, H. Theil, *Economic Forecasts and Policy* (Amsterdam: North Holland Publishing Co., 1961), Part 5, notes that changes to come are generally underestimated. If our mind tends to underestimate shifts in a continuous course, breaks in this continuity are even less acceptable to it.

objects about which it proposes to make statements of general and lasting validity, and therefore capable of being used for prediction, or anticipation. Nor is it necessary to advocate study of political behavior: this is presently the most esteemed compartment of political science.[7] Nonetheless something is to be said on this point.

"Behavioral studies," as they are called, are apt to deal with ordinary behavior: the word *ordinary* denotes at the same time, and very properly, what is not uncommon, and what fits into an order. Now times of trouble are characterized by extraordinary conducts: the behavior of the "force publique," when the independence of the Congo was proclaimed, came as a great surprise; no better, and no less surprising, was the behavior of the "gardes-françaises" on July 14, 1789. Some meticulous and respected German bureaucrats have been found out, to the shocked surprise of their colleagues, as the authors of most abominable actions in the days of the concentration camps: but for these historic events they might have lived irreproachable lives and no one would ever have imagined them capable of what they have done. Of course, saying that people would not have been criminal but for the occasion is not, as it is all too commonly taken to be, an excuse: the actions are their own and their features then made manifest were potentially there before. But it is a warning that the behavior we presently observe is not the only behavior of which the subjects observed are capable.

The instability of behavior is a great difficulty for political prevision. We know of course that a man's behavior is variable but in no realm is it as variable as in the political. And we get no inkling of behavior under "heated" conditions if we merely observe people under "cold" conditions, when they vote this way or that, attend meetings or not, move resolutions, or raise their hands. Under heating, we observe that the same people are not then behaving in the same way; and further we must note that it is not the same people who then claim most of our attention. At all times, if people are ranked according to their degree of political activity, we find that such activity is high only in a limited number and falls

7. See the ranking of the different compartments of political science given by Albert Somit and Joseph Tanenhaus, "Trends in American Political Science," *American Political Science Review*, vol. 57 (December 1963), 933, 941. The authors asked political scientists in what compartment of the science the most significant work was being done and "behavioralism" came an easy first.

off very rapidly as we consider greater numbers. "Heated" conditions are apt to increase the total surface included under such a curve, but they also substitute, for the most active minority under cold conditions, a minority made up of quite different persons.

Whatever the equality of political rights, so small is the share of total political activity performed by the great majority and so great that performed by a small minority, that the total hue and character of national political activity reflects that of the active minority. If that leading company then changes, the whole character of politics changes. And though the heat which changes behavior in the same people does pass away, the change in the people who impart their character to the total system may endure.

The great merit of an effective two-party system is that no man can rise to political importance otherwise than by a slow progress within one or the other party, a progress in the course of which he finds himself subject to screening by monitors at different stages of his rise. It is a major contribution to stability that the two parties conspire to persuade the public that between themselves they exhaust the possibilities. But the political scientist must be aware that, however salutary this belief, it does not correspond to reality: there are people floating in outer darkness who can, if the occasion arises, irrupt upon the scene, casting out both of the small armies that have been engaged in a civilized duel. The heads carried away in the baskets attending the French guillotine represented the whole spectrum of opinions preceding the Revolution (also those which appeared in its course); the same has been true in the concentration camps of Soviet Russia and of Nazi Germany.

All this pertains to the process of "heating." To this, political scientists have given, if I may say so, quite inadequate attention; they have been very prone to regard this as inevitable when it has happened and unthinkable where it has not. That where it has happened it had sufficient cause, is of course true, but uninteresting; what is useful is to pinpoint, if we can, what would have made a difference. It is now out of fashion for historians to stop their relation of events when they come to what seems to them a crossroads, and to note that, from a different decision or action at this point, a different course of things might have followed. It may be that such exercises are unbecoming to historical science; they are surely in the highest degree suitable to political science.

Our science stands in great need of a systematic study bearing upon the occurrence of these "changes of state" here called "heating." Unless I am much mistaken, such a factual study would not confirm the breezy theory that they occur when necessary to allow the coming forth of a predetermined new order—that is, if and only if they serve a providential purpose; strange indeed is the unquestioned providentialism of agnostic philosophers of history.

I have noted that studies of behavior tend to disregard changes in behavior which attend "heating," and that too little attention is paid in them to what leads up to such "heating." Another remark is now called for, relative to normal conditions.

Political phenomena have by nature a tempo different from that of social phenomena. Let us take, for instance, people's attitudes toward the consumption of alcohol. Let us suppose that over time the proportion of teetotalers increases from a small minority to a majority. As a social phenomenon this can be continuous and carried to any degree without a break. But now consider teetotalism as politically militant. Then, as soon as the teetotalers have reached a majority, they will forbid drinking to the minority: a discontinuity, a break, and an occasion of "heating." Thus the diffusion of a political attitude gives rise to distinct events, as it does not in the case of a social attitude.

But the above illustration assumes a perfect democracy, where decisions are made by a popular majority; such is not the practice of any modern state. Indeed, the present trend is to entrust the major decisions to a single person: thus in the United States, while the Congress decided on the President's proposal of how much financial aid should be given to South Vietnam, a military operation on North Vietnam could be decided upon by the President alone.

It follows therefrom that the political scientist, operating as "predictor," must pay to individual character an attention which is not called for in the case of the social scientist. A social phenomenon is the outcome of a very great number of individual decisions, an aggregate which reflects individual attitudes in proportion to their frequency. Social prediction can therefore safely neglect attitudes of a small minority—thus, for instance, Amish rejection of the automobile is insignificant for estimates of future automobile sales—and the social predictor need not (as, indeed, he cannot) pay attention to idiosyncrasies. If interested in estimating the number of divorces next year, he will wave aside as irrelevant a tidbit of information regarding John's disposition to quarrel with Mary. It is not so in politics: an attitude relatively infrequent, such as rabid antisemitism, acquires momentous importance if it pertains to a man who rises to the highest place. More generally, in the absence of any such extreme peculiarity, every little trait of the Prince's individuality acquires great importance, due to the "multiplier" of great power.

This has ever been recognized. We have centuries-old records of political forecasts in the form of diplomatic dispatches. While the ambassador owes his public character to his being the empowered spokesman of his sovereign, as soon as permanent missions abroad were established, they functioned mainly as listening posts, whence information was sent home, concerning political developments occurring or impending in the country of residence. These are the earliest "political surveys," of enormous value for the historian in that each describes a state of affairs, but also a source as yet untapped for the study of political surmising. The message of the political reporter is the more valuable the more it foretells; therefore, while conveying accomplished facts, the writer must also use them as raw material to convey a "transformed product," his surmise. The abundant diplomatic sources in existence are still to be used for the analysis of the surmising procedures they reveal. But it needs only the barest familiarity with them to remark the place occupied in such dispatches by the description of personal characteristics: the character of the Prince, those of his ministers and favorites, those also of possible successors.

What a change the simplest substitution of persons can make. Consider Frederick the Great in January 1762: he writes to the marquis d'Argens: "If Fortune continues to pursue me, doubtless I shall sink," and suggests that unless a turn for the better occurs, he may next month, take Cato's course: "Cato, and the little glass tube I have." But as he writes the turn has already occurred: Czarina Elisabeth has died, her nephew Peter has become Czar; a fanatical admirer of Frederick, he immediately relieves the pressure upon him by recalling the Russian troops. Peter's bare six months on the throne suffice to turn the tide.

Can we confidently say that personalities matter less in our own day? Why then did a shudder run through the West when the false news of Khrushchev's death was flashed? Even in the case of a liberal democracy, did we not find the very same men who intepret politics as a working out of impersonal forces, expressing the utmost alarm at the prospect of a Goldwater presidency in the mid-1960s?

Personalities always matter in politics, and never have they counted for more than in our century, which has, at one and the same time, tended to collectivize the individual and to individualize collective power. From this has come, as it seems to me, an improved predictability in matters pertaining to the social economy, and a deteriorated predictability in matters specifically political. Far be it from me to exaggerate the freedom of action of the man who sits at the top of a nation. He is always "riding a tiger," but the way he rides it makes a very great difference indeed.

From these remarks it seems to follow that the methods which serve us well in the prevision of social change, which is continuous and insensitive to idiosyncrasies, cannot be suitable for political phenomena, which have different properties.

VII

It is a great ambition of modern social science to study phenomena without "insight"; an understandable ambition, this being the way which has led the human mind to phenomenal success in the physical sciences, which serve as the model and basis of all others. Standing in the way of such progress was the "pathetic fallacy," our apparently innate propensity to lend quasi-human personalities to objects. It is not helpful toward the control of floods to regard them as fits of anger in the river genius, who should therefore be appeased by gifts, perhaps human sacrifices. Our knowledge and mastery of nature have progressed as we have ceased to regard natural objects as whimsical persons, who behave according to their mood, and have come instead to regard them as "things" which behave as they are made to by circumstances. Containing as it does a most vigorous repudiation of animism, a depersonalization of objects, the Bible can be said to have helped open the way for Western science.[8]

We find the eviction of "genii" historically associated with a

---

8. It is here beside the point that "the death of the Great Pan" or depersonalization of natural objects, has implied a great loss of reverence and sensitive enjoyment of them.

procedure of inquiry which seeks to ascertain how the object behaves under varying conditions, and to derive from observed regularities assertions of predictive value. The procedure has its utmost
practical value when it leads us to foretell with certainty how the
object will behave under certain future conditions as they occur,
and therefore also, what conditions we must create in order to
make it behave as suits us. These great practical rewards of the
method are fully attained when the object studied is a "thing"
which must perforce "behave" in perfectly passive compliance to
the conditions wherein it is placed. This being so, it is understandable that the method was extended to animals in consequence of
Descartes's assertion concerning their "machine" character, and
that Condillac and La Mettrie should have, by their views of man,
encouraged its extension to him.

Whatever historical role the inclination to regard man as also a
"mere thing" may have played in the extension to him of this
method of inquiry, it is surely a mistake to regard the validity of
the method, applied to his case, as dependent upon this ontologi-
cal assumption.[9] In fact the very first finding from such an application is that men do not display that uniformity of behavior which
we expect from "things." Thus an application, scandalous to some
who regard it as debasing man to the status of "mere thing," in fact
demonstrates that he is not such. But the method is not, in consequence, valueless: though we find in a number of men different
conducts in the same circumstances, if we note the distribution of
such conducts and its mode, and if we can find that over time this
distribution and its mode change but little or shift but slowly, we
have therefrom a predictive tool, as stressed by Quételet.[10]

Now a few words about "outwardness." The scientific method in
respect to things has substituted for interpretations of their "ge-

9. This mistake gives rise to heated quarrels between those who, being revolted
that man should be thought of as a "mere thing," therefore needlessly repudiate
the scientific method and those who, addicted to this method, therefore needlessly
champion the "mere thing" notion. Justification or condemnation of the method
does not rest thereupon but depends upon its efficiency. Here I would like to
digress to say that the true danger of a scientific approach, but shared with any
other form of intellectual outlook, is that excessive enthusiasm for general statements, however useful, should impair our appreciation of the particular and
unique.
10. A. Quételet, *Sur l'homme et le développement de ses facultés ou essai de
physique sociale,* 2 vols. (Paris, 1835).

nius" the examination of their performances. We attempt no sympathetic "understanding" of the thing's spirit but proceed by watchful "overstanding." In the metaphysical squabbles of social science, there is much argument for and against such "outwardness."

I can see no harm in observing a nation as one would an anthill; this just happens to be a hampering method. Were it the best, ethnologists who go out to investigate so-called "primitive peoples" should be strictly forbidden to learn the language of their hosts; for conversation conveys some insight into people's feelings, intentions, values. Thereby you lose the outwardness which some deem so essential.

Outwardness has indeed been used as a literary artifice by eighteenth-century wits, foremost among them Voltaire, to ridicule social behavior. If you look at conducts from an angle which annuls the values inspiring them and thus robs them of meaning, it is easy enough to make them appear nonsensical; thereby also they are made unpredictable. This is a clear warning not to press outwardness too far. The social scientist has to set the tangible behaviors he observes within the framework of prevailing beliefs and interests. An economist may dislike automobiles, he may, as a joke in the common room, describe weekends as an aimless buzzing of urbanites out of the hive, arising from a periodic perturbation of the regular courses therein: his forecasts must nonetheless rest upon men's known desires for cars. No forecasting is possible unless data about what people do are complemented with data about their feelings, wants, aspirations, judgments. These data may figure but implicitly in a model, which then assumes either their invariance over time, or that their changes will follow a certain ascertainable course.

But it is quite otherwise for the political forecaster: he has to focus upon feelings, attitudes, judgments, because these, in his field, undergo swift and vast changes, with major factual consequences. How soon, how very soon it was after Hitler's last stand in Berlin, that I heard an Americans for Democratic Action group in New York acclaim Mayor Reuter's* formula: "Berlin is the outpost and symbol of freedom!" What a reversal of significance!

*Ernst Reuter (1899–1953) was a Social Democratic politician, journalist, and municipal official. Imprisoned by the Nazis, Reuter was elected mayor of Berlin in 1949, and became famous for his pledge that "Berlin will remain a free city."—EDS.

Did it occur because the national interest of the United States demanded it? I have no patience with those who explain the emotional attitudes of actual people by the rational interest of collective entities: it is rather the other way round. Is it credible that the anti-Soviet revulsion of the United States soon after the end of hostilities was inspired by the national interest? If so, surely, in the last weeks of the war, the American troops should have been urged to gain as much ground in Germany and in Czechoslovakia as was possible, and to keep it. But no, the policy of containment came as an aftermath of a change in the affective valuation of Stalinist Russia.

History would be different—indeed there would be very much less of History as commonly understood—if policies corresponded to a relatively stable conception of the national interest. For instance, consider Britain's "war or peace" relations with Hitler over a period of less than five years. March 1936: Hitler's troops march into the Rhineland, demilitarized under the Locarno treaty, to which Britain is a party; all that Britain needs to do is to give backing and encouragement to the wavering French, who then can easily reoccupy the Rhineland, thus dealing to Hitler's prestige a possibly decisive blow. The British choose the opposite attitude. Summer of 1938: after the Anschluss, Czechoslovakia is threatened, the French make ready to march on its behalf, the British government invents the Runciman mission which leads to Munich, "peace in our time." The strategic situation is now much deteriorated, but the takeover of Czechoslovakia, which was made helpless by amputation, scandalizes British opinion and Britain waxes militant. No matter that the hoped-for alliance with Russia falls through, it is war; the now reluctant French follow unwillingly, and, as it proves, ineffectively. October 1940: France has been utterly overcome; the only power left standing in Europe, the Soviet Union, is Germany's ally; Hitler offers peace to England, at no cost to her—let her attend to her Empire, which Hitler admires. The offer is not even considered; by now the hearts of the British have been so turned against Hitler that, regardless of relative resources and chances, he must be fought, come what may.

The terrible ordeal was unnecessary; such mistakes will not be repeated: nonsense! Of course they are repeated all the time—though let us hope with no such dramatic consequences—and naturally so: because, at any moment, "the present situation" is ap-

preciated in terms of the present feelings and evaluations. It is not
like a chessboard problem which different onlookers can be un-
equally competent to solve but which they must all see alike; it is a
different situation according to the onlooker, not the same to
Baldwin or to Chamberlain as to Churchill. Nor are the policies of
a nation the outcome of one man's reading of the situation but of
an aggregate of visions. Doubtless the United States could have
prevented the Munich capitulation, and Roosevelt saw it should be
prevented; but if he expressed it as a private opinion instead of
throwing the weight of his nation in the balance, it is presumably
because he felt that the nation's mood did not allow him to do so.

What appears as a glaring mistake in a game of strategy may be
a natural outcome of a psychological context which "gaming" ig-
nores, and vice versa. The last war would have been won by Germany and Japan had the latter power attacked Russia instead of
making the capital blunder of outright aggression against the
United States fleet. It was so obviously good strategy for Japan to
make sure that Russia was counted out, and so obviously a bad
move to bring in the United States, that the unraveling of the
psychological motives for such conduct should be very instructive.

There is a political context to strategic situations; situations
which are much the same in strategic terms are very different in
political terms. Taking it as a datum that, throughout the period
considered, the United States has been interested in precluding
the spread of communism in the Indo-Chinese peninsula, we note
that in 1954 American aircraft carriers were in the Gulf of Tonkin,
available to the American President for an air strike. In the spring
of 1954, great results could be hoped for from an air strike at
Dien-Bien-Phu. Results then likely (not of course certain) were:
the French army saved, Giap's army (then offering a concentrated
target) crippled, the State of Vietnam (not then partitioned) re-
lieved for a time from communist pressure, and communist infil-
tration in Laos and Cambodia precluded. President Eisenhower
decided against making the air strike which might have had such
consequences; an air strike was made in early August 1964 when it
held out no such promises. In terms of strategy, it cannot be explained that it was done in 1964 rather than 1954. It has to be
explained in political terms; not of course in terms of formal politics, for an air strike in 1954 would have been made at the request
of a formally sovereign state on its own territory against those who

were formally rebels, while the air strike of 1964 was made against the territory of a sovereign state. The explanation is not then to be sought in "politics" understood as "public law." The explanation is to be sought rather in terms of a far different emotional context.

Explanation and a fortiori prediction are impossible in politics without understanding of affective attitudes. "The springs of politics are the passionate movements of the human heart," says Cournot.[11] Tragedy is meant to display the swiftness and amplitude of such movements, a lesson which statesmen forget to their undoing. It so happens that France in early 1848 had for Prime Minister an eminent political scientist, indeed the restorer of our Academy of Political and Moral Sciences, François Guizot. A rare feature in France, the parliamentary opposition acknowledged a leader, Louis Thiers, who was a distinguished historian. Neither of these men had an inkling of the revolution which was to sweep away the regime in a few days of February. What is more, neither of them took seriously the massing of a crowd on February 22—a crowd which indeed, according to students of those fateful days, showed as yet no signs of violent excitement.

Up to the last moment these eminent men did not foresee the revolution, and had they been told that within a few years Louis Bonaparte would be Emperor, they would have taken it as a joke. Now let me add that the history Thiers had written was that of the Revolution and Empire. He was familiar with such events as were to be repeated, but he must have felt, "It can't happen now"— another version of "It can't happen here." This instance stresses that *the political forecaster must guess how people will come to feel* (my seventh point) and also that this is no easy thing.

To this concern the study of public opinion corresponds, but it may be asked whether adequate attention has been paid to the dynamic of moods.

VIII

Consider "the body politic" as a vast army "making its way" in a literal sense; this raises a variety of problems, to be foreseen by a variety of social scouts, the political scientist a coordinator, wary

---

11. A. Cournot, *Traité de l'enchaînement des idées fondamentales dans les sciences et dans l'histoire* (Paris, 1861), para. 460, p. 525 of the 1911 edition.

of mix-ups which would generate excitement and anger. Such is
the rough sketch of the picture which has been presented in the
preceding sections. This so emphasizes policy expertise as to be
possibly shocking, relative to the established idea that the political
scientist is an expert on *institutions*. But far from there being a
conflict between the two conceptions, on the contrary the role of
the political scientist as detector of problems breathes life into his
role as student and designer of institutions.

Institutions are of instrumental value, good insofar as they efficiently cope with problems arising, and operate toward the achievement of social goods. If the machinery of government proves such
that no timely action can be taken to ward off some visibly impending harm, a vice in the institutions can be presumed. Of
course I do not mean that *any* bad policy is proof of bad institutions; none are so excellent as to exclude the possibility of foolish
decisions. What I do mean is that frequency of failure to cope or
achieve is a judgment upon what is in essence a coping-and-achiev-
ing machinery and nothing else.

Now this is precisely where institutional expertise is needed.
Left to itself, public opinion will be apt to reject the whole system,
throwing away what is good therein—and thus, for instance, turn
from a "government by discussion" regime which is not working
well, to a more efficient tyranny. It is for the institution's expert to
indicate the more modest adjustments required. But, as a forecaster on how people will come to feel (point seven), he must be
aware also that by the time public opinion has been aroused
against the inefficiency of the system, its disposition will be to
repudiate it altogether, so that minor adjustments, however well
they might serve, will not be acceptable to it. These therefore must
be made before the public has been aroused; and this is no easy
thing, as the public does not then demand it and the wielders of the
government machinery bask in complacency.

Indeed the political scientist should foresee the deficiencies of
the institutional system not only before these have excited popular discontent and brought it into discredit, but even before
these deficiencies have been made manifest by faulty performance. For this purpose he will rely to a considerable degree
upon the assumed stability of social trends, ask himself how
their estimated course will alter the demands made upon the
"coping machinery," seek to assess its adequacy to such differ-

ent demands, and thereupon look for the adjustments which can improve such adequacy.

To be sure, social change by itself has a direct impact upon the institutional machinery and tends to weaken or atrophy some institutions, to strengthen or hypertrophy others. Such direct impact may happen to work toward an improvement of the machinery: but it would be most unwise to take this as a postulate. Quite the reverse can be the case.

I do not propose to develop here my eighth point: *the political scientist should foretell the adjustments suitable to improve the adequacy of the institutional system 'to cope with changing circumstances.* Of the different points made here, this is the only one which is sure to be accepted by all; therefore the case for it need not be argued. If it comes here as the last point, it is because the institutional preoccupation is made most meaningful when derived from more immediate and concrete preoccupations. The future inflow of public business, its increasing volume, its new varieties, must be vividly pictured by the expert: only thus can he recommend adjustments in the public machinery, adequate to a liberal democratic handling of heavier and shifting burdens.

Any maladjustment enhances attitudes which amount to regarding political and private freedoms as conflicting with progress. It is for rulers who alone are far seeing, to lead their people in the way of progress, untrammeled in their decisions by lengthy discussions, and riding roughshod over individuals: such is the immanent doctrine sugar-coated in different ideological colors. This nefarious doctrine is rendered plausible thanks to the fact that the ancient bulwarks of liberty are often used as defensive fortifications by the very people who would in previous times have opposed their erection, and the character of such defenders provides an argument for the flattening out of these bulwarks. It seems a most urgent preoccupation for people committed to political forecasting to see what can be done for the progress of liberty in a materially progressing society, the features of which could not be imagined in the seventeenth and eighteenth centuries.

On the Evolution of Forms of Government

INTRODUCTION

The present mood of western opinion offers a conjunction of economic optimism and political uncertainty. During the fifties of this century, there occurred in western Europe a widespread awareness that the material condition of the common man and his life span had improved and were improving: such recognition was sharply demonstrated when the French Communist Party found its own followers unreceptive to the "doctrinal truth" that the proletariat undergoes progressive pauperization; this they knew to be untrue. Further, this improvement has been understood as coming from a continuous improvement in the productivity of labor; therefore it is not as if betterment for the many had its sole source in redistribution of a-once-for-all limited amount of wealth: it rests mainly upon the proven capacity of modern societies to get successively a greater abundance of goods from a given amount of work. The progress of energy procurement, of techniques, and of organization on which successive enrichment rests are accelerating rather than slowing up. Thence considerable confidence that, in the long run, the standard of life of the common man will improve further and further. And this confidence is now so solidly grounded that no temporary economic setback could shake it.

Knowing from experience that a low current standard of life can be remedied through the improved use of human effort, we feel therefore that the living conditions obtaining for the great number in the so-called "underdeveloped countries" can be remedied, and therefore ought to be remedied. About this we feel hopeful.

"On the Evolution of Forms of Government" is reprinted from *Futuribles,* vol. 1, ed. Bertrand de Jouvenel (Geneva: Droz, 1963). Used by permission of the publisher.

Our euphoria when we consider the economic future has no counterpart when we consider the political future. It is not only that we envisage the possibility of a disastrous conflagration (this I propose to leave out of account), but also that we have lost confidence in the general progress of mankind toward the best political institutions.

The disparity between our economic optimism and political uncertainty seems paradoxical. It exposes us to the question: "Does not your supposition of continuing and diffused economic improvement carry the implication that the political institutions will be such as to allow such betterment? So that in fact, you do assume political institutions, *good in this respect?* What more then do you ask for?"

This is a pregnant query. It leads up to two questions. One: when we suppose economic progress everywhere, we must realize that this belief implies that everywhere political institutions will present at least the qualities which permit such progress, that they will be instrumentally good with regard to this purpose. If we make this assumption, and still feel worried about the nature of political institutions, then we must make it clear what qualities we would demand of them, besides their capacity to promote material progress.

We have to realize that our worry about the political future lends itself to a very unfavorable interpretation. A Communist might analyze our attitude as follows: "Your Liberal forerunners had no doubt concerning the inevitable development everywhere of the institutions they deemed the best. You feel unhappy that you have lost such sanguine assurance. You ask yourselves whether the institutions which you regard as the best will spread to the countries where they do not obtain, and sometimes you even wonder whether they will endure in your own countries where they are more or less established. Such doubts and anxieties are indeed a new thing in progressives: but at all times they have been characteristic of Conservatives. If you are economic optimists, it is because, in that realm, you accept and welcome the trend of evolution. If you are, face the word, political *pessimists,* it is because, in that realm, you have tied your affections to outdated institutions, and are trying to buck the trend."

Our standards of self-criticism do not permit us to disregard such an attack. It is indeed possible that the forms of government which we were taught to regard as the best are superannuated. In five centuries of European history we have moved from custom-bound monarchy to absolute monarchy, thence to constitutional monarchy and from there to parliamentary democracy. Why should this be the *terminus ad quem,* the ultimate regime? There may be a better one. And thus we answer the communist critic: "Show us a better regime!" Here is the rub! The communist *militant* may praise the present political regime of communist countries: the communist intellectual would never be so incautious. The present political regime of Russia, he would say, is nothing but an ungainly scaffolding meant to serve the purpose of an economic and social change, necessary to achieve this transition, not desirable in itself. Therefore our finding them intolerable is quite irrelevant to the true problem of the political institutions of the future.

Let us play fair and accept that while the present political institutions and practices of the Soviet Union seem to us very undesirable by comparison with our own, yet the Soviet Union may move on to institutions far superior to our own. Which and how? This it seems legitimate to ask! As we get no answer, we turn to Marx: and in his works we find unmistakable indications that the political regime to be attained is a liberal democracy decentralized in the extreme. An excellent goal! But one which implies no originality relatively to our own objectives. The originality then resides in the way of reaching it. The claim is that private property applied to means of production disables us from achieving so excellent a regime, while the abolition of such private property solves the problem, bringing about the withering away of the centralized State with its coercive apparatus. Almost half a century after the Bolshevik revolution, and that is a long time, we see no sign of such withering away, and no indication that Russia has progressed very much toward the political goal of Marx, from which it stands notably further away than we do.

And thus we are caused to answer our communist critic: "You have nothing to show us which would at all validate your claim that there are better political institutions than those we cherish." This I say in no contentious spirit. I have little doubt that many of our fellow intellectuals on the other side of the Iron Curtain are worried about the political forms of the future, deeply disappointed that the abolition of private property has not led to the political goods which were supposed to flow therefrom. I think, or hope, that the day will come when a dialogue untainted by propaganda will arise between them and ourselves on the great theme of political progress.

As against the idea that the institutions we praise have "fallen behind the times," as was just discussed, there is another idea which has wide currency nowadays, and which stands in direct contrast to the former. "Your representative democracy is all very well for highly industrialized and rich countries, which can afford the luxuries of individual freedom and exhaustive discussions. But all this does not suit poor and struggling nations." This is a quite ludicrous argument which would not deserve notice were it not that one hears it so often. Athens was not industrialized in its days of direct democracy, nor were the thirteen colonies of America when they decided to rule themselves according to the representative system!

If representative democracy is not faring well today, the fact is not to be explained in such simple terms as that: "It is too late (or too early) for such institutions." The situation cannot so summarily be dealt with. It requires serious examination.

THE SHATTERING OF POLITICAL OPTIMISM

On the morrow of the first world war, Edward Beneš, then Foreign Minister of the newborn Republic of Czechoslovakia, thus eulogized the results of the war: It had "progressively become an episode of mankind's grandiose struggle for the progress of democracy in every realm of human activity"; it had finally "destroyed four great absolutist Empires,[1] three of which have turned into Republics, while the fourth, the Habsburg Empire, had given way to six new national States"; "It has swept away dynasties, the political preponderance of the aristocracy and the military, all remnants of the *ancien régime*"; he emphasized that "political institutions have been made democratic in all the new States and in the previously absolutist or only semi-democratic States; the dynastic notion has received a fatal blow; a number of new Republics have been born; not only have the aristocracy and the military lost all influence, but the last strongholds of feudalism have been de-

1. The German, Austrian, Russian, and Ottoman empires.

stroyed by agrarian reforms; the control of the Executive by parliamentary assemblies has been reinforced."

In short the war had indeed "made the world safe for democracy"
by bringing forward all states to the same form of government, and
such homogeneity of national institutions afforded a good working
basis for an international organization, all the members of which
professed the same principles and practised the same procedures.

To this international organization Beneš was to devote tireless
energy. But he was to see first the shift of an increasing number of
states to fascist or at least authoritarian forms of government,[2] the
paralysis of the League of Nations, a second world war, and he was
to afford in person a tragic illustration of disappointed expectations, since he fell twice, in 1938 and 1948 (and with him the
independence of his country), a victim to politics of brutal intimidation from two different sources.

I was privileged in my youth to live for a long spell with this
virtuous man, as if I had been his own son. He often discussed
Russia: while very sympathetic to its leaders, he deplored that their
regime was not shaping conformably to his ideal, but felt not the
least doubt that it would in time. As he saw it, parliamentary de
mocracy was the preordained *terminus ad quem* of political evolution. All of Europe had been inevitably moving toward that goal;
outdated prestiges had impeded the movement more or less effectively in different countries: they had to be overcome either gradually or at one blow, but, this being done, parliamentary democracy
was sure to come into its own, though there might be a short period
of revolutionary excess of power as a transition. Deeply convinced
that parliamentary democracy was the best form of government, he
felt no less assured that it was the one form of the future, and that
any other which appeared was a counteroffensive of the past,
doomed to failure.

We can today be faithful to the value judgment of Beneš: it is
hard to feel confident of the factual forecast which went with it. In
1936 Sir Austen Chamberlain expressed sadness in the following
terms:

> Consolidate democracy in the world! Was there ever a
> more striking illustration of the vanity of human aspirations

2. For example, Kemal, Pilsudski, the reassumption of authority by King Alex-
ander of Yugoslavia, and so on.

than the denial inflicted to this slogan by the history of post-war years! Of all the major Powers, only the United Kingdom, the United States and France have upheld their democratic traditions. Add the Scandinavian countries, Belgium, Switzerland, the Netherlands, and the present list of democracies is closed. Everywhere the parliamentary regime has fallen. We live in an age of dictatorships.[3]

To the testimony of a practical politician let us add that of a deep thinker, Elie Halévy, who, almost at the same time, presented to the Société Française de Philosophie a paper entitled: *The Era of Tyrannies*.[4] Quoting in part, Elie Halévy said:

The era of tyrannies dates from August 1914, from the moment when the belligerent nations adopted a regime which can be characterized as follows:

(*a*) from the economic angle, extensive *statification* of all means of production, distribution, and exchange; appeal of governments to union leaders for support in such statification, and therefore corporatism as well as statism.

(*b*) from the intellectual angle, statification of thought, assuming two forms: negative, by suppression of all unfavourable judgements, positive by what may be called the systematic organization of enthusiasm.

It is from this war regime, far more than from Marxist doctrine, that all post-war Socialism derives. The paradox of post-war Socialism is that it recruits adepts who come to it from hatred of war and disgust with it, and that it proposes to them a programme which consists in maintaining a war regime in peace time.

Let us to stop to admire the felicity of this formula: "maintaining a war regime in peace time," before we go on:

The Russian Revolution, born of a revolt against war, has organized, consolidated itself under the form of "war com-

---

3. I quote from an article published by Sir Austen Chamberlain in *L'Intransigeant,* October 14, 1936. I am sorry that I could not turn back to the English original, and merely "Englished" the French version.
4. The Halévy paper was presented at a meeting of the Society on November 28, 1936. I have used the form "statification" to render the French "étatisation." Cf. Halévy's book *L'Ère des Tyrannies* (Paris: Gallimard, 1938), pp. 213 ff.

munism" in the two years of war with the allied armies which cover the period from Brest–Litovsk to the ultimate victory of the communist armies in 1920. A new trait should here be added to those defined above. Because of the anarchic breakdown, the disappearance of the State, a group of armed men, inspired with a common faith, has decided that it was the State: Sovietism under this form is literally nothing but "Fascism" (Halévy 1936).

Halévy's historical acumen stands out in that, while speaking at a time when fascism was triumphantly advancing, he started from the Russian "tyranny" which he pointed to as the major and initial phenomenon, the fascist regimes being in his view derivative. He was of course attacked for grouping the communist regime with the fascist regimes under the generic name of "tyrannies": it was stressed against him that communism had a higher purpose. This, he answered, is not the question, we are discussing political regimes: who can deny that the political regimes are the same? Also he insisted that the name of *tyranny* was the suitable designation, the word not being used loosely as an insult but in a strictly scientific spirit: the Greeks coined it to designate arbitrary power, the holders of which claim to use it for the people and in fact appeal to the people, for support. Moreover, he stressed that while nationalism was the basis of fascism, and socialism that of the Soviet regime, yet fascism moved to socialism and communism to nationalism. "On the one side as well as on the other, the same conjunction of a proletarian ideology with a military ideology. Work camps. Labour Front. Battle of this or that. And the regime itself cannot be defined otherwise than a permanent state of siege, under the control of militias inspired by a common faith" (Halévy 1936, 245).

It was brought out in the discussion that socialism and nationalism, though historically associated with the progress of liberalism, both contained strong illiberal potentialities. But even though Halévy, for his own part, made much of the authoritarian streak of socialism, he refused to father upon Marx the form of government to be found in Russia. In his view it was the experience of the first world war which had "revealed to men of revolution and action that the modern structure of the State puts at their disposal powers almost without limit" (p. 249).

Of many interesting contributions to the discussion, far the most important, in my view, was that of the anthropologist Marcel Mauss, hereafter quoted in part:

> Your deduction of the two Italian and German tyrannies from Bolshevism is quite accurate. . . .
> The fundamental doctrine from which all this proceeds is that of "active minorities" as it prevailed in the anarcho-syndicalist circles of Paris, and especially as it was developed by Sorel, when I left the *Mouvement Socialiste*[5] rather than participate in his campaign. Doctrine of the minority, doctrine of violence and even corporatism were propagated under my eyes, from Sorel to Lénine and to Mussolini, as all three have recognized. . . .
> I lay greater emphasis than you do on the fundamental fact of secrecy and conspiracy. I have long lived in the circles of the active Russian P.S.R.; while I had less to do with the social-democrats, I well knew the Bolsheviks of the Parc Montsouris[6] and indeed I have lived with them somewhat also in Russia. The activist minority was a reality there: it was an unrelenting conspiracy. This went on through the war and under the Kerensky Government which it finally vanquished. But the form of the Communist Party has remained that of a secret sect, and its essential organ, the Guépeou, is the combat team of a secret society. The Communist Party itself remains camped in Russia, as the fascist and Hitlerian parties also camp, without artillery or fleet, but with a police apparatus.[7]

This statement focuses upon the decisive trait of twentieth-century politics. Here we start with a small group of men who dedicate themselves to the overthrow of the existing order. They wholly withdraw themselves, unless it be for camouflage purposes, from the peaceful pursuits of their contemporaries; they lead unattached lives; neither affective ties nor moral norms of any kind are allowed to impede their action; robbing, murdering, and lying are fully justified by the end sought; nor have they any scruples about

5. *Le Mouvement Socialiste* was a periodical.
6. The Parc Montsouris is a public garden of Paris where the Bolsheviks in exile used to foregather.
7. *L'Ère des Tyrannies*, pp. 230–31.

appealing in their difficulties to the sentimentality of the principles of those they wish to conquer. In short they try to benefit from the rules of peace to wage their war held to no rules at all. But further, when they have achieved victory, they do not disarm but "camp," as Mauss admirably put it, in conquered territory, maintaining the mores which afforded them their triumph. It is relevant to cite Sorel's regret that the barbarians who had conquered the Roman Empire allowed themselves to be civilized.[8] What all this calls to mind is the application to domestic politics of the spirit of Cortèz or Pizarro: ruthlessness to win, but the same ruthlessness when it comes to holding. In fact one might describe this attitude as extreme colonialist imperialism applied to one's own country.

This war spirit stands in direct contrast to that of constitutional liberalism. It is a principle of constitutional liberalism that any group may drive for a reform or bid for power, but such driving or bidding has to be done openly and according to well-known rules of the game. The activists are guilty in fact when they violate the rules, and they are sinful in purpose since they propose to repudiate the principle of free driving or free bidding once they have conquered.

It is true that the history of liberalism is rife with conspiracies, to which historians have imparted a dangerous glamour. Conspiracy can indeed be regarded as legitimate insofar as no opening is afforded for change pursued by open, public and peaceful means. Secrecy is then necessary, but the disregard of moral norms is unwarranted. Further, and far more importantly, men who have banded and armed to establish constitutional Liberalism, must logically disarm and disband when the constitution is put in vigor. If they sought to retain monopolistic control, this would be in direct contradiction to their proclaimed purpose of establishing a free competition of opinions and ambitions. Human nature being such that we do not readily obey the logic of our own principles, things did not always work out that way, but triumphant liberal conspirators, when clinging to power, felt at fault; not so twentieth-century conspirators.

I have dwelt at some length upon the discussion initiated by Elie Halévy in 1936, because it seems to me to formulate most clearly the political transformations we are faced with.

8. Georges Sorel, *Réflexions sur la Violence* (Paris: Librarie de "Pages libres," 1908), p. xl.

1. Modern war has proved that the energies of a whole people can be impressed in the service of a government purpose, provided opinion is managed, opposition silenced as treasonable, enthusiasm systematically fostered.

2. This has created a great opportunity for men fired with a purpose of social metamorphosis, or national grandeur, or both.

3. The condition requisite to take advantage of this opportunity is to regard the people as a conquest to be made and held by any means whatever, for their own good of course. Formal authority is to be thought of as a stronghold to be seized and made impregnable. Political participation is to be thought of as the recruitment of a vast network of auxiliaries, ceaselessly stirring up individual citizens in the interests of the public purpose.

4. The new tyrants have a new justification for unlimited and uncontrolled power: it is required for the fulfilment of purpose. Purpose is in fact the sovereign in whose name commands are uttered. However, the tyrants also claim that their regime is more truly popular than that of liberal democracies, since in the latter the rulers owe their position to the mere vote of a mere majority, while, in the tyrannic regime, every citizen in his daily business displays an active concurrence in the purpose of the community.

Be it noted that in the foregoing catalog "Marxism" does not figure at all. It is true that the tyrannical form requires an ideology, but it is obviously wrong to regard it as uniquely associated with what now passes as "Marxism": we have seen and will see non-Marxist tyrannies. Not only is the identification mistaken but it stultifies the very critique of Marxist tyrannies, which is then diverted to a largely irrelevant critique of Marxism, away from a more promising critique of tyranny.

It is our main problem that constitutional democracy, having cleared away the remnants of monarchic authority and aristocratic influence, has been successfully challenged by an unexpected, vigorous, and awful competitor: tyranny. While the most dangerous, tyranny is not, in our day, the only competitor of constitutional democracy, there is also caesarism. Caesarism is Hobbesian, not totalitarian. It has this in common with tyranny that it brooks no limit to or control of its authority. But it differs significantly from tyranny in that it distinguishes a public realm wherein Caesar is supreme and a private realm wherein citizens are left to their own choices, while tyranny requires that men in their daily lives should be inspired by the public purpose. In the *Pactum subjectionis* of caesarism, the citizen gives up his public role but retains his private freedom, while under a tyranny he must ceaselessly give proof of his civic spirit. Under caesarism public opinion is dulled, under tyranny it is stirred up and channeled. At worst, caesarism requires of us a passive "faith" in Caesar, while tyranny requires that our "work" prove our dedication to the purpose of the tyranny, as defined by its leaders.[9]

Both these regimes claim to be democracies. According to their leaders, not only do they govern "for the good of the people" (a principle of all governments, not specifically democratic), but they exercise their authority in the name of the people, they draw their powers from the people (recourse to universal suffrage) and wield them with popular approval (attested in the case of caesarism by way of referendum, in the case of tyrannies by a stream of applauding resolutions voted by gatherings of citizens). Now the word *democracy* is so ambiguous that contesting this denomination would lead us into a semantic discussion, which is quite unnecessary.[10] We have no doubt that such regimes are bad. When we talk of democracy, we have in mind something quite different which I shall call by an old name: constitutionalism. Our trouble is that we now feel uncertain about the spread of this excellent regime to countries where it does not obtain, and ill-assured of its maintenance in some of the countries where it does obtain. Why? What has gone wrong?

A RETROSPECTIVE OF CONSTITUTIONAL DEMOCRACY

It would obviously be unwise to embark here upon a description of constitutional liberal democracy: either I would form a composite

9. For a different formulation of the contrast, cf. Robert Waelder, "Authoritarianism and Totalitarianism," in *Psychoanalysis and Culture,* ed. George B. Wilbur (New York: International Universities Press, 1951).
10. While revising this paper, a book has come to hand which quite competently describes the various meanings attached to the word *democracy:* Giovanni Sartori, *Democratic Theory* (Detroit: Wayne State University Press, 1962). See also my paper "What is Democracy?" in *Democracy in the New States* (Rhodes Seminar Papers) (New Delhi: Office of Asian Affairs of the Congress for Cultural Freedom, 1959).

image from the features of different countries, and it would be blurred, or I would form a clear archetypal image, and it would be too simple and probably very subjective. But it does seem relevant to our preoccupation to recall certain dominant features; and, for this purpose, I shall make use of the grossest, most unscholarly historical review. While this must be a mortal sin in the eyes of a serious historian, others will forgive me on the plea that I am merely substituting for reality a simple model building.

1.   A man of our time cannot conceive the lack of real power which characterized the medieval king,[11] from which it naturally followed that in order to secure the execution of a decision he needed to involve other leaders whose say-so reinforced his own. Whatever the unsuitability of analogies and the scandal of anachronism, it seems to me not unmeaningful to refer to the president of AFL-CIO in the United States of today and suggest that he wants to make a decision to be carried out by all industrial workers. He has not the least chance of success unless he calls together all the leaders of important unions (lords) and a representative sample of people influential with the lesser unions (knights), and gets them after discussion to concur with him in the promulgation of the decision. Even so, he may run up against the effective defiance of some great lords (e.g., the Teamsters Union).

2.   The *State* is quite a modern word, reflecting a major innovation in European structure; the rise of a disciplined *apparatus* of state servants, available to carry out and enforce the decisions of the ruler. I must say that I deem it a cardinal blemish of political science that so little attention has been paid and so little emphasis laid upon the rise and development of the apparatus. No matter in what hands it is placed, and in what name it is exercised, public authority is the more independent of its subjects the stronger its apparatus.

3.   The modern state arose under monarchic rule. It could not have been otherwise: the despotic spirit of barons had to be curbed by a strong and constant will. True, Northern Italy, which was far ahead of the rest of Europe in material civilization and intellectual

---

11. I plead guilty to the absurdity of speaking of "the medieval monarch" as if there had not been many highly differentiated "ages" in the so-called "Middle Ages."

culture, had republics: but they were doomed by factional strifes; one by one they slipped under Caesarian rule. Monarchic rule could confer its benefits only if there were no struggle for the Crown. It is telling that three great and glorious countries, which had a system of elective monarchy, in turn lost their independence: Hungary, Bohemia, and Poland. It is clear that the so-called "Salic" rule of succession, firmly established in France at the beginning of the thirteenth century spared the country the equivalent of the English Wars of the Roses. It is absurd to regard hereditary monarchy as based on theology: it was a prudential rule which served its purpose.

4.   An unquestioned and effective authority can do much good: but also much harm. How to prevent the latter? The spiritual power, the Church, had been tireless in its exhortations against the misuse of power. It is easy to forget that it was dealing with barbarian chieftains, to emphasize the evils it did not prevent or even condoned, and to under-estimate the good it did.[12] But however much good it had done in the Middle Ages, it was afterwards disabled from controlling the absolute kings, by the moral disaster of the religious strifes.

When the Church was divided in the sixteenth century, both sides vied with one another in urging monarchs to take, for religious interests, measures which the united Church would previously have, with one voice, condemned as abominably oppressive. However much it is stressed that the duty of government is to protect the rights of subjects, the power afforded to protect can always be used to injure, and at no time have rights been quite safe. But there is a world of difference between misbehavior of the rulers which all moral authorities condemn, and offensive behavior of the rulers, authorized, incited, demanded by moral authorities. This sin has been repeated in our own day by part of the secular intelligentsia: it was then a sin of the clerical intelligentsia (even worse in men of God) and, whatever the outcome of the struggle, whatever form of Church triumphed locally, the spiritual authority in temporal matters was discredited.

12. Need I point out that when we, today, describe the proper spirit of magistracy, we use formulas of ecclesiastical origin: "for the good of the people," "according to well-known rules," "after having taken the best counsel," and so on. Turning power, potentially a beast of prey, into a watchdog, is always the same problem.

5. While the royal administration was developing its capacity to serve the nation, it was indispensable to find practical devices precluding the royal authority from arbitrary practices.[13] Let me begin with a device that failed: the French *veto* of the judiciary.

English being nowadays the main medium of the noncommunist world, it is hard to remember that the abandonment of the Latin medium (largely due to the Reform) had cooped up English culture in the seventeenth century. Very few foreigners understood English and even fewer visitors to England troubled to master it,[14] while French was fast becoming the international medium as the language of the greatest power.[15] English thinking and English events were known abroad only through translations or relations in French, and they were known quite unfavorably. The political writings which were circulated in France, and thence in Europe, were those of James I and to a greater degree, of Hobbes. Different though they were, they were deemed of an excessively despotic bent. It seemed in keeping with their tone that the English Revolution against Charles I, which was regarded with horror, eventuated in the excessive power of one man.[16] The first efforts to control the increased royal power in France thus owed nothing to English inspiration.[17] Of what nature were these efforts?

The great lords of France had ever opposed in a disorderly manner the rise of the administrative state. They were not foresighted enough to accept the "nationalization" of their regional powers and to seek a collective restraining authority upon the exercise of a centralized authority in exchange for the loss of their

---

13. The expression once current in America "an economic Bourbon" implies a total misunderstanding of the character of the Bourbon Administration, which was active, interfering, dynamizing, concerned with road and canal building, with the implanting of new industries, the planning or replanning of cities. While often balked by resistances, its reforming and progressive character is clear to any reader of administrative documents.

14. See that admirable work of erudition: Georges Ascoli, *La Grande-Bretagne devant l'Opinion Française au XVII*ᵉ *siècle*, 2 vols. (Paris: J. Gauber, 1930).

15. See Ferdinand Brunot: *Histoire de la Langue Française*, T. VIII (Paris, 1887).

16. And that even by the "Frondeurs." It is characteristic that an *Histoire des Troubles d'Angleterre* (Monteth de Salmonet, Paris, 1649), which was very hostile to the revolutionists, was dedicated to "Monseigneur l'Archevêque de Corinthe," that is, to the man who was soon to play a very important part in the Fronde, and who is now remembered as the "cardinal de Retz."

17. Such inspiration can be said to begin with the translation of Locke's "Essays on Civil Government" in 1691.

individual autonomous powers. After the collapse of the Fronde, they were systematically mustered in the resplendent "concentration camp" of the Court, where they had no function but were available to worry the ministers, who almost always were earnest men of humble origin.[18]

The effort to build up a restraining authority came from the judiciary. The judges of Paris sat (as they still do) in the ancient Royal Palace; though the great number and variety of causes had brought about a multiplication of chambers, this division of labor within the judiciary body did not impair its traditional unity. It was a "sovereign company" which had formerly sat with the king himself, the members of which "talked over" with the king the sentence to be uttered: and therefore the company retained the name of *Parlement:* there were twelve other such in twelve different French towns. The attributions of the Parlement gave it immense potential power.[19] No royal ordinance or bursary edict went into force until it had been registered by the Parlement, which had the right (and, as the Parlementaires preferred to put it, the duty) of remonstrating to the king that the measure was ill-advised: this could be used as a suspensive veto. Resolutions were voted by the Parlement, messages came back from the ministers, giving rise to new resolutions and so on until the King sent *lettres de jussion* which were a command to register, itself often laid aside.

Being the only check to what was called (with much exaggeration) "ministerial despotism," the veto of the Parlement became very popular. A good thing in principle, it was not always so good in practice.[20] It contributed to the popularity of the Parlement that it opposed obdurately, blindly, any new taxes, an attitude which drove the monarchic government to worse and worse financial

18. The duc de Saint-Simon's memoirs display the resentment of the nobility against Louis XIV's "long reign of the ignoble middle class," the author's efforts to restore a political role of the grands seigneurs, and also his discouragement caused by their incapacity.

19. No royal appointment took force before it was registered; actions by officials could give rise to injunctions and impeachment.

20. Also it seemed admirable to see men, without any weapons but their robes and awareness of their dignity, stand up to the might of a great monarch, and this with the utmost politeness: indeed they forever urged that it was out of respect for the king who can do no wrong that they could not let through a measure unsuitable to the royal character.

expedients. It did even worse: it turned down a number of excellent reforms, in particular it balked and destroyed Turgot.[21]

For this reason the *philosophes* were of two minds regarding the *Parlement,* liking it as an obstacle to discretionary power, disliking it as a stumbling block of enlightened administration: many of them, indeed, came out for "enlightened despotism."

6. The conjunction of an active administration with a vigilant, but understanding and flexible controlling power had not been achieved in France. The attitude of the parlementaires was far too juristic, they had little understanding of the substantial requirements, there was practically no communication between them and the ministers, the physical distance between Paris and Versailles being an image of the lack of common ground. Moreover their attributions bade them intervene at too late a stage. A far happier combination of activity with control had been achieved in England. Though himself an eminent parlementaire, and though praising the role of the institution to which he belonged, the President de Montesquieu found in England the model of a good political system. His account thereof is sketchy and Delolme's is far more comprehensive.[22] The Genevese writes:

The Doctrine constantly maintained in this Work, and which has, I think, been sufficiently supported by facts and comparisons drawn from the History of other Countries, is that the remarkable liberty enjoyed by the English Nation is essentially owing to the impossibility under which their Leaders, or in general all Men of power among them, are placed of invading or transferring to themselves any branch of the Governing Executive authority; which authority is exclusively vested, and firmly secured, in the Crown. Hence

21. The battle was joined on two main Edicts of Turgot which were evidently good. One of them abolished the *corvées,* that is the obligation of laborers to contribute a limited number of days of work to the building and upkeep of roads, and substituted a land tax laid on all proprietors. The other abolished the *jurandes,* that is the self-government obtaining in a great majority of trades and professions, and whereby access to any such activity was controlled by those presently exercising them, which, among themselves, saw to it that no one of them "spoiled the trade."

22. Delolme's book was originally published in French in 1771. I quote from the fourth English edition of 1784: "*The Constitution of England or An Account of the English Government, in which it is compared, both with the Republican form of Government, and the other Monarchies in Europe,* by J. D. Delolme, advocate, member of the Council of the Two Hundred in the Republic of Geneva."

the anxious care with which those Men continue to watch the exercise of that authority. Hence their perseverance in observing every kind of engagement which themselves may have entered into with the rest of the People.[23]

Delolme argues that the unity of the executive power is necessary for its efficiency, and that it must be placed beyond the reach of factional strife: so far, he follows Hobbes. But immediately he goes on to add: "The Executive Power is more easily confined when it is ONE."[24] This, at first sight, seems untrue, nor is Delolme blind to the perils of tyranny. His argument is that if the power of one is always visible in the same seat, if it cannot be transferred or divided, then it happens as it has occurred in England:

[T]he indivisibility of the Public power in England has constantly kept the views and efforts of the People addressed to one and the same object: and the permanence of that power has also given a permanence and regularity to the precautions they have taken to refrain it.

Constantly turned towards that ancient fortress, the Royal power, they have made it, for seven centuries, the object of their fear; with a watchful jealousy, they have considered all its parts—they have observed all its outlets—they have even pierced the earth to explore its secret avenues and subterraneous works.

United in their views by the greatness of the danger, they regularly formed their attacks. They established their works first at a distance, then successively nearer, and, in short, raised none but what served afterwards as a foundation or defence to others.[25]

Every member of the Legislature plainly perceived, from the general aspect of affairs and his feelings, that the Supreme executive authority in the State must in the issue fall somewhere undivided, and continue so; and being moreover sensible, that neither personal advantages of any kind, nor

23. Chapter 17, p. 387 of the edition cited.
24. Title of the second chapter of Book 2.
25. Op. cit., 217–18.

the power of any faction but the law alone, could afterwards be an effectual restraint upon its motions, they had no thought or aim left, except the framing with care those laws on which their own liberty was to continue to depend, and to restrain a power which they, somehow, judged it so impracticable to transfer to themselves or their party, or to render themselves independent of.[26]

According to Delolme, the English were wise enough to recognize it as an inevitable fact that the actual business of government is always in the hands of a few,[27] or one; that no few or one should ever be trusted blindly; that those actually governing should be jealously watched; that such watching is the easier the more unchanging the seat of power and the source of possible excesses; and that the watch is best kept by those who have no hope of assuming the very powers they have to control. It does seem that Delolme had clearly perceived the practical principles of English institutions since his reading almost perfectly suits the description of the institutions set up by the American Founding Fathers. Indeed L'Enfant's ground plan of the town of Washington, setting up the White House and the Capitol on rival heights, illustrated the idea.

7. However important the sweeping *social* reforms brought by the French Revolution, it certainly afforded no useful political innovation. The assemblies which successively exercised sovereignty were bullied by small cliques and terrified by the increasing irruption of blustering petitioners. It all ended up in Caesarism: the dreaded *Conventionnels* turned to abject *Tribuns* praying Napoleon to establish a hereditary Empire, arguing that in the same manner the crown had been transferred by the nation from the Carolingians to the Capetians!

Thus, after the fall of Napoleon, the eyes of all progressive-minded men were turned to England more than ever. An ardent spokesman of liberalism, the abbé de Pradt could in 1821 point to

26. Op. cit., pp. 437–48.
27. Delolme, in Book 2, chapter 5, proves an early theoretician of "political activism." He explains how a popular assembly is inevitably managed by "the few who are united together" and "can at all times direct, at their pleasure, the general resolutions," an oligarchy the worst for its being occult.

the successes of revolutionaries in Spanish America, to the obtention of a constitution by Brazil, and exclaim that the whole of the continent was following in the footsteps of the United States, obtaining independence and establishing a constitutional order.[28] Such an order was established already in one half of Europe, but Europe could not subsist half slave and half free; the constitutional order must apply everywhere: it was sure to come!

As Pradt saw things, the holding of regular parliaments caused the whole intellectual life of the nation to reflourish. He wrote:

> Formerly the regular recurrence of legislative assemblies was peculiar to England. Now the same feature is established in France, in the states of Germany, and throughout the south of Europe. Every new meeting of political assemblies renews, as one might say, civil life itself, infusing into it a new activity, sometimes giving it a new aspect. Both London and Paris do not seem the same whether Parliament is sitting or not; in either city, there is a thousand times more life during sessions than in between. Held in the season when nature is stilled, these meetings seem devised to draw the mind away from such immobility, and turn it to the notions of stirring and growth.[29]

Here is enthusiasm indeed! Almost we are moved to think of the end of the session as the dismemberment of Osiris and the opening as the rebirth of the God! But men must have that sort of feeling for their institutions if these are to flourish and endure. Their mere rationality does not suffice to inspire the loving respect which procures allegiance; and those who operate them

---

28. Pradt (born in 1759) had a most eventful life. In 1789 he was a deputy to the States-General (thereafter Constituent Assembly). He emigrated in 1791. He was one of the members of the aristocracy whom Napoleon inducted in his service, became the Emperor's chaplain, a bishop, and an archbishop after his success in conducting in 1808 an unsavory negotiation with the King of Spain. He was Ambassador to Warsaw, then disgraced, took part in the Restoration of Louis XVIII, was great chancellor of the Legion of Honor. Fortunately for us he was soon dashed from such eminence and thereafter turned out in rapid succession a great number of books dealing with current developments in Europe and America, books which constitute the first series of "Surveys of International Affairs."

29. Abbé de Pradt, *L'Europe et l'Amérique depuis le Congrès d'Aix-la-Chapelle* (Paris, 1821), vol. 1, 19.

must bring to it the purifying awe of participation in sacred rites, if they are to display the *pietas, auctoritas, gravitas,* required in public magistrates.

It was that sort of sentimental, indeed mystical, belief in parliament which procured the geographic diffusion of the institution during the century which followed Pradt's eulogy. A century marked by the sinking or disappearance of monarchic prestige, a century marked also by the powerful development of the French metaphysic of popular sovereignty, which up to a point served the heightening of parliamentary power but was just as apt to destroy it, since this sovereignty might be delegated to One or a Team.

In that century, constitutionalism changed a great deal. When Tocqueville published in 1835 the first part of his *Democracy in America,* he compared the position of the American president with that of a constitutional monarch in Europe, and found the royal power much greater than the presidential. Among the many points of superiority of the constitutional monarch he found some which were of a legal, others which were of a practical character.

On the first score he stressed[30] that both president and king were entrusted with the execution of laws but that the king could veto laws while the president could not;[31] that the king could nominate members of the upper house, not so the president; that the king could dismiss the lower house, not so the president; that the king shared legislative initiative, not so the president; that the king was represented in parliament by his own agents who expounded his views, argued for his opinions, and advocated his maxims of government, while the president and his secretaries were excluded from Congress.

On the second, practical score, he pointed to the great number of public servants owing their mandate to the executive power: "This number has, in our country (France), passed all known precedents, it has risen to 138,000. Each of these 138,000 appointments must be considered as an element of strength. The president has not the absolute right of appointment to employments the total number of which does not exceed 12,000."[32]

De Tocqueville went on, with great prescience, to suggest that

30. After noting that the presidential power is related to that part of sovereignty which is federal, while the king's power is related to national sovereignty.
31. Of course I reproduce Tocqueville's views as formulated.
32. *Democracy in America,* First Part, chapter 8.

the presidential power increase in time.[33] He did not suggest that the monarchic power would decrease in Europe. In fact, while the American president grew to be a full-sized constitutional monarch, the constitutional monarchs of Europe disappeared or became mere figureheads, the independent executive vanished from the European political map.

The acting chief executive was in fact the prime minister, or president of the council, who formed a team of ministers, drawn like himself from the ranks of parliament, and this government endured in office as long as it held the favor of parliament. This was in fact an executive commission of parliament, which sat well with the powerful idea of popular sovereignty. This sovereignty, entrusted to parliament, and more and more exclusively to the lower house, popularly elected, was delegated in part to an executive at all time dependent upon its grantor.

So great a shift in the system would have been regarded with horror by the constitutionalists of the late eighteenth or early nineteenth century. Sharply aware of the dangers of power, they felt that its holders should be watched over jealously by assemblies wherein mistrust of government was an institutional feature. Now it would be unnatural in members of a house to feel such mistrust toward some of their own colleagues, temporary occupants of executive offices, from which they can be recalled when the house so

---

33. "If the executive is less strong in America than in France, this is perhaps to be explained more by circumstances than by the nature of the laws.

It is mainly in relationship to foreign States that the executive power of a nation finds occasion to display its skill and strength.

If the life of the Union were constantly threatened, if its major interests were involved daily with those of other powerful nations, the executive power would have enhanced prestige, because of what would be expected of it and because of what it would actually do.

It is true that the President of the United States is head of the army, but it is an army comprising 6,000 soldiers; he commands the fleet but the fleet numbers only a few ships; he controls the Union's affairs in relationship to foreign countries, but the United States have no neighbours. Since they are separated from the rest of the world by ocean and are too weak as yet to have control of the seas, they have no enemies, and their interests only rarely come into contact with those of the other nations of the globe.

This clearly illustrates that the practice of government should not be judged theoretically.

The President of the United States enjoys almost royal prerogatives which he has almost no occasion to use, and the rights he has been able to exercise hitherto have been severely circumscribed: the law allows him to be strong, but circumstances keep him weak."

chooses. Constitutionalists would have said that such a relationship was sure to abolish the vigilance of the legislature and to favor the development of executive powers, which in time would lead to a recovery of predominance by a now untramelled Executive.

Such indeed was the development in England thanks to party organization.[34] A general election which gives the majority to a party, at one and the same time establishes the leader of the party at 10 Downing Street, and gives him in the House a majority which will steadily back him on every occasion. It seems strange that so much was made in Walpole's day of his mustering votes by the promise of personal advantages, while so little is made nowadays of the threat to the backbencher that he shall lose the party label and his seat at the next election if he fails to support his government on a voting day. It would be both insulting and untrue to regard voting discipline as obtained mainly through such intimidation: such discipline has come to be regarded by members as a moral duty, which I regard as a deplorable change in the conception of a representative's duty.

In France the older conception endured longer, according to which the individual member owes it to the nation, of which he is a representative, to side on each issue as his best personal judgement bids him to. Any good principle can be appealed to in favor of conduct which is not inspired by the highest motives, and I would not say that the French freedom of voting was always used according to the dictates of conscience, but it did have a strong moral basis, too often overlooked. Therefrom followed the multiplicity of groups and the easy shifting from one to the other. In consequence, the man called upon to form a government had to assemble a team which could win a vote of confidence; he had to accept on a footing of equality colleagues who might leave him if they disagreed with a government decision; the executive had therefore a collegial character. The President of the Council lived

---

34. M. Ostrogorski, in his famous work *La Démocratie et l'Organisation des Partis Politiques*, 2 vol. (Paris: C. Lévy, 1903), described the rise of party organization in Britain, the Chamberlain-Schnedhorst drive to control the Liberal members of Parliament. Whatever their past services members calling themselves Liberals were requested, before standing again, to make an act of submission to a self-appointed committee which required of them disciplined voting in the Commons. Thus, while the control of the country was increasingly entrusted to the Commons, the control of members of the Commons was being monopolized by a small outlying clique. Surely this was a turning point in political history.

in fear of losing decisive votes, which led him to respect minority opinions.

The French system is said to have worked disastrously; to this I cannot agree. The Third Republic worked reasonably well until it encountered the challenge of the Depression, which economic prejudices did not allow it to counter effectively: in foreign and military affairs, French governments of the thirties proved inept, but not more so than British governments. The great weakness of the system was the ridicule cast upon it by the frequent falls of cabinets, but only because so much was made of them: if one counts the "separation rate" of ministers from fallen cabinets and the "accession rates" of new ministers in the incoming cabinet, one finds that throughout such falls a great stability was maintained: this was no more change than the reshuffling of a national football team over a period. The danger which threatens such a system, as the event has proved, is caesarism.

But then there is also a danger inherent in the British device of party control of the legislature, a danger perhaps incapable of being activated in England, or in countries with a population of English origin and tradition, but most serious when the system is transferred elsewhere. What indeed, other than moral reasons, is to hold back a government quite assured of an absolute majority in the House from governing oppressively? And the temptation is great to "rig" the following election so as to permit the development of tyranny: the Hitlerian tyranny started with party control of the Reichstag.

Thus the development of parliamentary democracy in its British and French varieties offered openings toward tyranny and caesarism. This should be noted, but it should also be stressed that, as such, parliamentary democracy worked reasonably well: indeed its performance in both countries up to 1914 may be called brilliant. It was then naturally taken for granted that this was the regime of the future, and even some Americans looked toward it.

THE DECLINE OF PARLIAMENT

Today there are very few countries, other than Britain, without a written constitution. But on the other hand, there are very few countries, other than the United States, where the constitution is known and cherished by every citizen. Parliaments are to be found in a great many countries; but as to their being the vital center of public life, the cases are fewer; and fewer again the cases of parliaments observing a self-discipline sustaining their moral character and influence. Constitutions and parliaments have to a surprising degree become mere hulks: reality does not correlate with what is written down in the constitution, and the speeches delivered in the House are without echo or consequence.

How has such a state of affairs come about? Where am I to seek data, and of what kind, to study such "emptying of content"? This I found a puzzling problem until it suddenly dawned upon me that practically all the men who played active roles in Europe after the second world war (the Nazis offering a notable exception), or in Asia and Africa after the second world war, had shared in the intellectual life of Paris or London, either during their formative years, as students, or later in life as refugees. It then occurred to me to wonder whether I could not find in the Parisian and Londonian intelligentsias some propensities which had led to the disfavor of constitutionalism. And finally I asked myself whether my own involvement in such discussions, during the interwar years, did not make me a witness to such propensities. Obviously no individual's set of conversations can be congruent with another individual's, and there must be a subjective tinge in the testimony as to what "people" talked about.

While international organization was discussed with eagerness and passion (but this falls outside my subject), as far as I remember domestic political institutions were never mentioned: parliamentary democracy was taken for granted. All the discussions I remember (other than those centered on the League of Nations) bore upon social and economic progress. To give our preoccupations their later names, they were social security, full employment, planned growth, generalized education. Indeed they are most aptly summarized in the statement attributed to Confucius: "When the Master went to Wei, Jan Chhui acted as driver of his carriage. The Master observed: 'How numerous the people are!' Jan Chhui said: 'Since they are thus numerous, what more shall be done for them?' The Master replied: 'Enrich them.' Jan Chhui said: 'And when they have been enriched, what more shall be done?' The Master said: 'Educate them!' "[35]

Successive improvement of the average worker's condition was

35. *Lun Yü*, XIII, IX. Quoted in Joseph Needham, *Science and Civilization in China* (Cambridge, Eng.: Cambridge University Press, 1956), Vol. 2, 9.

our central preoccupation. Even then, enough statistical information was available to prove that the most complete redistribution of existing incomes could have made but an insignificant contribution to our object. We were sharply aware that overall production was inadequate to procure the average standard of life we deemed decent; even the provision which we felt should be made immediately for the handicapped and the burdened could not be rendered adequate if we did not press forward toward more production. Convinced as we were that there "was not enough to go around" we had been deeply shocked by the 1920 crisis of "overproduction." Most of us were familiar, to different degrees, with Edgar Milhaud's gigantic *Enquête sur la Production* (done for the International Labor Office), which displayed the inadequacy of world production. "Overproduction" was therefore to us, as it has ever remained to me, a sinful word, camouflaging sheer mismanagement.

A most scandalous consequence of mismanagement was unemployment. This we saw as a cause not only of material want but of moral humiliation: a man is degraded in the eyes of his family if he cannot support it, he is degraded in his own eyes if he has to go round humbly begging for a job. We deemed it essential to the dignity of the worker that he should be sought after, that a condition of full employment should obtain. And to this day I cannot read without revulsion learned dissertations on the "adequate ratio of unemployment," apt to slow down price increases.

Not only full employment but increasingly productive employment. Of course we had a sentimental bias against "capitalism" and delighted in "exposures" of capitalist misbehavior. Nonetheless we felt the merits of a market economy and the advantages of enlisting personal interest in the service of general welfare. Our attitude was reformist rather than revolutionary. What we asked of the system was that it should "pay off" in a rising standard of life. And we deemed it indispensable that public policy should stimulate and guide economic development. Therefore, of course, we were enraged by the Great Depression and the inadequacy of policy reactions to it.

It would be irrelevant to say more.[36] One may indeed ask in

---

36. Otherwise valueless, my little book of 1928, the title of which coined the expression *L'Economie Dirigée,* may acquire some interest as revealing a state of mind.

what manner what I have said is relevant to my present theme. I shall now make it clear. Of all the objectives we had in mind, only one, social security, could be achieved *by means of law,* and even then the measure of its implementation must depend upon the general progress of the economy. Full employment and economic growth were objectives which could not be achieved by the promulgation of once-for-all edicts but only by the ceaseless *adjustment of policy* to their attainment.

It is telling that of all the western states who, after the second world war acknowledged full employment as an imperative, one only, the United States, wrote it into law.[37] But it is a very strange sort of law, in that it gives no definite instructions for the attainment of its stated object. I am no jurist and my understanding may be faulty, but I expect an act of legislation which prescribes, to prescribe well-defined conducts, in short, *routines,* so that those to whom the command is specially addressed can be said to obey the law if they conform to the stated routine, and to disobey it if they do not. In some minor part, the Employment Act of 1946 follows this model: it creates a new body, the Council of Economic Advisers and definitely instructs it to report once a year to the President. This, no doubt, is a good thing in itself, but, by itself it does nothing to achieve full employment. This achievement requires government moves which remain undefined in the Act, and must perforce so remain, since the suitable actions depend upon circumstances.

It was said in America in the early 1960s that "Prosperity cannot be legislated." True, and the same holds of full employment and uninterrupted economic growth. But if they cannot be legislated, they can be managed. This suffices to explain a major shift in political institutions. If there are important goals of government which should be achieved, and if the ways to achieve them cannot be boiled down to routines prescribed by the legislative to the executive, then *the law is consequently devalued and the executive upgraded.*

Inevitably situations must arise wherein the executive points to some existing laws as impediments to the attainment of the policy goals, and the legislature must then choose between revoking such

37. The Full Employment Act of 1946. Stephen K. Bailey, *Congress Makes a Law* (New York: Vintage Books, 1950); also Bertram Gross, *The Legislative Struggle* (New York: McGraw-Hill, 1953).

laws or placing itself in the position of a stumbling block to the achievement of generally desired objectives; more than that, if the executive is to remain straitly bound by laws, then the legislature must respond to every demand of the executive for new adjustments of the "straitjacket" required to permit the moves which present circumstances call for. This means at the very least that legislative initiative passes to the executive. It further implies that a proud and independent legislature, unwilling to be rushed, may, by its very virtues, seriously handicap the attainment of generally desired objectives.

Such, as it seems to me, is the situation which has arisen of late in the United States, and I find it most worrying. The U.S. Congress is the only parliament, as far as I know, which is not "led" by the executive. Affectively I am very much in favor of its retaining its independence, I greatly admire the high sense of dignity of its members, and indeed, to me, seeing an American senator is the way to understanding a Roman senator. But the fact cannot be balked that the care taken by Congress to tie down the executive by bonds of law is on many occasions most inconvenient. And here is a problem.

Locke's ideas do not fit the present situation.

> [I]n a constituted commonwealth, there can be but one supreme power, which is the legislative, to which all the rest are and must be subordinate. . . .
> But because the laws that are at once and in a short time made, have a constant and lasting force, and need a perpetual execution, therefore 'tis necessary there should be a power always in being, which should see to the execution of the laws that are made, and remain in force.[38]

This power which "sees to the execution" is conceived as "subordination," a subordination stressed in the choice of its name: "the executive." A significant and momentous denomination. An executioner is a man who kills, pursuant to the sentence passed by another; an executor is a man who conveys property, pursuant to the last will of another; generally in law, execution is the carrying out of a judgment passed by others. Similarly the executant of a concerto, though he bring to its performance the genius of Menu-

---

38. Locke, *Second Essay on Government*, paras. 149 and 144.

hin, still is performing faithfully the design of another, the composer. No doubt is permitted that such was the conception of Locke: the legislative designs, and the executive performs.

Now such a conception is tenable if, and only if, the legislative can provide a set of instructions so adequate that the executive need not (and should not) do anything but follow them. This then is completely "government by laws alone." At no moment do subjects obey anything but the laws, which the executive magistrates are carrying out. Characteristically, foreign affairs have been excluded from this model by the most rigid champions of government "by laws alone." It was acknowledged that in this sphere the executive had to cope with the unexpected, to vary its designs on account of incoming information, and that it should therefore have freedom of decision, discretion.

In domestic affairs, by contrast, it was assumed that a good architecture of laws could cover all situations likely to arise. Significantly, it seemed sufficient that the legislative should sit once a year, nor was it deemed useful that the same men should be called to the lower house with any continuity (the two-year term of American Representatives is a remnant of this ancient viewpoint). It was postulated that substantial and earnest citizens knew enough, while journeying to the capital, to devise in concert adequate instructions to their executive magistrates. Reasonable laws were deemed to require no special information, but only a thoughtful understanding of human nature: a very sound view, but while laws so devised are a necessary *basic* framework of society and check to arbitrary government, they are quite inadequate to provide a complete set of instructions for the executive magistrates, and the more inadequate the more rapid the transformation of society.

The faster the pace of change, the more difficult it becomes to provide the executive magistrates with a complete set of instructions for their future operations. If this is to be done, then the lawmakers must be sharply aware of changes in progress, and so devise their instructions that they will prove salutary relative to new situations and problems arising or apt to arise. This requires much more than common sense, it calls for a great deal of information and careful assessment, for want of which legislators may pass laws which seem to do some present good and prepare great future harm (e.g., the French rent control acts).

As it is in the nature of things that the government first encounters the new situations and problems, therefore also it is within the government that the measures to cope with them are designed, and slowly, very slowly indeed, governments have set up agencies[39] to foresee and to prepare forward-looking measures. It naturally follows that laws are written within the executive and submitted to the legislature. This still is, in a not unimportant sense, government by laws, but surely they have lost any claim to the capital letter. This or that law is necessary, says the executive, to implement our general policy objective or to cope with this or that specific situation or problem. The executive writes its own instructions and parliament has a veto, like the *Parlement de Paris,* which it may also misuse, misunderstanding what the present trend requires.

The dominant position of the legislative was linked to the dominant position of the law. Obviously the position of the law declines if instead of asking in a given situation: "What does the law allow me to do or require me to do?" one asks: "Given that such situation, such outside pressure, or such intention of ours calls for a certain conduct, what law do I need to authorize and require it?" The "modern" regimes had been devised to tie down the active power, they were pictured as nomocracies where the law, made independently of the active power, prescribed and circumscribed its operations. Quite different must be telocracies, where the active power, pursuing objectives in changing circumstances, demands from the legislature ad hoc rules as required to implement policies.

The point I wish to make here is not that such a shift from nomocracy to telocracy had happened to any great degree in Britain or France during the interwar years, but merely that the views which were then "in the air" all militated in its favor. At no time did one hear in the political discussions of intellectual circles any

39. The U.S. Congress is the only parliament which has had the wit to set up its own expert bodies to check the findings of the experts serving the executive. Indeed there is more to be said: Westminster (and the same was true of the Palais-Bourbon when it was still throbbing) uses the same plant and the same auxiliary personnel as it did when the whole of the executive was housed in a few buildings and employed but a tiny fraction of its present personnel. The U.S. Congress alone has enlarged its plant and auxiliary personnel. Even in Washington, however, the physical growth on Capitol Hill is insignificant compared to the growth of executive departments and agencies.

complaint that the government was inadequately controlled or restrained, but on the contrary complaints that it was inadequately
enterprising and active: complaints which of course rose to fever
pitch when governments did nothing to combat the Depression[40]
and showed no reaction to the challenge of Hitlerism.[41] Historians,
I think, will agree that the inept governance of these years was not
due to the resistance of parliaments but to the mere ineptitude of
the executive leaders, and in part to their fear of the electors.[42] But
in any case the demand of public-minded circles was in favor of
more initiative and vigor in the executive. Therefore the impression made upon youths from other countries, steeped at that time
in the atmospheres of Paris or London, was that the thing to want
was a strong driving executive. There was nothing in the then
prevailing climate to make them value a "jealous" parliament,
keeping the executive on a short leash.

But more than that, the "Idea of Parliament" seemed to have
lost weight in the minds of members themselves. Sitting in the
House, whether at Westminster or at the Palais-Bourbon, was
indeed an object of eager desire. But such a position was less and
less desired for the dignity, activity, and responsibility which it, by
itself, implied; and increasingly as a prerequisite of access to semi-
ministerial and then ministerial office. The English expression
backbencher has an unpleasant and ominous sound. It conveys the
impression that the man "back there" is awaiting advancement,
promotion by steps, to the ultimate full glory of the front bench.

Here is a very complex problem. It is beyond doubt that the

40. An anecdote is to the point. In the winter of 1932–33 I was urging upon an
eminent French senator the absurdity of pursuing budgetary equilibrium in the face
of a Depression. He told me: "But surely budgetary equilibrium is a rule, and we
have to see that rules are observed."
41. A very striking example was of course the lack of reaction to Hitler's remili-
tarization of the Rhineland, on March 7, 1936. As this was a violation of the
Locarno Treaty, France was entitled to take immediate military action and to call
upon Britain to implement in kind the guarantee it had given under the Locarno
Treaty, and such behavior would have put a stop to the Hitlerian adventure.
However, the French Government chose to go to London and ask Britain what it
was prepared to do to implement its guarantee, and the answer being "Nothing,"
the French Government itself did nothing.
42. In the aforementioned case of March 1936, what caused the fatal hesitation
of the French Government was that general elections were to be held at the end of
the Spring, while Sir Austen Chamberlain told me on the evening of March 7 that
the British Government would not take action because there was no popular feeling
to support it: he did not for a moment suggest that the obstacle lay in Parliament.

body which exercises control over the active power gains very much from the previous executive experience of its members, and it is relevant to stress that the Roman Senate was formed of men who, each and everyone, had held executive magistracies. Lack of such executive experience is a defect in a parliament. But on the other hand, the judicial majesty of the controlling body is much impaired if its members aspire to positions in the executive whose judges they are. Walpole had been taxed with corruption of the legislature through the offer of executive jobs. The French National Assembly had decided that none of its members could accept an executive position not only during the legislature but for a subsequent period of four years (April 7–8, 1791). Of course there could not be the same reasons for such a prohibition once the executive was not regarded as alien to the legislature. But the fact remains that while parliamentarians look forward and look up to ministerial positions, by implication they look down upon the "mere" position of member of parliament. I am not concerned here to pass judgment upon the system, but only to point out the devaluation of parliament inherent in the attitude described. Already in my youth, a representative deemed himself unsuccessful, and was so adjudged by his electors, if he had not been called to some ministerial office. This certainly implied that the executive was a greater thing than Parliament, and such an implication could hardly inspire foreign spectators of the system with that profound respect for Parliament as such, which had obtained at an earlier stage.

I am not concerned in this section to criticize the evolution of parliamentary democracy, but merely to bring out that the current attitudes and practices in London and Paris, and the intellectual moods there obtaining, were not apt to imprint upon the minds of alien visitors a clear picture of a majestic controlling power, but rather to convey to them an impatience with the lack of dynamism of the active power. Far be it from me to suggest that the climate described, by itself, was propitious to the fostering of tyrannical tendencies! All I mean is that it was inadequate to imbed into minds a wholesome concern for restraints.

The lesson which foreign visitors must have derived was that general elections to a lower house were a means of conveying to it the full sovereignty of the people, the exercise of which then fell to the government, which thus had a popular mandate. This was an *authorizing* view: now add to this an ideology, which brings a *demanding* view; add the notion of a "sect" devoted to the ideology and seeing to it that the government serves it; and we are well on our way to tyranny, which however also demands a certain brutal-mindedness. There are thus many other components indispensable to tyranny other than the mere depreciation of control.

EVOLUTIONISM AND CONSTITUTIONALISM

I propose to examine the relation between liberalism and evolutionism. I shall first show that in the preevolutionist stage of thought, there was no political optimism, but rather the reverse; that liberal doctrines were mooted independently from any evolutionism, but that optimism as to their triumph was aroused by the stirrings of evolutionism; that, however, evolutionism is no warrant of political progress as we understand it.

Our earliest authority, Plato (to whom we owe in *The Politics* the definition of the three "pure" forms of government, where decisions are respectively taken by One, the Few or the Many), stressed the inherent tendency of any good form of government to change into its corrupt and harmful variety, requiring the shift to another good form of government. Polybius attributed the impressive success of the Romans to their "mixed" form of government. All the great Latin authors, however, writing at later dates, described and mourned the corruption of the republic which had finally caused its fall to Caesarism. The theme of *institutional deterioration* was absorbed by Europeans from ancient literature.

Aristotle had stressed that the institutions he, after Plato, was discussing were those of the *polis,* which should be of limited size: "If comprising too few, it would be incapable of self-defence and that is essential; but if made up of too many, then it is a nation, not a *polis,* and it is almost incapable of constitutional government."[43]

This emphasis on size provided the basis of what we may call *The Dimensional Law of Political Forms,* which was developed in classical Europe, and which can best be introduced by a more general statement, quoted from D'Arcy Thompson:

> [Galileo] said that if we tried building ships, palaces or temples of enormous size, yards, beams and bolts would

43. *Politics,* Book 7, chapter 4.

cease to hold together; nor can Nature grow a tree nor construct an animal beyond a certain size, while retaining the proportions and employing the materials which suffice in the case of a smaller structure. The thing will fall to pieces of its own weight unless we either change its relative proportions, which will at length cause it to become clumsy, monstrous and inefficient, or else we must find some new material, harder and stronger than was used before. Both processes are familiar to us in Nature and in art, and practical applications, undreamed of by Galileo, meet us at every turn in this age of cement and steel.[44]

Both Montesquieu and Rousseau have made famous statements of the dimensional law of political forms. Montesquieu's occurs in Book VIII of the *Spirit of Laws,* where he says bluntly:

It is in the nature of a republic that it should have but a small territory: else it cannot subsist as such [chapter 16]. . . . A monarchic State should be of limited extent [chapter 17]. . . . A great empire requires a despotic authority in the ruler [chapter 18]. . . . If it be the natural condition of small States to have a republican government, that of the middling States to be ruled by a monarch, and that of great empires to be under the domination of a despot, it follows that in order to conserve the established form of government, the State must retain the same size; and its spirit must change as its limits either shrink or expand."[45]

Montesquieu took little care to offer proofs of the dimensional laws, which, in his formulation, seem based mostly on the extent of territory. Rousseau's formulation, which refers to population, is far more careful and precise. As his demonstration covers a large part of Book 3 of *The Social Contract,* I must summarize it. A citizen bears two figures: he is a subject entirely bound by the laws; he is also a member of the sovereign people, which is the sole legitimate author of laws, and in this second quality, he is coauthor

44. D'Arcy Wentworth Thompson, *On Growth and Form* (Cambridge, Eng.: The University Press, 1942), p. 27. The reference is to Galileo's *Discorsi e Dimonstrazioni matematiche, intorno a due nuove scienze. . . .*

45. My own translation; the same holds true of other quotations from French authors.

of the laws that bind him. But what is the measure of his coauthorship? One-ten-thousandth if the sovereign people comprises ten thousand citizens, one-tenth of that if the body rises to a hundred thousand citizens, and so on. Whatever the number of the citizens, the individual as subject always bears the full burden of the laws, but as the number of the citizens increases, his part in the making of laws declines to a vanishing point where he ceases to value his diluted share of sovereignty, and comes to regard himself only as subject, burdened by laws, which he no more recognizes as the expression of his own will. As awareness of personal participation in sovereignty thus wastes away, so does the sense of personal responsibility for the enforcement of laws, and the greater the need for and the role of enforcing agencies of government. "Thus the Government, to be good, must be the stronger, the greater the number of the people."[46]

Rousseau then goes on to ask what is conducive to the strength of the government. He argues that if the governing authority is entrusted in part to a large body and allocated in parts to a variety of special authorities, a great deal of the energy of these many governors will be spent on agreeing between themselves and combining their moves, and the less energy will be available for the total action of government upon the subjects. And he comes to his conclusion: "I have just now proved that government is the weaker the more numerous those sharing therein, and I previously proved that the more numerous the people the greater the repressive force needs to be. It follows that . . . the greater the number of the people, the fewer must be the chiefs."[47]

No writer ever stated more clearly than Rousseau that true popular participation in government requires a small community, that in a large state it is a myth; that men in a large state are in fact, and must inevitably be *subjects,* on which score he of course rejected the large state as incapable of a good form of government; just as Aristotle had said. Observing that the historical trend was toward the large state, he felt that it was away from a morally good form of government.[48]

Most liberal writers accepted the dimensional law, started from

46. Book 3, chapter 1.
47. *The Social Contract,* Book 3, chapter 2.
48. Cf. my essay, "Rousseau the Pessimistic Evolutionist," *Yale French Studies,* 28 (Fall–Winter, 1961–62): 82–96.

the admission that the individual citizen in a large state could not personally participate in the exercise of sovereignty, was in fact a subject and that his interest lay chiefly in the guarantee and development of this civil liberty.

Such was the position taken by Benjamin Constant in his famous lecture of 1819, "The Liberty of the Ancients Compared to that of the Moderns" (my own translation):

> Let us first ask what it is that an Englishman, a Frenchman, a citizen of the United States of America, in our day, understand by the word *liberty?*
>
> It is for each one the right to be subject only to the laws, the assurance of being neither arrested, nor detained, nor put to death, nor in any way mistreated, by an arbitrary act of will of some one individual or of many. It is for each one the right to express his opinion, to choose his occupation and ply it in peace; to dispose of his property, be it abusively; to come, to go, without any permission and without rendering any account of his motives or steps. It is for each one the right to assemble with other individuals, either to confer with them upon common interests, or to practice the religion of his choice, or merely to use his leisure conformably to his inclinations or indeed to his fancy. Finally it is the right of everyone to exert some influence upon the administration of public officers, be it by contributing to the choice of all or some officials, be it by making representations, petitions, requests, which authority is more or less bound to take into account. Now to the liberty thus described, let us compare that of the ancients.
>
> It consisted in the collective and direct exercise of many parts of sovereignty: in deciding in the public places on issues of war and peace; in including with foreign states treaties of alliance; in voting laws; passing judgments; examining the accounts, the actions, the performance of public officers; in citing them before the whole people, accusing them, and condemning or absolving them. This, all this, was comprehended in the term *liberty* by the ancients. But in the meantime they regarded as compatible with this collective liberty the complete subjection of the individual to the authority of the whole. You will find among them practically none of the

enjoyments that, as we have seen, are inherent to liberty among the moderns. All private behaviors are subject to a severe watchfulness. Nothing is granted to individual independence, whether it be in the realm of opinions, occupations, or especially of religion.

Thus among the ancients, the individual, while he was habitually sovereign in public affairs, was a slave in his private affairs. As citizen, he decided on peace and war; as private man he was circumscribed, spied upon, repressed in his every movement. As a part of the collective body he interrogates, dismisses, impeaches, despoils, banishes, condemns to death his public officers or superiors; as subjected to the collective body, he may in turn be shorn of his status, stripped of his dignities, banished, put to death by the discretionary will of the whole to which he belongs. Among the moderns on the contrary, the individual, independent as to his private life, is, even within the freest commonwealths, sovereign only in name. His sovereignty is a power almost ever in abeyance; and if, at some infrequent and fixed moments he is allowed to exercise this sovereignty, in a way that is carefully specified and limited, it is only to commit it to others.

The idea that modern liberty was something new had already been advanced by Sismondi:

We shall never sufficiently stress that new theories on liberty have been invented in our times, that our philosophers, seeking to assess its consistence, have aimed at a goal widely different from that of the ancients; that the liberty of the Greeks and of the Romans, of the Swiss or of the Germans, as well as that of the Italians, was in no way that of the English; that, in short, up to the eighteenth century, the liberty of the citizen was always thought of as a participation in the sovereignty of his country, and that it is only the example of the British constitution which has taught us to think of liberty as a protection of the security, the happiness and the independence of daily life. . . .

The Italians, knowing only political liberty, and having no precise idea of civil liberty, we should not be astonished to find them calling free government that which admitted no limit to the powers exercised in the name of the nation. The citizen exposed to arbitrary measures, did not regard himself as less free, if the arbitrary act which victimized him came from a magistrate which he could regard as his mandatory.[49]

Whatever the historical accuracy of the Constant–Sismondi theme, the emphasis is unmistakably upon civil rights and their guarantee,[50] which is understandable enough after the excesses of the French Revolution, and the domination of Napoleon, accredited by plebiscite. As a consequence of such emphasis, a liberal constitution was thought of not as a means of "incarnating the sovereignty of the people,"[51] which could lead, through the theory of mandate, to tyranny or Caesarism, but first and foremost as a guarantee against abuse of power, in whatever hands it lay.[52] A mixed form of government was thought to afford such a guarantee, together with an independent judiciary. And the constitution affording an elected Parliament openly discussing public affairs, since civil liberty comprised the right to utter and propagate opinions, it was felt that the citizens had thereby ample opportunity to

49. This appears in vol. 10 (p. 330) of my 1840 edition of Sismondi's *Histoire des Républiques Italiennes du Moyen Age.* I have not checked whether it had appeared in editions anterior to Constant's lecture.

50. Cf. Daunou's important, *Essai sur les Garanties Individuelles* (Paris, 1819). Therein the great jurist, who had actively participated in public life throughout the Revolution and Empire, maintaining at all times a striking independence, gave a valuable definition of tyranny. Having recalled that the basic, fundamental function of public authority, not the only one, but to be sure, the very first and most essential, is to secure persons against the aggressions of others, he goes on to say that tyranny obtains whenever and wherever the public authority commits on its own account those very aggressions for the repression of which its powers are primarily meant: violences, spoliations, extortions, outrages; and individual guarantees consist in the commitment of public authority to abstain from such aggressions and in the institutions which in fact force it to renounce them.

51. Benjamin Constant, who had known the tyranny of the Terror and the despotism of Napoleon, wrote:

When you assert that the sovereignty of the people is unlimited, you create and fling into human society a power which is in itself too great, and harmful in whatever hands it falls; entrust it to one, to several, to all, you will find it equally evil. You will then accuse the holders of this power, and according to circumstances, you shall thus arraign monarchy, aristocracy, democracy, mixed government, representative government. You will be wrong, it is the degree of power you have accepted and not its occasional grantees that you should blame. Benjamin Constant, *Principes de Politique* (Paris, May 1815).

52. Need I point out that the weakness of the doctrine lay in the development of a proletariat which, as it was said, "had nothing to lose but its chains."

influence the conduct of public affairs, which could not in fact be in their hands, and therefore should be said therein to reside.

However different the views of Stuart Mill, yet he shared what may be called the "defensive" view of Constitutionalism:

> Among the tendencies which, without absolutely rendering a people unfit for representative government, seriously incapacitate them from reaping the full benefit of it, one deserves particular notice. . . . There are nations in whom the passion for governing others is so much stronger than the desire of personal independence that, for the mere shadow of the one, they are found ready to sacrifice the whole of the other. . . . The point of character which, beyond any other, fits the people of this country for representative government is that they have almost universally the contrary characteristic. They are very jealous of any attempt to exercise any power over them not sanctioned by long usage and by their own opinion of right; but they in general care very little for the exercise of power over others. Not having the smallest sympathy for the passion of governing. . . .[53]

Now for the impact of evolutionism. In the same work, Mill, after mentioning that "government altogether [is] only a means," comes to discuss its functions and here he states: "The proper functions of a government are not a fixed thing, but *different in different states of society: much more extensive in a backward than in an advanced state.*"[54] Here we have in a short sentence, two important propositions: (1) the functions of government (therefore also its form) depend upon the state of society; (2) as the state of society advances, the functions of government recede.

If the second proposition is true, then we can face with equanimity Rousseau's argument that a mixed and composite government in which many share is inadequately strong for a large nation. That may be true in a rude state of society, but Mill suggests that the functions of government recede as the state of society advances; thus a large nation, in an advanced form of society, as it does not then require a great activity of government, does not need an unpleasant concentration of authority: it can enjoy a

53. *Representative Government,* chapter 4.
54. Op cit., chapter 2.

mixed and composite form with ample participation. And this then can be regarded as the terminus *ad quem* of political evolution.

But now let us listen to what Auguste Comte had to say as early as 1822. He makes a statement in full agreement with Mill's first proposition:

> The best minds . . . feel the absurdity of conceiving the political system in isolation, and of regarding it as the origin of the social forces from which indeed it is nourished. In short they recognize already that the political order is and can be nothing but the expression of the civil order, which means that the more important social forces must of necessity become those which direct. There is only a step therefrom to acknowledge that the political order is subordinate to civilization. For, as it is clear that the political order is the expression of the civil order, so it is that the civil order itself is nothing other than the expression of the state of civilization.[55]

This is a plodding way of saying the same thing as Mill, but agreement ceases when we go on to what we have called Mill's second proposition. In the very heyday of liberal theory, Comte attacks these doctrines, which he regards as having had their use in a critical capacity for the destruction of the "feudal and theological system," but as quite useless as "organic principles" for reorganization.

> Government which, in any regular state of affairs, is the very head of society, the guide and agent of general action, is by such doctrines shorn of any principle of activity. Deprived of any important participation in the overall life of society, it is reduced to a purely negative role. Indeed they go so far as to regard the action of the social body on its members as limited to the maintenance of public tranquillity, which has never been more than a minor object, further belittled by the progress of civilization which renders the maintenance of order ever easier.

55. Auguste Comte, *Plan des Travaux Scientifiques Nécessaires pour Réorganiser la Société* (published in May 1822 in an edition of one hundred copies). It appears as the third part of the Appendix of vol. 4 of *Système de Politique Positive*, in 1929 edition, p. 88 of Appendix.

They will not recognize in government the chief of society, with a vocation to bunch[56] and direct towards a common goal all the individual activities. It is represented as a natural enemy, camped in the midst of the social system, against which society must fortify itself by acquired guarantees, holding itself against it in a condition of permanent vigilance and defensive hostility, ready to react to the first symptom of offensive.[57]

Comte then explains how the Government must promote the preordained march of civilization, blithely accepting that the masses cannot be won over by scientific demonstration, but that their passions have to be appealed to:

In the determination of the new [social] system, it is necessary to omit any consideration of its advantages and inconveniences. The main question, indeed the only question should be: "From our observation of the past, what is the system which the march of civilization now tends to establish?" It would be confusing . . . to concern ourselves with the goodness of this system. We had better take it as a postulate that the idea of goodness and that of conformity with the state of civilization [can be identified]. . . .

Thus we can institute truly positive politics, in real harmony with social needs. But while the new system should be determined in that spirit, this is not the best way of presenting it to society for final adoption, as such a presentation is not the most apt to obtain assent.

For the establishment of a new social system it is not enough that it has been well conceived, it is necessary that the mass of society should be impassioned for its achievement. This condition is indispensable to overcome the resistances which shall be opposed by decadent classes. But it is moreover necessary to satisfy this need for moral exaltation which spurs man in a new path. . . .

The only means of obtaining this awakening of passion consists in offering to men a vivid picture of the improve-

---

56. Comte uses the expression "unir en faisceau," which Mussolini was to popularize.
57. Comte, op. cit., 52.

ments which the new system can bring in human condition, under a variety of aspects. . . ."[58]

What all this adds up to is that while Mill regarded social evolution as bringing a decline in government functions, on the contrary Comte regarded it as implying an energetic governmental impulse. We do not have to look far to find out which of the two men was right. Indeed men of our day find it easy to harbor in their minds both Mill's doctrine that the backward nations are not ripe for constitutional liberal government, and Comte's doctrine that it does not cover the organic needs of the advanced nations!

THE NEED FOR DESCRIPTIVE TERMS

When discussing that most ancient problem of politics, the form of government, it comes naturally to draw upon the great authors of the past. Whatever the advantages thereof, there are also important drawbacks. The authors of the past addressed themselves to different circumstances. For instance the Greeks thought in terms of a small township and, what is no less important, they had no idea of a permanent body of professional civil servants. The authors of classical Europe thought in terms of nations which seemed to them far-flung on a vast territory, implying difficulties in holding the commonwealth together.[59] Most of the great liberal authors certainly underestimated the degree of economic dependence of each upon all others which would result from the developing division of labor. Moreover, the prolonged use of the same abstract terms obscures the great shifts which have occurred in their connotations, due not only to material changes but to changes in the affective pictures they connote.

It may therefore be useful to attempt a new start from the conditions we are familiar with. For this purpose I propose to use terms devised to represent phenomena of our own life, which may indeed have also some retrospective value.

When I look at a state in our day, the first thing which strikes me is the very great number of professional public servants who carry out the laws of the legislature and/or the instructions of the gov-

58. Op. cit., 104–105.
59. A preoccupation clear in Montesquieu's formulation of dimensional law.

ernment. These I propose to call the *Agentry*. If we are looking for an evolutionary trend in government, we can find none clearer than the successive development of agentry. From the rude state of Europe which obtained after the fall of the western Roman Empire to our day, the progress of agentry has been irreversible, though, on examination, this progress is found to have been arrested in some periods, precipitated in some others. To my mind, there is no more glaring gap in political science than the want of good histories of agentry.

The growth of agentry has important political consequences. The belief that such growth of itself abridges individual freedom is absurd. There is an obvious increment of what the individual can do if the agentry builds bridges for him, and an obvious increment of what he can do without hazard, if the policing of the streets allows him to walk through them at night in security. It is a clear gain to the individual peasant to have in his neighborhood good experimental stations and good schools. Generally, a well-administered state affords to the individual opportunities which he would not enjoy otherwise, and increases rather than diminishes his freedom of choice. Indeed the agentry can be used oppressively, but it is not oppressive by its very nature. It can validly be claimed that the administrative state is the service state.

The incidence of the agentry upon political liberty is more systematically unfavorable. This is easily proved. Let us assume that public decisions rest only with One, but that this One has no agents to execute his decisions or see to it that they are carried out by the subjects. Then the execution of the decision depends entirely upon the willingness of each and everyone to carry it out. The decision can be carried out only if the unwilling few are carried along by the great willingness of a great majority. Therefore, while the outward appearance of such a regime is monarchic, since the decision is taken by One, its substance is extremely democratic, since the people have it in their power to validate by their actions, or invalidate by their mere neglect, the decision which has been taken. The One, in such a position, can take only decisions to which the great majority not only "consent" but are so agreeable that they will freely lend their energies to their implementation.

Rude societies are naturally democratic because there are no means of procuring the execution of any decision other than persuasion. Their character, now brought out by careful anthropologists, was mistaken by hasty early visitors who saw an honored person, useful to solemnize the proclamation of a command, and did not stop to consider that the substance of the command had to be thrashed out by a prolonged talking-over, making it clear what command, to be uttered by One, was agreeable to all. Where there is no agentry, there is no *government,* in our sense of the word, there is a "sense of the meeting" proclaimed by the chairman.

It is clear by contrast that the more agentry there is, the less the government is dependent upon citizens for the carrying out of decisions, the greater the independence of government. If we ask of modern laws or executive instructions *"Who* is required to do *what?"* we shall find that in a great majority of cases the private citizen is not required to do anything (the command is addressed to public agents), and that when he is so required, watchful public servants urge him to do it, control his performance, and arraign him for noncompliance. In short, specific acts of government are, by increasing reliance upon agentry, increasingly independent of the specific willingness of citizens.

However annoying bureaucracy can be, it would be hard to maintain that many social advantages now enjoyed did not require the development of agentry. And it would be most unfair not to acknowledge that the intellectual and moral standards of agentry in our Western countries are very high indeed. On the other hand it can be claimed that while modern governments have come to rely increasingly upon an ever-increasing agentry with a high sense of responsibility, conversely it has come to rely less upon its citizens and not to expect from them too high a sense of responsibility. This seems to me a general phenomenon of our times. As performance with public regulations is more and more overseen by officials, as management of collective interests is more and more taken over by professionals, the individual feels less a "citizen" and is more prone to act as a "private man."[60] And while this is probably unavoidable, it sits ill with the moral idea of democracy.

As I have said already, though an extensive agentry can be used as a means of oppression, it is far from true that it is necessarily

60. The French have a word for this: we say *le particulier* as against *le citoyen.* The Greeks also had a denomination, but which has with time acquired a different meaning.

such, and indeed the high principles of public servants can offer a powerful obstacle to such use. Nor is an extensive agentry of necessity associated with a strong government. France of the Third and Fourth Republics offered a striking instance of an agentry admirable in its intellectual and moral qualities, indeed the salt of the nation and the backbone of the community, on top of which sat indecisive Governments.

Nor does the government of a large modern state need to be strong, notwithstanding Rousseau's demonstration. A good agentry does not only see to the execution of laws in vigor but also takes care of new situations arising: similar in this to the silver-haired steward of the inexpert heir, it guides ministers in adjustments which are required. The government needs to be strong only when it wants to break down powerful resistances. And this brings us to the subject of notables.

In any conceivable state of society there are men who stand out as possessing some social power or influence. Such in our day are, on the national scale, business leaders and trade union leaders, while there are others in localities. Nothing is more natural for a government than to seek for a national policy the active support of such notables. When the medieval kings called the lords spiritual and temporal to sit with them, advise them, and concur in their decision, they certainly had the purpose of thereby committing these words to the decision reached and obtaining their active contribution to its execution. When Mr. Selwyn Lloyd* conceived the idea of assembling business and union leaders in a National Economic Development Council, he obviously had the same end in mind; that is, to obtain their active cooperation in keeping prices and wages from rising too fast. Any prudent rulers must feel that they can spare themselves unpleasant displays of coercion if they can involve in their objectives notables who are in positions to further the governmental purpose. And it is clear that such involvement requires ceremonious invitation to participate in the shaping of policy. A most masterly achievement of this kind has been French *planification* of the fifties, in which magnificent civil servants managed to obtain the willing cooperation of industrialists and syndicalists.

---

*John S.B. Selwyn-Lloyd (1904–1978), Chancellor of the Exchequer (1960–1962) and Chairman of the National Economic Development Council (1962–1964) in the Macmillan Government (1959–1964)—Eds.

Just as it saves a great deal of force to work through notables, it requires a great exertion of force to break them. Imagine an American President feeling that corporations and unions should be broken. Obviously he could not attempt both at once, but only successively. Moreover he could not attempt either without overpowering Congress. Even in Britain, where power is more concentrated in the Prime Minister, a Labour Prime Minister seeking to destroy the joint stock companies or a Conservative Prime Minister seeking to destroy the unions could not embark upon such ventures without assuming a dictatorial character. We can therefore easily understand that at any time when the government turns against established notables, it requires a great concentration of authority. And thus we can easily understand that while the growth of agentry is a long-term trend, on the contrary the hardening or relaxation of government is a more fluctuating phenomenon. Obviously the government must harden when it takes the offensive against established notables, obviously it can relax when it works with and through established notables. Just as obviously, the government cannot undertake to destroy the notables unless the people are disaffected from them and there are rising social forces which can be used against them; and again obviously, government finds it advantageous to work through notables only if they do have influence and are not unwilling to use it in harmony with the government's purpose.

The worst political situation obtains when the existing set of notables have lost the respect and confidence of the people, and the government uses its power to uphold their positions and attributions. Then that government is bound to perish with the outworn notables to whom it has unwisely tied itself, and triumphant mutiny ushers in the arbitrary power of the boldest. The best political situation is that wherein trusted and diligent notables share the vision of progress which inspires the government, and lend their specific activities and prestiges to the furtherance of a well-inspired governmental policy.

This latter position is of course eminently favorable to representative government, because then the notables, being liked and trusted by the people, are its natural representatives, available to oppose in their assembly those governmental decisions which are bad or inopportune, and not only to approve in a body the good decisions, but also individually to promote in their specific constituencies the active acceptance of these measures.

It is clear that notables are best able to play this useful role if the popular credit they enjoy is currently earned by them, if their present notability is the fruit of current merit and services, and least able to play it if their notability is a crystallized status, not currently deserved, which is not nourished by popular roots which have died out, and is therefore uneasily suspended in the air. Such notables will then inevitably be hangers-on upon the government to which they should be bringing vital forces and to whom they have instead become a burden.

In any society there always occurs a desiccation of some notables who become deadweights, while new notables are surging up from the people; and the government must be attentive to blow its wind upon the old and shine its sun upon the new. A liberal government will take account of all self-made notables, a totalitarian government will want no position to arise which it has not itself made and filled: a major difference! While a liberal government will welcome vital notables and seek to work with them, it must combat their inherent tendency to generate a hard shell around the position they have established, thus securing the position for a succession of men who may not have the same active contacts with their basis: in this respect all "privilege" laws, such as those which now obtain for "fictive persons" (e.g., corporations and unions), are not without danger.

This theme of notables casts much light, I believe, upon the history of parliamentary government in France during the twentieth century. At the beginning of the period, we find both Houses of Parliament solidly rooted in the nation. The men who sat in either the Senate or the Chamber were there because they had achieved local reputations in their constituencies. The senator or deputy was, for instance, a doctor, whose professional services had been appreciated, who had become the mayor of a locality and whose administration had given satisfaction, who had then been elected as a member of a local council,[61] and there again had displayed activity. Not only his name but his face was known throughout the constituency long before he stood for the Chamber or Senate. He came to Paris assured that he understood the disposition of his constituents. Moreover, every weekend he went back to his constituency, which he knew so well that he could rapidly conduct his own "Gallup poll" on any pendant issue.

---

61. *Conseil d'Arrondissement* or *Conseil Général.*

Therefore he did not hesitate to tell the President of the Council himself: "My people, back home, will not stand for this." Therefore also it was well worth the President's while to have a conversation with this individual member, wherein the President tried to convince the member of the merits of the measure demanded by the government. If the member was persuaded, then the confidence he enjoyed "back home" made him an effective propagandist for the measure. He did not only give his vote to it, he promoted popular understanding thereof.

As the French system has been derided, I feel I must testify that French parliamentarians displayed enormous zeal in understanding the wants and dispositions of their people on the one hand, the justifications of government schemes on the other, and were extraordinarily active and conscientious mediators.

These men truly deserved to be called "representatives" since they represented to the government the wants and wishes of the people in their constituency, and represented to the people in their constituency the needs and requirements of government. While they at times impeded the government and overthrew it if it persisted (or, to be more accurate, caused it to be reconstructed on lines taking account of the resistance encountered), on the whole and in general they served the government by explaining to the electors why this or that measure seemed necessary.

This representative character was lost with the long ballot (*scrutin de liste*) and proportional representation. Instead of a locally well-known figure being chosen by a small constituency (which created a strong link between the deputy and the people), the elector of a large constituency picked one of several lists on the basis of political color and, after the counting of votes, each large constituency found itself with a medley of deputies, none of which was personally known, none of which was personally familiar with the large constituency he formally represented. This man, because he had no close contact with his constituents, could not oppose the government on the grounds that "my people do not want this," but neither could he serve the government because he enjoyed no personal credit "back home." He was a footloose fellow to whom nobody would listen: the electors because he had no personal reputation in their eyes, the President of the Council because he knew that the deputy had no personal weight.

The extreme example is of course the UNR deputy of the so-

called Fifth Republic, who has ridden into the Chamber by clinging to the coattails of General de Gaulle. He could not justifiably
stand up to the General: in whose name? He has no constituents;
the votes which were given to him were intended for the General.
Therefore he may not oppose; but neither can he effectively support in the country, because he has no audience of his own: the
General is well able to speak up for himself, the UNR deputy is
unable to add any weight of his own.

This is an extreme case, but it seems to me significant of the
trend which sets in, when elections apply increasingly to party
rather than to the individual. Ask how many votes an individual
member would still muster if he lost the party label and there you
have the measure of his independence from the leader of the party
and of the positive support he brings to the Government.

These thoughts pose a very interesting problem for new states.
In most cases it is difficult for their governments to constitute an
extensive and competent agentry. This makes it almost a necessity
for them to work to a considerable extent through acknowledged
notables, who enjoy effective prestige in various parts of the country. These then might normally be thought of as the people to be
called to the capital to receive explanations of governmental
schemes, to subscribe to them and, thereafter, to procure their
implementation thanks to local prestige and authority. On the
other hand, however, many new governments want to undertake
fundamental social transformations, to which the existing notables
are deemed to be opposed, and a strong element of hostility to
them indeed commonly colors these projects. A general popular
mandate can be obtained for these schemes, but it will fill the
house with men elected on the basis of belonging to the reforming
or revolutionary movement, not on the score of personality. Such
men have no basis of their own on which they can take their stand
to control the government formed by their leaders.

Now there is yet another notion which I want to denote by a
specific term. It is obviously not true that all the citizens endowed
with the right to vote participate in the running of public affairs. In
the not so distant past when franchise was restricted to a minority,
members of this minority were often distinguished by the adjective
"active": they were the "active" citizens, while those who did not
have the vote were "passive" citizens. But this was a very inadequate manner of speech because not all those who were "entitled"

were in fact *active,* and some who were not entitled could in fact be active. I look not to the right but to the fact. I am concerned to mark out those people who are effective *participants* in the conduct of public affairs.

Obviously the mere casting of a vote is not participation. By participant, I mean a person who currently and continually devotes a good deal of time to public affairs, a good deal of effort to promote certain policies. This sustained expenditure of time and effort is what here defines participation. The lobbyist therefore is a participant as well as the militant for unilateral disarmament, the political journalist as well as the member of a constituency party, the high-ranking public servant as well as the elected representative.

How many people thus participate? A great many, but a very low percentage of the eligible population; how low depends upon the "minimal" expenditure of time we use to delimit participation.[62] I am afraid that any reasonable minimum would put the percentage around 1 percent in the large countries, while it would be higher in Switzerland.

But whatever the extent of participation, two very important points can immediately be noted, relative to our democratic countries. Participating circles are not a "closed shop." Anyone can participate, speak, write, petition, assemble, and so forth. In so doing he does not have to cleave to any line. The notional "set" of participants admits an endless variety of actual "sets" at variance with one another.

The second point is that, while joining the participants implies no commitment to any line, it does in practice imply a certain commitment to manners. The man who attends a public meeting and calls for the extermination of any group will generally be silenced, and if any subset is formed wherein such an extremist position obtains, all the other subsets will join against it.

The participating population may be regarded as a sort of "bath" in which the levers of command and their holders are immersed. The liberal authors thought of this "bath" as "public opinion" urging the government to a progressive course, holding it back from rough practices. If, however, there is a "closed shop" of

---

62. Experienced American political scientists or sociologists would, I am sure, find it easy to devise questions which, being posed in sample investigations, might allow a rough distribution of population according to degree of participation. And possibly this has been done already, and I am displaying my lack of information.

participation and if the monolithic set has a rough character, then you have a tyrannical and brutal system.

The notion of a limited number of active participants casts, I believe, a great deal of light on sharp political changes of the so-called "national temper." The French *philosophes* put their trust in "public opinion" which they pictured from the polite conversation of enlightened circles. The horrors of the French Revolution cast great discredit upon sovereign assemblies and awoke a great distrust of "the people, fundamentally savage." But none of these conclusions was warranted: at no time was there a free majority of any elected assembly in favor of terror, and at no time was a majority of the population of that disposition: what did happen was that the assembly, besieged by a limited circle of extremists, deliberated under pressure from blustering so-called deputations which came in arms.

Those people who "ring" around the politicians constitute in effect "the people" in the concrete sense of the expression; that is, *the people who are there* (which was obviously the way the Greeks thought of it: "the people" were those people who effectively came to the assembly, however small their proportion of the entitled citizenry). Now "the people" so defined (in the sense here used, i.e., the active participants) have indeed all that effective importance which democratic theory attributes to "the people" at large. Under any liberal regime they are much divided among themselves, far more than either the people at large or the politicians in the arena (think for instance of the divisions within the British Labour Party). At the same time they are committed to the procedures and manners essential to the liberal conduct of affairs. But here is the threat: that this "people" can be driven out by another. Think of Weimar Germany and of the people who participated in politics: these people you find a few years later driven into exile or pushed into concentration camps, or at least silenced. Another "people," with quite different mores, then camps around the political offices.

How superficial it is to say then that "the character of the German people has changed" or that "the German people have revealed their true character"! All that has indeed happened is that a different tiny percentage of the nation has pushed out that which previously ringed the political scene, and given it a different character!

Now surely a phenomenon of this kind is not to be thought of as a function of long-term social evolution. Probably we can regard the development of agentry as correlated with social complexity; certainly we can regard the concentration of government as corresponding to moments of social problems, and, for instance, the same degree of unemployment in the United States as in Germany does bring such a concentration in the hands of Franklin Roosevelt as well as in those of Hitler: but in the case of the United States you do not see a change in the manners of government, you do not see a substantial change in the participants of politics: in my view this "moral mutation" is the really awful phenomenon we should understand.

It has happened in France when she was the *Patrie des Philosophes,* it has happened in Germany when she was the paradise of the professors; therefore no degree of "enlightenment" by itself is a guarantee against it; it can easily happen in a new state, and we should certainly discriminate between the concentration of government which may be necessary there and the control of the nation by a political army, which is horrible. Conversely, the political army may in time lose its warlike character, and this would fundamentally transform the totalitarian countries, if it occurred.

No government by itself can exercise tyrannical domination if it operates in a milieu of public participants who, whatever they may severally advocate, jointly detest tyrannical domination. Any government, whatever its form, by whatever name it goes and whatever principles it invokes, can exercise tyrannical domination if it is served and spurred by a standing army of partisans. The militant party is the great source and condition of tyranny.

Thus the great problem to which political scientists should address their utmost attention is the moral mutation which occurs in politics and government when moderate and diverse partakers in public life are driven out by an invading party which occupies the country. When, why, and how does this occur? And how can it be prevented?

Up to now, there is no evidence that this terrible occurrence, however common in our century, is in any way correlated with social evolution: it occurs in countries very differently placed on any "scale" of social evolution; it has not occurred in any English-speaking countries.

Therefore we cannot inscribe it in any evolutionary model, though it is far more important than any evolutionary change.

CONCLUSION

Can we find any phenomena which seem common to all countries in our day? Indeed we can. One is the prodigious growth of agentry, linked to the great increase in the functions of government. Another is the decline of parliament, linked to the decline of law, and the more pronounced the more members are cut off from a local basis and the lesser the vitality of local communities. Yet another is the personalization of authority, which is visibly displayed in the hopes which public opinion puts in "summit meetings" which are fundamentally undemocratic.[63] All countries today have a *Princeps,* the combination of which with an extensive agentry is reminiscent of Imperial Rome. This principate may be a psychological necessity in an age when the state plays a major role in the lives of individuals, in direct opposition to liberal Whig forecasts, and this pervading anonymous presence probably must for the great number bear a recognizable figure: this agrees with the "star cultus" which has developed in modern society, unforeseen by the men of the enlightenment.

Back of this publicized figure of *divus Caesar,* there is an invisi-

---

63. Indeed when one imagines Krushchev and Kennedy settling the problems pendant between their countries by a face-to-face talk, this implies that they are both regarded as enjoying a great *autonomy of decision* in their respective countries, a great freedom from all other national authorities. To make this clearer, let us picture the "positions" of the U.S. and U.S.S.R. governments as lacking any point of coincidence, which, if it existed, would of course be easily reached by both governments, doing away with the conflict. These positions being thus distant, what one imagines, when one expects things to be settled by the top-level meeting, is that either Krushchev or Kennedy, or both, move away from their respective national positions to reach agreement. And this assumes that the national position is not binding upon them, that they can change it at their personal discretion. But further I can point to the fact that, up to 1914, summit meetings occurred essentially among the three Emperors (Austrian, German, and Russian) who had retained some measure of personal power, that they occurred between the leaders of the democratic states only in the course of the first world war, when the state of war had conferred on them an unusual degree of personal power; that, during the interwar period, summit meetings were characteristic of Hitler's methods ("Axis" meetings) and that he sought to impose them on democratic leaders for their undoing: the Hitler–Schussnigg summit meeting leading to the Anschluss; the Munich summit leading to the dismemberment of Czechoslovakia; the Hitler–Hacha meeting leading to the "Protectorate" over Czechoslovakia. Summit meetings are fundamentally foreign to a collegial executive subject to an independent parliament.

ble and informal senate. In France, to quote what I am familiar with, earnest civil servants have formed circles where policies are discussed and shaped. It seems to me beyond doubt that to a large degree the invention of policies lies with these and not with the politicians. It may be that the real initiative in democratic states lies with the permanent executive (i.e., the civil servants), whose suggestions are then to some degree espoused by ministers and later ratified by parliament. In France the *Conseil Economique* and the *Commissariat au Plan* both are formal institutions which put civil servants or "experts," their analogues and allies, in contact with "representatives" of "constituencies" more real in our day than local constituencies: union leaders, farmers' leaders, business leaders. This displaces discussion of policies from the formal parliament to "talking-over" places which enjoy little publicity and are entitled to no part of sovereignty.

In such talking-over places every feature is to be found which one would like to see in representative government. There is a very high degree of qualification and information, there is an earnest concern for the general welfare, there is much mutual respect, the good will of colleagues is taken for granted, one expects to learn from their statements, there is no speaking for effect, and so on. Whether these pleasant traits are somehow related to the fact that there is no power to be won there, I leave the question open.

The biggest issues, however, and the more truly political, fall outside the scope of such circles. They are decided by the Prince, and the trend is toward his using the mass media to address the people directly, thus short-circuiting the ancient role of members of parliament. The impressive television presence, seen by millions, makes both a more extensive and a more intensive mark than any newspaper article, and indeed determines a climate which political journalists have to take into account and to which, in no small measure, they come to defer.

With these traits, democratic countries do not offer a sufficiently striking formal contrast with the nondemocratic to inspire a vigorous, principled, dynamic liberalism. The formal institutions for which liberals have fought can now be adopted without producing the effects which were thought inherent to them. You can have a parliament, but it can be so party controlled as to offer no resistance to the executive; you can have universal suffrage but it can be handled in a plebiscitary manner. These ways have been found[64] in democratic countries themselves and if there they have not been driven to the extreme, it is a matter of moral restraints which may be lacking elsewhere. I may be wrong, I hope I am wrong, but I feel that a wise man coming to us today from a new state, earnestly searching for political institutions which, on being transplanted to his country, would fully guarantee it against arbitrary power and the invasion of personal freedom, would not find in our countries any definite institutions sure to procure such results.

The United States and Switzerland may be held up as exceptions. But in the United States our wise man would find all the progressives complaining of the independence of Congress and calling for a strict party control of Congress which would put its majority votes at the discretion of the White House occupant. He would be struck by the fact that while in Switzerland there is great care to proceed at different times to the election of different bodies, in the United States there is already a disposition to spare the electors the "inconvenience" of several elections by holding very different elections at the same time, which is an important step toward monolithizing the system of authorities, and an important departure from the principle that the interest of citizens in public affairs should be stirred up as often as possible.

It seems, therefore, that at this moment of history, so critical for the fate of freedom, we do not have any clear recipe of free institutions, such as our ancestors felt possessed of. And this is extremely disquieting.

It may of course be said that there exists no such recipe, a position which is apt to enjoy intellectual vogue because of its sophistication. But I come increasingly to think that no intellectual with a sense of social responsibility should allow himself to take such a position, because it must leave you without any principles you can advocate and champion against arbitrary government. And no mere dislike of arbitrary government, however intense, will serve you as well as institutional barriers. Indeed mere dislike

---

64. The idea of *safeguarding procedures* has been essential to liberal institutions, and the modern idea of *efficient* process, very good in its proper sphere, has invaded the political sphere where it is immensely dangerous. Admittedly safeguarding procedures can be hampering. When you are trying to get things done as fast as possible, safeguarding procedures come to be regarded as obstacles which you find means of nullifying.

of one arbitrary government may often cause you to lay down your life for what turns out to be the establishment of another and a worse one.

My conclusion would then be that the Whig restraints upon domination have crumbled or been by-passed, and that we have to devise others which would perform, under different circumstances, similar services.

The Principate

I

To lessen the share of any *one* in the conduct of public affairs, such was the chief concern of the political thinkers, from Locke onwards, whom we currently acknowledge as our teachers. However unproven and unlikely that Louis XIV actually said "*L'Etat, c'est moi*," this legendary statement serves to represent in the form of an aggrandized shadow the reality which our mentors meant to expose, denounce, and oppose. Personal rule has indeed undergone a process of decline in European states, beginning according to countries, sooner or later after the 1680s when Louis XIV shone and Locke wrote. This we can properly call *demonarchization.* This term is here taken to imply, not only that power slips out of the hands of anointed kings, but that it does not accumulate in the hands of any *one,* however labeled. For we must be mindful, as Algernon Sidney so aptly put it, "that the most absolute Princes that are or have been in the World, never had the name of King: whereas it has frequently been given to those whose powers have been very much restrained."[1]

In this process of demonarchization we can distinguish two successive and quite different stages: in the first, monarchic authority is limited, circumscribed, by the attribution to parliament of legislative power and the power of the purse: the structure of the federal government in the United States perfectly pictures the accomplishment of this first stage. In the second stage, ministers fell into complete dependence upon parliament, so much so that

"The Principate" is reprinted from *Political Quarterly,* vol. 36, no. 1 (January–March 1965). Used by permission of the publisher.

1. Algernon Sidney, *Discourse concerning Government,* 2nd ed., chapter 3, sect. 32 (London, 1704), 368.

they became its own revokable commissioners, holding office by its favor and as long as this favor endured. It was at the height of this second stage that a man of my age found things opening his eyes to take in the political scene on the morrow of the first world war.

From Parliamentary Government to the Principate

There was then a striking uniformity in political institutions: this indeed was frequently referred to, during the first years of the League of Nations, as a promise of mutual understanding and a guarantee of international order.

It should be stressed that in none of the parliaments then existing was there an absolute majority of one disciplined group: this feature suffices to build up enormous personal power in the hands of the prime minister, whose colleagues in the cabinet thereby become mere lieutenants, whose backbenchers become mere soldiers, striving, by faithful service, to attract their general's eye. It was quite otherwise when the parliamentary system was in its heyday. Having to make up his majority from diverse groups, none of which was disciplined, and having to make up his governmental team from colleagues who brought him some contingent of votes, the chief executive was impeded from personal rule. The political élite was most hostile to such personal rule: it was this feeling which led to the eviction of both Clémenceau and Lloyd George despite their great war services, or rather because of the great popular prestige such services had earned them.

To those who have witnessed parliamentary government so widespread and so undisputed, the change that has come about in the past forty years or so seems enormous. Looking down the list of states that are now members of the United Nations, how many do we find where power is not concentrated in the hands of a single man? It is unimportant whether or not this monopoly of political power is written into the constitution: Octavius did not have to change the outward forms of the Roman Republic to empty them of all substance and to inaugurate the Principate.[2]

2. "Insurgere paullatim, munia senatus, magistratuum, legum in se trahere," says Tacitus, *Annals,* Book 1, section 2.

Problems for Discussion

Principate is the generic noun I have proposed to designate all our
contemporary régimes where the body politic is in fact vested in
one man.[3] I have chosen this term because it seems to me the most
neutral, equally acceptable to those who approve of such régimes
as to those who disapprove of them.

This being our subject, it seems to me that discussion falls naturally into the three divisions of time: in the past, *explanation* of the
phenomenon; in the present, *appreciation;* in the future, *prognos-
tication.* To put it another way:

1.   What are the sources and causes of the phenomenon? How
and why has it developed?

2.   Just what is the nature of the phenomenon and what value-
judgments can be passed upon it?

3.   What evolution thereof can be plausibly foreseen? And
what are the conditions for alternative deflections of its course?

Positive Causes of Monarchization

There is no lack of explanations of the phenomenon: they could
even be said to abound. First, there is the rapid extension of
governmental activities in the twentieth century, which has materially swelled the state bureaucracy and psychologically increased
the prestige of the executive. The more the work of government
involves initiative, the less it is the simple, routine execution of
laws passed by the legislature—and the more so-called "executive" power springs from the limitation which was implied in the
very name given to it by Locke and which continued in practice
well into the nineteenth century. The importance which is in fact
given to the executive focuses attention upon its head: as the executive becomes more active it is also more personalized.

"We can predict with assurance," wrote Gabriel Tarde in 1899,
"that the future shall offer personifications of Authority and
Power outshining the figures of Caesar, Louis XIV and Napoleon."[4] But must the rise in the importance of the executive so

3. The flatterer Gallus says to Tiberius: "Ut, sua confessione, argueretur unum
esse reipublicae corpus, atque unius animo regendum." Tacitus, *Annals,* Book 1,
section 12.
4. Gabriel Tarde, *Les Transformations du Pouvoir* (Paris, 1899), 219.

benefit its head? It seems that we are prone to regard the executive as naturally of a monarchic complexion. The idea never seems to have been questioned in European history. It has been put very clearly by Léon Blum: "I like work to be well done and I know that all collective work requires fixed rules and single direction. This direction must be exercised by the President of the Council. . . . We must get used to seeing him for what he is and what he should be: a monarch. . . ."[5]

I found this quotation from Léon Blum in the very interesting work that Léo Moulin has devoted to the constitution of religious orders, in which the author shows to what extent the governmental practices developed within these bodies, with their highly selective "citizenship," have influenced the political practice of states.[6] These constitutions demonstrate that the fundamental tendency of the European mind has been to contrast an assembly that legislates and controls with the strictly *unitary* character of the executive: action is monarchic.

One is reminded that, in the period from the fifteenth to the seventeenth century, when it was felt socially necessary to increase the intervention of the central government, this took the form of *the rise of absolute monarchy.* On the other hand, the reaction against absolute monarchy coincided with the rise of ideas that have usually been associated with the slogan *"Laisser faire, laisser passer."*

But if the twentieth century was to be a time of great socialist transformation, did this necessarily involve a strong resurgence of personal power? Louis-Napoléon affirmed as much in his very revealing book of 1839, which deserves careful study. There is a great deal of historical truth in his formula: "Just as public opinion had demanded the weakening of Power, regarding it as hostile, it favored its heightening, having come to regard it as protective and constructive."[7]

However, the nineteenth-century socialists, whose ideas were to be put into practice in the twentieth century, hated personal power

5. Léon Blum, *La Réforme Gouvernementale* (Paris: B. Grasset, 1936). It should be noted that Léon Blum adds: "A monarch, whose field of action is laid out in advance, a temporary, constantly revokable monarch, but one entrusted nevertheless with the entire executive power." It is the reservations expressed here that have tended to disappear.

6. Léo Moulin, *Le Monde vivant des Religieux* (Paris: Calmann-Lévy, 1964).

7. *Des Idées Napoléoniennes,* by Prince Louis-Napoléon Bonaparte (Paris, 1839).

no less than that of the capitalists, and did not think that the former was necessary to curb the latter. Any contrary opinion attributed to Marx is founded upon an erroneous reading of his formula of "the dictatorship of the proletariat," by which he meant no more than a temporary suspension of the division between the legislative power and the executive power, the undivided power going to a multitude of workers' councils, not to a single man. Elie Halévy has tried to show that authoritarian government had no original connection with the idea of socialism, but that the experience of the "militarization of Society" brought about during the Great War of 1914–18 inspired a militarization of politics and government. This thesis gave rise to a discussion of very great interest and deserves to be taken up again.[8]

The connection between single leadership and war is too well known to need emphasizing. Is it necessary to recall that the Romans never had the slightest notion of the unity of the executive power? On the contrary, government was spread out over several different magistratures, of which each had at least two titularies at any one time, with *par potestas*. It was only during a military campaign, over the army he commanded and in the field of operations assigned to him, that the consul enjoyed any undivided power. Undivided power upon the whole people was granted only to a dictator, nominated in times of exceptional danger. He alone was accorded an *imperium*, that was to be exercised not in some specific place outside the territory, but upon the people itself. He was *magister populi*, without any sharer in his power, since the "master of cavalry," who also appeared in such circumstances, was nothing but his coadjutor, appointed by himself.[9] Reference to Roman political genius makes the association of single leadership and military function quite clear. It would also be interesting to trace the gradual introduction into politics of a military vocabulary—something which, incidentally, attracted the notice of Baudelaire.

After Saint-Simon, almost everyone took up the contrast he had drawn between the military concern and the industrial concern as

8. A discussion which is taken up in Elie Halévy's still relevant book, *L'Ere des Tyrannies* (Paris, Gallimard, 1938).
9. The character of the Roman dictatorship is particularly well brought out by L. Lange, *Histoire intérieure de Rome jusqu'à la bataille d'Actium*, Appendix to vol. 1 (Paris, 1888).

principles of political and social institutions. The contrast that this difference of principle brought into political institutions seems to have been overshadowed in our own time by the likening of the enterprise of economic progress to a military enterprise, not only in the name of the "struggle" against social reaction, which is plausible, but also in the sense of a "war of conquest" directed "against nature," which is entirely metaphorical. It is the head of government who has benefited from the notion of the "generalissimo."

Moreover, in the case of the huge and confused category of "underdeveloped countries" or "new States," a great many reasons for the personalization of power are cited. They can be drawn from the "distant" past or from the "recent" past, from immediate needs or from long-term projects. Thus it is said (invoking the "distant" past) that peoples without education can picture government only in the shape of a chief, or (invoking the "recent" past) that a struggle for independence has identified its achievement with some leading figure; or again (now invoking a present and future requirement) it is said that in order to "integrate" disparate peoples into one nation, a "founder" is necessary, as represented in ancient mythology; or further that rapid modernization is a species of *social mobilization*,[10] a term which naturally suggests a "generalissimo."

Here are many impressive reasons: nor do I quote all those given; but this very abundance arouses suspicion. Are we then to think that parliamentary government is "not yet" suitable to economically retarded countries, and "no longer" suitable for economically advanced ones? Are we to regard personal government as called for in the case of the first to remedy the dearth of administrative personnel, and in the case of the last to overcome its weight? It seems to me that we are burdened with all too many explanations for the same phenomenon: would it not then be a simplification to reverse the terms of our problem?

On the Probability of the Monarchic Form

If we assumed at the outset that the monarchic form of government is the most probable, then we could not be surprised to find it

10. A very significant expression coined by Karl Deutsch. Among many important pieces of work by this author stressing that theme see his "Social Mobilization and Political Development," *The American Political Science Review*, vol. 55, no. 3 (September 1961).

associated with very diverse circumstances: indeed it would then seem unreasonable to look for the conditions of appearance of this most common alternative, and more in accordance with the principle of intellectual parsimony to inquire into the conditions of appearance of the more uncommon alternative: the nonmonarchical form.

Now this assumption, that the monarchic form is the most probable, is one to which we are strongly induced by the study of history, which, at least, establishes beyond doubt that this form has been by far the most frequent. Omitting human societies so small and rural as to do without any command institutions, we find the phenomenon "state" strongly correlated with the phenomenon "monarchy." This can be strikingly displayed if, taking the states with known histories during the last twenty centuries, we roughly estimate therefrom the percentage of human lives which have been lived under a monarchic régime: this percentage will appear quite overwhelming. Or again one could make a kind of historical film composed of successive shots, decade by decade, of maps of the world meant to bring out the positions and population weights of republican states: these would be seen to gain some ground at times, as in the fifth century B.C. But such gains have not proved irreversible.

It would be unwarranted to take the enormous preponderance of the monarchic form in the past as the a priori measure of its probability in the future: but neither does its marked decline during a few generations offer any guarantee of a continuing process of gradual extinction.

When parliamentary régimes stood at their height, two prejudices were very widely held that later proved to be unfounded: a general prejudice that a phenomenon "of the past" could be regarded as "surpassed," and a specific prejudice that only the descendants of past kings would be prone to restore a monarchic power. These two prejudices undermined the vigilance that the republicans of Rome had ever exercised: these Romans were ever ready to suspect one or other among themselves of aspiring to the *regnum,* to *dominatio,*[11] the monarchy being considered as always restorable by any ambitious man exploiting favorable circum-

---

11. Cf. J. Hellegouarc'h, *Le Vocabulaire Latin des Relations et des Partis Politiques sous la République* (Paris: Les Belles Lettres, 1963).

stances. Not only was any attempt at restoration a capital crime among the Romans, but the institutions were so arranged as to prevent its ever coming about.

"The laws of Rome," says Montesquieu, "had wisely divided public power into a great number of magistratures, which supported, checked and moderated each other: as then each had no more than limited power, each citizen was apt to participate in them; and the people, seeing several personages pass before it one after another, never became accustomed to any one of them."[12]

The political institutions of Rome were assuredly complex. But the Roman republic lasted for four and a half centuries, while the English republic, which succeeded the very limited monarchy of Charles I, soon developed into the unlimited rule of Oliver Cromwell, and the French republic brought down the limited power of Louis XVI, only to be replaced by the imperial power of Napoleon. History repeated itself in the same way with the second French Republic: Napoleon III had more power than was ever exercised by Louis-Philippe.

The Prevention of Personal Rule

If we regard personal rule as inevitable unless sufficiently strong measures are taken to prevent it, we are soon led to a consideration of the factors that make for its prevention.

The most natural and most important of the factors that go to prevent the monopolization of power by *one* man is the desire of the *others* not to relinquish power. This could be seen at work in a cabinet of the Third Republic, in which each minister considered himself master of his own department, and was not in the least disposed to see himself as a mere lieutenant of the President of the Council appointed by this leader to act under his orders. It was to be seen in the French Parliament of the same period, when the deputies were unwilling to let a head of government escape their control. This is perhaps the place to note, as the most gradual mode of progression to the Principate, the change that has occurred in the status of the parliamentary deputy.[13] If the parlia-

---

12. *Considérations sur les causes de la grandeur des Romains et de leur Décadence,* chapter 11 (Paris, 1736).

13. The origin of this process has been admirably described by M. Ostrogorski, *La Démocratie et l'organisation des partis politiques,* 2 vols. (Paris: Calmann-Lévy, 1903).

mentary deputy no longer owes his seat to the confidence that his electors have in him personally, but gets it from the party on condition that he votes for the government of his party, a Chamber or a party with a disciplined majority is no more than a rubber-stamp Assembly; and when the head of the party is the true head of the government, his ministers are reduced to the rank of lieutenants that he can dismiss as he wishes, as Harold Macmillan dismissed seven of his principal ministers at a single stroke. Indeed, the British prime minister has in fact become far more powerful than the president of the United States, though at the turn of the century the position was the other way round.[14]

Generally, the monopolization of power meets its greatest obstacle in the political élite. As an example of the phenomenon in general, I shall take one from outside the field of government properly so called—from the American trade union movement. Since the AFL and the CIO merged, there has been a general president of the whole union movement: but he has no personal power over the whole "people" of the unions. The different parts of this "whole people" are severally ruled by the leaders of the particular unions, such as the president of the Automobile Workers, the president of the Steelworkers, the president of the Teamsters. Here is a striking analogy with the situation of the medieval king; just like the medieval king, the general president has direct authority over some people, the membership of his own union, but he cannot directly move the members of the other unions: this lies with their respective leaders or "barons"; so that no movement of the "whole unionized people" can be brought about by the general president alone: as discrete parts of the "whole people" acknowledge no other direct authority than that of their respective leaders, therefore, it is only with the consent and participation of these various specific leaders or "direct lords" that the whole people can be moved. Indeed, a powerful "union lord" can defy not only the general president but also a coalition of this "overlord" with a great majority of "other lords," as Charles the Bold of Burgundy did relatively to Louis XI, as the president of the Teamsters has done in recent years relatively to the general president of the AFL–CIO backed by a majority of the union

14. This fact was brought out by Max Beloff in a correspondence in the *Daily Telegraph* in 1960.

leaders. It is clear that, in the AFL–CIO or even in the British Trades Union Council (TUC), the existence of a general president or a general secretary in no way implies that these men are in fact the "monarchs" of the trade union movements: it is the individual "barons" who hold power, and it is the congress of union "barons" that takes decisions, by which, moreover, a dissident "baron" is not effectively bound.

Starting from such a weak position, the medieval monarch moved up to absolute monarchy, because he succeeded in transferring to himself the psychological allegiance of the barons' constituents. Why should the Teamsters so transfer their allegiance to the general president? Whatever can be said against their specific leader, it cannot be gainsaid that he has advanced their interests? The word *constituency* is charged with meaning: wherever there is a solid following, a power thereby is constituted, and the overall constitution of power depends upon the distribution of followings. There is no place for a power monopolist where many people "matter" in the political field, thanks to the backing they personally obtain from their several constituencies, and provided these people who "matter" jointly operate in an effective manner. To rob them of their power, the would-be monopolist must tempt away their following: he has to "concentrate upon his own head the hopes of the nation" as the youthful Bonaparte wrote in his *Souper de Beaucaire*. The political set help him to this if they behave selfishly, as the Roman senators did when Tiberius Gracchus proposed his reforms; by their obstruction, they drove him to courses which they could call tyrannical but all they gained was to make people wonder whether perhaps *dominatio* was not the condition of reforms: which stacked the cards in favor of Marius, Cinna, Catilina, and finally Caesar. But it need not be for selfish reasons that the political set ceases to satisfy: it may perform inefficiently out of mere loyalty to now untimely routines.

Whatever the cause, if the people become dissatisfied with the performance of the political set, then the assertive fellow who promises to break the obstruction gains their ear. Indeed, belatedly and suddenly aware of such discontent, the political set is apt to panic and throw itself into the arms of a savior. Thus a loss of confident contact between the political notables and the people provides two roads to personal power. Jean Bodin has worked out these two ways with perfect clarity.[15] An aspirant to the Principate might very well use both ways at once, at one moment the sword of the people, at another the shield of the *optimates*. Such was Octavius's plan: sometimes he posed as Caesar's inheritor, at others as the defender of the Senate.

II

Reviewing in 1792 the work of France's Constituent Assembly, Necker deplored that the ruling spirit in such recasting of institutions has been to present "each successive defeat of the Executive power as a victory for liberty."[16] The French legislators, he said, had been eager to outdo, to outshine the English: as the English had wisely laid the foundations of liberty, in order to surpass their reputation and reap the glory of originality, something quite new had to be done: what offered itself was the complete abasement of the executive power. "But wise men cannot fail to perceive that where the English have sought to restrain the abuses of the Executive while maintaining its activity, we clumsy legislators have struck out blindly and, to prevent the abuses of the Administration, have destroyed its power to serve." "Things having been brought to this pass, it is idle to complain that the National Assembly usurps the functions of the Executive."[17] For, as he goes on to explain, public action is necessary, and if the so-called "executive" has been incapacitated, then this action must be taken by that other power which is free to move.

Necker's analysis presents a remarkable parallel with those which, in America, had preceded and prepared the Convention of 1787. At first the insurgents had also sought the belittling of the executive, an attitude the more understandable in that the executive power had been, until the rising, exercised by governors nominated in England. But very soon they discovered the serious disad-

15. Jean Bodin, *Les Six Livres de la République,* Book 2, chapter 4 (Paris, 1576).

16. Necker, *Du Pouvoir Executif dans les Grands Etats,* 2 vols. 1792 (no date of publication mentioned), vol. 1, 343. I would like to mention that I regard as regrettable the fall into almost complete oblivion of this very interesting book by a man of great experience.

17. *Ibid.*

The Principate

vantages of such abasement, and found that the State of New York, where wide powers were left to the Governor, fared far better than the other states. It was in the light of these facts that the presidency of the United States was constituted as we still know it today.[18] It is very significant that the champions of a strong executive have always tried to maintain, against the overwhelming evidence of history, that the word *monarchy* is applicable only in the case of hereditary rule: this was to avoid a reaction of "psychological allergy," as we now say, to the truly "monarchical" concentration of power which seemed to them to be necessary. An elective monarchy, no doubt, but one that was in fact all the stronger for being so, since the election was in practice, if not juridically, popular. On the other hand, a monarchy to which all legislative power was refused, and whose action was, by the "power of the purse," to use the forthright expression dear to the Genevan Delolme,[19] submitted to the control of Congress.

Though it differs from the Roman formula, which divided the executive into magistratures, while conferring on them the right to *agere cum populo* and therefore a certain initiative in the matter of laws, the American system has this in common with the Roman system—they both lasted a long time and brought their republics to leadership of the world in which they lived.

However great the power of the president of the United States may be, recent developments in the world have been such that it now appears to be the *minimum* form of the principate, so much so that we can use it as cut-off point: the régimes of our time can be arranged according to their effective degree of personal power and divided into two classes. Where the actual power of an individual is, in his own country, greater than that of the president of the United States, we shall call it a principate.

The Intellectual Vogue of the Principate

Not only are principates very numerous today but, what is more surprising, in the older democracies the tendency of political journalists or theorists seems to work in that direction. It has always been a "progressive" doctrine in the United States that Congress

---

18. Charles C. Thach, *The Creation of the Presidency 1775–1789, A Study in Constitutional History* (Baltimore: Johns Hopkins University Press, 1922).
19. Cf. J. L. Delolme, *La Constitution de l'Angleterre* (Amsterdam, 1771).

should be "reformed," "reconstructed" so as to afford to the president a "faithful," a "reliable" majority. Some toy with the idea of suppressing "midterm" elections (a change which would of course imply a change in the duration of mandates), many look for ways of submitting senators and representatives to voting discipline; in short, moving toward the abolition of the separation of powers is deemed "progressive."

It is indeed understandable that "liberals" should be annoyed by the resistance of Congress to such reasonable measures as Medicare, but must such annoyance lead to structural changes leading to absolute power? Again it is understandable that fear of such concentration of power should be dulled by reference to the British experience; for who would call the British government domineering and oppressive, although a disciplined parliamentary majority is available to vote any laws which the government deems necessary? But the fact that the potentially unlimited power inherent in such arrangements is not realized in this case does not mean that this is also the case elsewhere; for example, in Ghana, where the same institutions have been set up. It seems to me that the political journalists and theorists of the old democracies should be aware that the institutions they recommend also serve as examples in quite different circumstances.

Are we to believe that the absence of constitutional precautions is dangerous in the case of "new" nations, while it is not so in the case of "experienced" ones? It is a matter for discussion, but my own opinion is that there is a danger in both cases.

Such was the feeling of the "constitutionalists" who made their views known with such force after the collapse of the "Caesarism" of Napoleon I. They never said that institutions to limit the exercise of power were necessary in Russia but not in England. According to them, "constitutional charters" were necessary everywhere. Napoleon had brilliantly demonstrated that the proclamation of the sovereignty of the people was in itself no guarantee against *dominatio*. Indeed, the opposite can be argued. Call sovereignty the attribute of One: we shall not then be so rash as to conceive it unlimited; but it seems safe to do so if it is called the attribute of "We All"; but "We All" cannot exercise it; allow it then to pass into the hands of One: his power, reared upon the basis of popular sovereignty shall rise far above that of any king. When used to build a monarchy, the popular principle outbuilds the monarchic principle. This was carefully explained by Benjamin Constant, who had to look no further than the events of his own time.[20]

The lessons learned from the Napoleonic experience had then brought almost the entire world of letters to "constitutionalism," to a belief in institutions that limit personal rule. It is very strange that the experience of Hitler—and how much worse *that* was!—did not start a similar movement!

Politician in Disfavor

Let us try, however, to understand. But first let us follow Titus-Livius, who makes us witnesses of the exchanges between the Roman consul, Titus Quinctius Flamininus, and the tyrant of Sparta, Nabis.[21]

> Nabis says: I am called a tyrant for having freed the slaves and given land to the needy. Our institutions, it is true, are not yours. In your country, one serves in the cavalry or in the infantry according to one's income, and you wish the plebs to be dominated by the rich. Our law-giver did not wish to entrust public-affairs to the small number of men you call the Senate, nor to a dominant class in the state, but he sought a levelling of fortunes and dignities, so that the nation would find a greater number of men willing to defend it.

After this apologia, Nabis listens without interest to the Consul, who blames him for bloodshed, for not holding free assemblies in which an opposition could make itself heard, and finally enjoining him to produce, in their chains, all those whom he has had arrested, so that their families at least will know that they still live.

How much of this dialogue would have to be changed in order to place it in Cuba, for example? To how many contemporary in-

20. These developments are to be found at the beginning of his famous work, *Principes de Politique applicables à tous les gouvernements représentatifs et particulièrement à la Constitution actuelle de la France* (Paris, May 1815). Moreover, in his pamphlet, *De l'Esprit de Conquête et de l'Usurpation dans leurs rapports avec la civilisation européenne* (Hanover, 1813), he had developed another connected theme: that emergent monarchies are far more vigorous than hereditary ones, which he presents as "softened by habit, surrounded by intermediary bodies that both sustain and limit it," appeased by a self-confidence "which makes power less shadowy."

21. Titus-Livius, Book 34, sections 31 and 32.

stances would it not apply, representing exactly the arguments used against each other now? The intellectuals of today are for the most part on the side of Nabis. This attitude is not as new as it might appear. Bodin writes:

> Tyranny can also be that of a Prince against the nobles, as always occurs during violent changes from an Aristocracy to a Monarchy, when the Prince kills, banishes, or confiscates the possessions of the greatest; or a needy and poor Prince, who knows not where he may obtain money, often asks it of the rich, rightly or wrongly; or again, a Prince may wish to free the common people from the servitude of the noble and rich, and by so doing obtains the support of the poor. For of all tyrants, there is none less detestable than he who, attacking the rich, spares the blood of the poor.[22]

If I have spoken of tyranny, it is not to identify all principates with tyranny. This would be to employ one of those rhetorical devices, by which Louis XVI was called a "despot." But I had a perfectly valid reason for beginning with tyranny: for it represents in its strongest form the conditions, in some ways "organic," that lead to a principate. It is a state of crisis in the relations between the ruling class and the people which leads the latter to desire a liberator, or the former to accept a savior. Such a crisis may be described from different points of view.

The rise of Bonaparte provides a particularly interesting case. The ruling class of the ancien régime was divested of power, dispossessed, and finally guillotined without offering the least resistance. It is an incontestable historical fact (though often slurred over) that the victories won from the privileged classes after the convocation of the States General were obtained from adversaries who made no attempt at resistance: this can be seen very clearly in the notes of Arthur Young, who predicted a violent reaction on the part of the aristocracy, a reaction that never took place in any form.[23] Finding no adversary, the Revolution had no need of a leader. But some years after the Revolution, with the notables of

---

22. Jean Bodin, *Les Six Livres de la République,* Book 2, chapter 4, "De la Monarchie Tyrannique."
23. Arthur Young, *Travels During the Years 1787, 1788 and 1789,* 2nd ed. (London, 1794), vol. 1, 138 et seq.

the ancien régime quite eliminated, others had arisen in their
stead, politicians who had survived the various purges, or new
rich, who had bought for a song the land confiscated from the
Church or the émigrés, who had sold supplies to the armies,
creditors of the state. At present they rode high, but they did not
feel safe. They were anxious to stabilize their acquired situations;
and for this purpose they wished to be preserved as well from a
further wave of revolution as from any reflux. The revolution had
to be stopped and consolidated. This is why the new ruling class
appealed to Bonaparte. The result was entirely to their advantage. One has only to read the declarations in favor of hereditary
monarchy made by the "Tribunes" in *floréal* of the year XII: it is
from the mouth of the parvenus of the Revolution that one hears
the cry for measures which "will deliver us from the dangers that
must threaten to destroy and to devour the fruits of this
revolution. . . ."[24]

The Change of Elites

Bonaparte consolidated the results of the Revolution. The work of
Beau de Loménie[25] shows how those who rose with the Revolution
formed a class of "lords" who reigned over French politics under
the July Monarchy and over the French[26] economy for a century
and a half. The cemetery of Père-Lachaise is a very good place to
follow, from the inscriptions on the tombstones, the dynastic histories of this "new" ruling class: member of the Convention, prefect
under the Empire, peer under the July Monarchy, and chairman of
a large company under the Third Republic.

This historical example reveals how a revolutionary upheaval
destroys élites only to create others, as Pareto pointed out;[27] the
consolidation of the position of the new élites presents a problem,
which can result in a strong man being called as "consolidator,"
but also, which is more important to our present concerns, once he
has consolidated the position of the new élite, they no longer have

24. Speech by Costaz, in the session of 10 floréal, year 12.
25. Emmanuel Beau de Loménie, *Les Dynasties Bourgeoises,* 3 vols. (Paris,
Sequena, 1942).
26. The fusion of the political and economic élites under the July monarchy is
the subject of a report by A. J. Tudesq to the Table Ronde de l'Association
Française de Science Politique, November 15–16, 1963.
27. See especially the Introduction to his work, *Les Systèmes Socialistes,* 2 vols.
(Paris, 1902).

any need for personal rule. It may be presumed that the eliminated élite was "unfunctional" and was eliminated for being so. It may also be presumed that the élite which was formed by and benefited from the revolution is the result of "natural selection," was "adapted" to the period, and capable, after a difficult transition period, of obtaining fairly lasting popular acceptance. Finally, strengthened by this popular acceptance, it could fight and defend the monarchy. This is what happened in England with the Whig aristocracy and in France with the "grande bourgeoisie" created by the Revolution and the Napoleonic régime.

These observations would suggest that there is Bonapartization in periods in which one élite replaces another: when the established élite is strong and accepted, it prevents the concentration of power in the hands of one man. When it ceases to be strong and accepted, it sees a concentration of personal power form against it, or relinquishes power to a single protector. Rising élites, according to the circumstances, need personal power either to direct the conditions that give rise to them, to pave the way for them, or to consecrate their arrival. Once established, a new, dynamic, and fairly popular élite can dispense with personal power.

Despots, in the true sense of the term, have never allowed themselves to be surrounded by a group of men of recognized merit. They have always filled the highest posts with men whom the prejudices of the time have prevented from acquiring a great personal following (such as freed slaves, eunuchs, foreigners); often they have been clever enough to retain members of the old élite, sometimes its most vicious examples, as stalking horses. Certain of the Roman emperors used members of the senatorial nobility in this way—thus lending them an artificial survival. It is the height of despotic cleverness to keep on discredited "leaders" to prevent the appearance of men of real merit.

Of course, these ruses of the despots are ruinous in the long run, since they deny the state and society the cadres that are really needed. It is probably by this very impoverishment of the cadres that the Roman and Ottoman Empires perished, while the French monarchy flourished for so long by favoring the rise of élites, by rewarding merit, and by breaking the power of decadent and "unfunctional" aristocratic groups.[28] It is for having slackened in its

28. This is the theme of Augustin Thierry in his *Du Tiers État* (Paris, 1853).

role of "liquidator" that it perished. By allowing itself to become paralyzed by ancient "unfunctional" élites, the monarchy aroused the antagonism of the people and then, by an astonishing volte-face, became their champion, and in the end shared their fate.

Our Period as One of Changing Élites

The correlation suggested between Bonapartization and change in élites would explain the frequency of the first phenomenon, the second being a characteristic of our time.

First, on account of the strength, of the new nationalisms. A country that has lived long under colonial rule has seen its leading elements associated with the ruling power and tends to reject one with the other. In certain ways, this has been prepared by the colonial power itself, which has usually consolidated and extended the power of traditional élites in order to provide itself with cadres. At the same time, it has formed new intellectual élites, without providing them with jobs. Nationalist emotion will be particularly strong if the struggle for independence has been hard and the old élites can be charged with "collaboration." But the same phenomena are to be seen in countries that have long been independent, as in Latin America where opinion is ranged against foreign companies that exploit the natural resources of the country and, by association, against natives who are involved with these companies.

Moreover, the landowning class is always an object of attack, since their fortunes arouse a resentment all the more justified when their large share of the national revenue is spent on consumption and on the consumption of foreign goods. The case of Japan, where the landowners, in the Meiji period, converted their income from agriculture into industrial equipment for the development of the nation, is rare.[29]

It should be noticed that the changes in élites now taking place in a third of the world are not necessarily stable. In fact, the intellectual élites that succeed the social élites are often characterized by ability in *expression* rather than in *action*. In this case, the feeling that they discuss rather than fulfill the promises they have made—which cannot in any case be fulfilled very quickly—aids the rise of a Prince. In cases where independence has been

---

29. "Aspects politiques et sociaux du développement économique." *Futuribles* no. 28. *Bulletin S.E.D.E.I.S.* (April 20, 1962).

achieved only after armed struggle, the élites forged by this struggle no doubt possess practical abilities; but either the struggle gives rise to a single leader, or the dissensions of the leaders after victory call forth a single leader to discipline the others.

The change of élites in European countries presents aspects that are less striking but no less important.

Not only in the social field is there a shift from owners to managers,[30] but in the political field there is an even more pronounced change. Traditionally, the representatives of the people have been drawn from the liberal professions: men of literary or legal training, well qualified in argument. Théremin explained enthusiastically, in 1796,[31] that the political tendency of the French Revolution had been to transfer government to men of letters, and that this transfer, suddenly or gradually, was taking place throughout Europe. And he was right. However much society developed into a plutocracy, it is true that in the political field it was members of the liberal professions that predominated.

The reputation of the abilities of these men is now declining. Independents in a world of large-scale industry, possessing a classical education in a period of scientific fashion, the members of the liberal professions suffer from a loss of prestige and are quite plainly being replaced in popular esteem by "scientists" and "experts."[32]

But at present the injection of scientists and experts into the apparatus of government is only the work of the executive, and by their recruitment the executive gains in prestige over assemblies which remain in the hands of an élite that is less and less valued by popular opinion. This is a phenomenon that can be observed in the press, where journalists show far more interest in the opinion of an expert than in that of a parliamentarian.

One may wonder if the growing prestige of scientists and experts will one day allow them to inherit the role played until now by lawyers and men of letters. It may be thought that the difference in

30. M. M. Postan, "The Economic and Social System in 1970." *Futuribles* no. 10. *Bulletin S.E.D.E.I.S.* (September 1, 1961).

31. Charles Théremin, *De la Situation Intérieure de la République,* pluviôse, year V (December 1796–January 1797).

32. Robert C. Word, "The Rise of an Apolitical Élite," in Robert Gilpin and Christopher Wright, *Scientists and National Policy-Making* (New York: Columbia University Press, 1964).

the nature of these abilities might present an obstacle. They are not orators capable of inspiring an assembly or writers capable of persuading public opinion.

The Polysynody

Consequently this technocratic élite must make its influence felt in some other way: in the committees.

The network of interministerial committees that are to be found in every modern administration is a system of communications by means of which strong personalities in the civil service can spread their influence throughout the administration. A civil servant in charge of a rich department, who propagates his views through a network of communications, is a "lord" of our time. His weakness is that he is confined to one place. But in practice even this is hardly so. It is with such lords that a modern Caesar in fact shares his power. Is an increasing autonomy of the civil service conceivable? Easily. Can we conceive of problems to be solved by Caesar being presented by civil servants in a way that suggests a particular answer? Even more easily. Can the civil service be said to exercise upon the head of the government a restraining and guiding influence less visible than but possibly as efficient as that previously exercised by parliament? It is no way inconceivable: it is still fictitious to speak of a "Senate of Civil Servants" but it could become a reality. It also seems to me to be wrong to associate the terms *caesarism* and *bureaucracy* as I have often seen done. Bureaucracy may be a corrective to caesarism rather than an instrument of it.

III

I do not think anyone will deny that the tendency of our time is in the direction of the principate. I could wish for no other proof than the welcome given to the thesis of Benjamin Akzin on "the rebirth of monarchy."[33] When I was young, the essay that appeared with this title would have been taken by all readers as an apology for personal government. In our time, not a single reader, to my knowledge, has seen in it anything but a desire to limit personal government by regularizing its status. It was plain to all that the author, contrasting what had been the royal power with the power

---

33. *Futuribles* No. 13. *Bulletin S.E.D.E.I.S.* (October 1, 1961).

now exercised by the Prince, was concerned to confine the second within the limits of the first. He probably thought that if the concentration of power in the hands of one man was *formalized,* it would at the same time be limited; since nobody would be so foolish as to assign unlimited power to one man, such a monopoly of power could only occur if it were not formally recognized. It is certainly permissible to think that personal power gains much from the confusion created between Prince and people, whereas if the distinction is well marked, the people is far more vigilant. Keynes spoke of the "monetary veil": there is a veil in politics, too, a veil which can hide the Prince, if he can say that he is merely obeying something which is in fact only an echo of what he has himself initiated. Akzin thought that in tearing aside the veil, the grandeur of personal rule would be unmasked, and that the process so well described by Delolme of building trenches against this rule would be facilitated. But just as it is significant that readers recognized in the thesis of Akzin an intention to restrict personal power, so it would seem unlikely that things would happen as he imagines. For in giving a crown, the peoples believe they are giving too much, while dictators see it as a means of circumscribing their power.

While Akzin's thesis deserves extensive discussion, it is here mentioned only as a symptom of a widespread belief among political writers in the progress of the principate.

A New Constitutionalism

This calls for a new doctrine of constitutionalism. The old doctrine, which we associate with the name of Locke, and which has served so well, has now lost its appeal almost everywhere. The crying danger is that we should be left without any constitutionalism because the ancient one does not suit the new role of government. The old idea was that (foreign affairs set apart) good government consisted in the faithful application of sensible rules. The rules were thought of as obvious enough to be laid down by representatives elected for a single brief session. Seeing to it that the rules laid down were observed, such was the necessary but subordinate role of the government, therefore given by Locke the telling name of "Executive." This structure could suit a purely "policeman" state which had merely to provide a framework for the activities of private individuals, regarded as the sole source of movement in the social body. An illustration of the system can be offered, if we think of traffic on a given road network. The representatives of the motorists meet from time to time, and revise the rules governing the traffic. The road police enforce the rules.

But this will not do if we have to foresee the rise in volume and the shift in direction of motor traffic, taking into account the increase of wealth, the displacement of employment areas and of residential dormitories. It is then necessary to draw up a long-term program for the reconstruction of towns and ways of communication. This is the theme of the British Buchanan Report.* Who ordered such a report? A minister. Who drew it up? Experts. Who will choose, among the various "solutions" proposed, the one to be implemented? The British Cabinet. Parliament will be asked simply to vote the funds necessary to carry out the measures.

This example clearly shows how the initiative has fallen to the executive (therefore now misnamed). And yet the example chosen concerns so individualistic an activity as motor circulation. The purpose of the government here is to let the people use the cars procured with their own means, according to their own wishes, with minimum impediment to each other. It is otherwise when the Government devises a policy concerning scientific research. Here the assumption is not that individual scientists will build with their own means their individual laboratories, and the problem is not merely how to prevent the smells from laboratories inconveniencing neighbors. Here there is a concern to increase the volume of research and to induce it into directions which are deemed most profitable to human welfare. These are two different examples of *policies*.

It seems obvious that *policies* are becoming a major feature of modern government. As one thought of laying down laws, one now thinks of planning policies. And for the planning of such policies, it is not enough to be a sensible man, chosen as such by his neighbors. Anyone who desires to maintain as far as possible the importance of parliament should be eager to equip deputies with all the means (experts) and procedures (subcommittees) enabling them to take some efficient part in the elaboration of policies: this has been done for the United States Congress, but, to my astonishment, nothing of the kind has been attempted in Europe (many a time did I, under the Fourth Republic, stress its desirabil-

---

*A report to the Minister of Transport on highways, by a team chaired by Prof. Colin Buchanan (1963)—Eds.

ity). I am not sufficiently informed to state whether the challenge of "policy construction" has been satisfactorily met in the American Congress, but as for Europe it seems to me that it has not even been faced, and the European parliaments (I do not exclude the British) seem to be sinking in importance, a process which gives rise to heated denials rather than effective remedies.

If we now turn to the public servants, it is clear enough that carrying out policies is something quite different from attending to the execution of laws. It is a matter of conducting operations with a given goal, taking the initiatives and decisions which seem necessary, adjusting measures to circumstances. The men who are in charge of such policies are somewhat like field commanders. From this it follows that such public servants are important magistrates, while they are not mere executors of parliamentary laws, neither are they mere subordinates of the Prince. The very volume of the functions assumed by the executive makes it impossible for the head executive to control them. He must let policy operators forge ahead. This leads to an actual division of executive magistracies, those effectively holding important magistracies more often than not being civil servants rather than ministers. While the Prince obviously has a decisive say-so the nature of things seldom allows it to be more than an instruction to slow down or speed up a policy or deflect it somewhat.

At the height of absolute monarchy the king would say, through his chancellors: "The fundamental laws of our kingdom put us in a condition of fortunate powerlessness to. . . ." This expression, which has always fascinated me,[34] has its modern equivalent, or may have it. The fundamental laws above mentioned were not laws as we understand them but agreed principles, and our long-term policies are in fact future obligations that can seem no less fortunate. I am far from believing that "policies" can replace principles, and I should like to see the Prince bound by principles before being bound by policies: but I can see that the power of the first is in decline and therefore I vest my hopes in the second.

State Power and Personal Power

Already in 1835 de Tocqueville was writing: "Everything seems to combine to increase indefinitely the prerogatives of the central

---

34. I have spoken of this in *Sovereignty,* part 3, chapter 3 (1957).

government."[35] Yet this was at a time when the doctrine of complete economic liberty was at its height, McCulloch *regnante*. Tocqueville invited the reader to observe "that, during the half-century that has just passed, centralisation has grown everywhere in hundreds of different ways." That this process of centralization was not foreseen by Locke, one can well understand, but that it was not perceived by the constitutionalists of the French Restoration is more surprising. In fact, if they were not unaware of it, they believed it to be connected either with circumstances, great wars, or with monarchy, especially of course in its Napoleonic form. Tocqueville, on the contrary, found that the phenomenon had, among other reasons, "a single great cause . . . this cause is the development of industry." He anticipates in an amazing way, by saying of the state: "It is not only the greatest industrialist, it tends more and more to make itself the leader or rather the master of all the others." But at the same time the position of the monarch is weakened. The state becomes stronger, its head becomes weaker: this is illogical, "and I do not doubt that at the end of all these throne-shaking disturbances, sovereigns will be found to be more powerful than they were before."

More powerful than ever before—that is easy to understand. To recover no more than the same degree of monarchization of state power as existed before means a much greater power of the monarch over society, if, in the meantime, the power of the state over society has much increased. This, if I may be allowed to recall it, was the central idea of a work[36] which has often been interpreted as a single denunciation of the increase in the power of the state, whereas its essential purpose was to warn that, in proportion to this increase, the seizure and control of the state power by a single will presents greater dangers. This "single" will can never, of course, be the will of all (which is not single and which has, in the singular, only a mythical existence).

Supposing that our predecessors, liberal political thinkers like Benjamin Constant, Simonde de Sismondi, and Alexis de Tocqueville, found themselves thrown into present circumstances. Anxious above all to combat *dominatio,* they might take up two very

---

35. This and the following quotations from de Tocqueville are taken from *Democracy in America,* part 4, chapter 5.
36. B. de Jouvenel, *On Power* (Boston, 1962).

different positions. The first would consist of combating to the
utmost the extension of state power, which they would see as a
means of domination: this attitude would lead them to defend in
principle all forms of private power, whatever it may be, not for
itself, but as something different, and consequently as a refuge.
Whatever the vices of "the other Power" it has the virtue of being
"other." Consider Grotius who, however much he preferred in
principle the institutions of the United Provinces to those of the
French monarchy, was happy to find a refuge in the latter when he
escaped from his imprisonment in the United Provinces. Of the
powers whose increase we applaud, hopeful of their beneficent
use, we can never be assured that they shall not fall in the hands of
persecutors: and when such evil days are upon us, any realm to
which these powers do not stretch becomes to us a haven: it is the
foreign power then which appears as a protector, indirectly, only
because your own country's policemen must stop at its frontiers.[37]
Similarly, it is a useful precaution to maintain in your country
realms which are secured from the possible frenzies of public authority. If, according to a presently ruling political mania, you are
unfit for public employment, as "a security risk," or on any other
grounds, it is a good thing that there are other employers who are
in a position to take independent action. No less a person than
Trotsky made this point. It is on such grounds that there being
besides the public power other powers which are independent,
whatever they may be, is of great value.

The second attitude that our liberal thinkers could adopt would
be to accept the ever-growing role of the state, but to organize it in
such a way that the apparatus developed to provide social needs
could not become an instrument of domination in the service of a

37. This is why—and not for reasons of nationalism—the idea of a world government seems to me appalling. Its supporters, moved by the most praiseworthy
intentions, seem unconscious of the risk. They sacrifice the ultimate recourse which
the diversity of states affords us against tyranny. How precious seems the low wall
of a foreign frontier that lets through the refugee and stops the pursuer! So many of
us have had this experience that surely we should draw conclusions from it. Before
speaking in favor of a world government which would admit no such walls, one
should imagine Hitler's or Stalin's régime spread upon the planet. But a world
government, you may say, could not take on such a character. Are you sure, I mean
absolutely sure, that there is no possibility of this ever happening? For it needs no
more than a slight possibility of so great an evil to weight toward a negative value
the "mathematical expectation" of world government, and to make a choice in its
favor an insane bet.

single will, either of a man or a group. So many desirable things seem possible in our time only by state action that a limitation on this action would also limit their realization. It is understandable that the great majority of intellectuals should be in favor of an extension of state power. But what is surprising is that they make no mention of the precautions necessary to prevent the oppressive use of this extended power. It is only in specific cases that the problem is seen to exist at all. Thus it is permissible to think that the educative possibilities of radio and television would be better served by making it a public service. But it is obvious that it also provides the government with a powerful instrument for propagating its policies. In this case, it is seen to be necessary to organize a public service in such a way that its employees are not used as servants of the government.

The greater the state machine and the more completely it penetrates society, the more important it is that it should not become an instrument of domination for whoever happens to have got into the central control cabin. It is not an easy problem. The most immediate solution is the autonomy of the public organs. But it must be recognized that popular feeling works against it and quite understandably. It is a plain fact that whenever a service becomes "public," thereby it escapes the direct, day-to-day pressure of the public. It is not the motto of public services that "the customer is always right." Conscious of a moral superiority in working for the nation, and not for profit, executives high and low, earnestly concerned to provide the best possible service, are also convinced that the ignorant customers are the worst possible judges of performance, and are seldom prone to recognize as an obligation this responsiveness to current complaints or demands which is a necessity in the case of a private service. Therefore members of the public usually lodge their complaints with parliamentarians; if these become ineffective, the public turns to the head of the administration and set him up in their minds as a sort of overall "Tribune of the People" against the bureaucratic system. Thus popular protests against "bureaucracy" tend constantly to strengthen the power of the Prince over the state machine, which is the very thing we were trying to avoid. It could hardly be otherwise unless the public (in the concrete) found in public bodies the same immediate sensitivity to its demands that "private" bodies, without the benefit of "royal" prerogative, are subject to. We find within the state the same situation we have been discussing. The growth of the state creates a class of administrative "notables." In order to resist personal rule, they must themselves have built up a basis of goodwill with the general public. It is certain that the prestige of the great civil servants in France[38] is a factor in the limitation of personal rule: for they constitute a body of accepted "notables" that can temper a personal rule that the body of political notables who had lost their following are unable to prevent.[39]

The Basis of a New Constitutionalism

The more society is dominated by the state, the less it is possible for the state to remain monolithic. It must acquire the natural complexity of what it absorbs. But traditional "Constitutionalism" no longer meets the needs of the present situation.

The great liberal thinkers wished to reduce the role of the state to that of a general supervisor. The rules governing the actions of individuals were laid down by a legislating assembly: the servants of the state (the executive) were inspectors who supervised the application of those rules. But the state has completely changed its character: it is now a general employer.

A reconstruction of the state in alignment with its new role will logically follow. The less one thinks about this reconstruction, the more dangerous its absence becomes. The term *lettre de cachet* has remained synonymous with arbitrary rule: yet it was nothing more than a personal letter from the king, giving orders that did not pass through the normal channels, just as evocation was the withdrawal of a case from the normal juridical process. Practices of this kind are not necessarily mere caprices: they could be symptomatic of a lack of adaptation of the regular system to the needs of the time. But it would be preferable to reorganize the state system than to have a duality of heavy routine and sudden decisions. There is a strong tendency to such a duality in the old states of today: the dynamism of the Prince compensates for the inertia of the departments. As to the political danger, it is manifestly untrue that personal omnipotence is less dangerous when armed with a popular

38. Bernard Gournay, *Les Grands Fonctionnaires,* Table Ronde de l'Association de Science Politique, November 15–16, 1963.
39. Léo Hamon, *La Latitude d'Action des Catégories Dirigeantes: Réalités et Limites,* Table Ronde de l'Association de Science Politique, November 15–16, 1963.

mandate; on the contrary, it provides greater latitude. It is also untrue that an organization as cumbersome and complex as that of the modern state can be well directed by the "boss": we have only to refer to the experience of the great industrial corporations (and how much smaller and simpler they are than the modern state!).

Organization, Decision, Information

It is no doubt because the state is surrounded by mystery that one does not apply to its structure the remedial reflection that has already been applied with profit to the structure of organizations in general: but we are coming to it.[40]

If the problem of organization were clearly posed, taking into account the objectives recorded to the state and the "products" which are expected of it, a re-division of the powers of decision would result. It is the weakness of political theory that rights of decision are attributed en masse to subjects who cannot exercise them in practice. It is the starting-point of a practical theory that a union of "All" can take only very few decisions, and these must be reduced to a simple, prearranged (yet how important and influential!) alternative, while on the other hand "One" is quite unable to take all decisions. It follows, therefore, that there must be a redivision of decisions.[41]

In fact, the notion of decision allows us to give a wider meaning to the concept of constitution. For the effective constitution of a nation (constitution without a capital "C") can mean the total structure of the powers of decision, both private and public. First, there are the decisions that individuals take for themselves and which involve only their own means: to protect the area of these decisions was the purpose of the classical declarations of the rights of man, which assuredly have not lost their relevance. Above this area, there are decisions which involve collective means, either private or public. It is important to recognize explicitly that deci-

40. Cf. C. J. Friedrich, "Organization Theory and Political Style," in *Public Policy,* vol. 10 (Cambridge, MA: Harvard University Press, 1960); Herbert Kaufmann, "Organization Theory and Political Theory," *The American Political Science Review,* vol. 58 (March 1964); there are numerous other references that could be given.

41. Cf. Jacob Marshak, *Efficient and Viable Organisational Forms and Theory of an Efficient Several-Person Firm,* Cowles Foundation Paper no. 150 (New Haven, CT: Yale University Press, 1960).

sions involving collective means are but rarely a matter for "collective decision": fictions here conceal reality and dissipate responsibility. Almost all so-called "collective" decisions are in fact, and must be, taken separately by a small number of individuals, who are not the same for all. This must be admitted, if we are to be lucid, and we must determine whether the effective decision makers are the best informed, and what results accrue from exposing them to the limitations of reality, including the material day-to-day pressure of the public.

Nonauthoritarian Planning

For me, the great merits of the French system of planning are first of all political. It recognizes, in the economic field, a wide variety of effective decisionmakers, from the governor of the Banque de France to trade union leaders, including the heads of public and private industry. There is no question of ordering all these "officers of society" to obey an authoritarian plan, even less of replacing all these autonomous officers by docile agents of the central authority. But they have all been presented with a vision of a possible future, reasonable and attractive enough for each one to make it his own, and to apply his own particular authority to its realization. Pierre Massé has been concerned to impart to such a common vision a longer range than the four or five years of a Plan, and a wider extent than that of quantitative growth.[42] Some of us would like to see a "surmising forum" where the possibilities and hazards of the future would be continuously discussed.[43] The fundamental idea, of course, is to expel as far as possible the need for command, thanks to the increasingly far-seeing co-operation of free agents. It is unfortunately all too obvious that one must take into account what Cournot called "the impassioned movements of the human heart."[44] However, in certain conditions, these impassioned movements can no doubt be arrested at source. Three conditions come to mind immediately. First, that in all fields a sufficiently rapid renewal of the effective decision makers should prevent, on the one hand, a loss of dynamism in the system and, on the other, an accumulation

---

42. It is for this purpose that he established the "1985 Group" of the Plan.
43. This is a main theme of our *Futuribles* venture.
44. Notice the remarkable contrast he makes between the rationality that can be imported into the social economy and the resorts to passion that occur in politics. *Traité de l'Enchaînement des Idées Fondamentales dans les Sciences et dans l'Histoire*, sections 459 and 460, p. 525 of the edition of 1911.

of young, inadequately placed talent.[45] Second, that all neglected or adversely affected interests should be able to make themselves heard, which presupposes great concrete progress in representation. Third, that the judiciary be placed on an equally honorable footing with the other powers to protect the weaker members of the community not only against arbitrary decisions but also against certain shocks inevitable in a dynamic administration.

Returning to the second point, I would note that one of the greatest causes of the decline of the European parliaments is the loss of their representative function. Even in England the parliamentary majority in the Commons is no more than the tail of a comet of which the Cabinet is the head. Now that parliamentary elections are substantially the election of a government, it is this government, springing from a popular election, that represents the nation, and those members of the victorious party who do not get seats in the government are no more than its pale and passive aspect, the reflection of the representation of the nation which in its active aspect is formed by the government. If the representatives are to have a function to equal that of the government, it must be a different one. Against the government, that represents the nation in its entirety, the assembly must represent the nation in its diversity, in its constitutive parts, either in terms of region or socioprofessional group. Each of its members should make himself the advocate for the cause of some social group (not forgetting either the young or, more important, the old, who are becoming the submerged class of our dynamic society).

The great weakness of the representative political system today is that everyone claims to speak in the name of all. This is all very well during elections, but once the majority has chosen the team which will have the right to act in the name of all, the voices henceforth useful are those raised in the name of discrete parts of the public. The chosen rulers must not think in terms of fifty million times "the average Frenchman" (or Briton, etc.), but in terms of a great diversity of people. Serving "the people" means in fact serving many kinds of people, and for this, you must know how each kind is faring. And it is a representation so broken down according to discrete sections, which provides this information.

---

45. There are very interesting ideas on this subject in the book by Michael Young, *The Rise of the Meritocracy* (London: Thames & Hudson, 1958).

Each group must have its speaker: such seems to me the mode of representation toward which we are moving. This is to be seen in the case of discussions on a "national incomes policy." The "representatives" are not the "elected of the people," but the spokesmen of particular groups. And it should be noted that the growing complexity of society can only multiply these particular groups. Those with whom one must "parley" constitute the parliamentary reality.

I shall say no more, as neoconstitutionalism is not my present subject. This theme has appeared in a discussion of the principate only because the principate itself seemed to me to be a permanent possibility in any political system, which occurs whenever a fault in the system provides it with an opportunity.

Personal Power and the Personalization of Power

It is an incontrovertible fact that countries have returned to the practice of being represented by a single man. The practitioners of politics are well aware of this: look, for example, at the strong criticism that rose within the British Conservative Party against the nomination of Sir Alec Douglas-Home as Harold Macmillan's successor. What was the nature of these criticisms? It was felt that the personality of the new Conservative leader was insufficiently attractive to the general public. The term *attractive* is particularly apt here, as it is on the whole a question of attracting interest, sympathy, . . . and votes. The victory of the party is therefore regarded as dependent to a considerable extent on the personal popularity of the man at its head, a man whose "image," to use the language of advertising, plays a leading part. Some years before the same question was asked within the Labour Party: all those who knew Hugh Gaitskell have retained the memory of a man who combined the highest qualities of heart and mind, of a sensitive and noble character: but was this exceptional personality also the most apt to make an impact on the electorate? It was complained that he was not, and a most interesting inquiry[46] revealed that the electorate votes for "the man," that is, "the image."

In France, there was an explicit recognition of this tendency of the electorate after the defeat in 1962 of the *Cartel des Non.* The

---

46. Mark Abrams and Richard Rose, *Must Labour Lose?* (London: Penguin Books, 1960).

Cartel des Non was a coalition of the politicians of the Fourth Republic against a new advance of personal power. The lesson of the defeat has been learned: the young elements of the opposition started to look for "a man" who would have the necessary qualities to become accepted by the electorate. This way of thinking could not be better revealed than in the process adopted, which consisted of describing first a "Monsieur X" and only naming him afterwards.

The singling out of one man as the nation's guide, or as his "challenger" is a characteristic of our time. It has been explained in terms of television and the other mass media: but, at bottom, all that can be said is that these media give form to what is a deep tendency in society. It is probable that power has always been conceived as personalized. But in the great days of the French Third Republic, the person who embodied the idea of power was the deputy, who was to be seen in the marketplace, to whom one addressed a multitude of requests, and the power that he was supposed to possess in Paris increased his local credit, which in turn provided him with a real basis of power for the political intrigues of the capital. It is true that the decline in the local activity and standing of the deputy, together with the establish-ment by newspapers and television of the image of the national leader have enormously aided the transfer of attention and popularity from the deputy (and consequently from parliament) to the national guide. But it must be repeated that this concentration of interest on a single leader has been too frequent an historical occurrence for it to be useful to seek particular causes, and the ones worthy of study are rather those which in certain times and places have presented an obstacle to this phenomenon.

But as Georges Vedel has very rightly remarked, the personalization of public power does not necessarily involve the grandeur of personal power. Thus the monarchy of the ancien régime presented a complete personalization of the state and yet the degree of personal power was very low.[47]

It is easy, therefore, to sympathize with the position taken by

47. It is telling that Louis XIV regarded conscription, which would have been so well in line with his endless war-making, as an institution he was powerless to establish. And here we are dealing with a king who carried monarchic power to inordinate lengths: calling them inordinate I refer not to our present-day standards but to those of royalist tradition and doctrine.

Akzin. If I rightly understand it, he accepts the personalization of power, which answers a psychological need, and is concerned to limit the effective concentration of power in one hand. Such limitation can be obtained if, and only if, the public gives to others than the Prince other forms of confidence and allegiance. Speaking of others, obviously I do not mean this or that other who would in turn be Prince, but others who would not be Prince, who play and are content to play different roles, and who, being trusted in these roles, thereby constitute a limiting environment.

But let us examine this problem: What does the public want in our day? Movement. Therefore the people who are looked up to, who enjoy public credit, are those who contribute to movement, not to conservation. If then the "others" whom we would want to use as limitators of princely power become identified with conservation, all their attempts at resistance will do nothing but swell the popularity of the Prince, promoter of movement. If we wish to limit his role, we must turn the tables: the "others" must appear as the bearers of movement. The Prince then would no longer be the leader who initiates movement, but he, who, in the midst of movement provided by others, appeases anxieties, stabilizes, reassures, is in one word the *guarantor*.

Countervailing Power

Is such an evolution feasible? What makes it seem improbable is that we naturally see the "others" here mentioned in the form of those "notables" who have been and are losing ground: capitalists whose power is sapped by the progress of public authority, parliamentarians whose role is dwindling. The "others" I have in mind are neither survivors nor ghosts but newcomers, among them the very companions of the Prince, the parvenus of the princely régime, eager to consolidate in their hands that portion of power which he has entrusted to them. Many countries which show us an extreme of princely power also show us the promoted companions making ready to defend their acquired positions against any inroad by the Prince's successor. And if they are capable men, if they have built up their own credit with the general public and especially with the members of the agency which they head, then their position may be secured against the successor Prince. There is more than one side to Napoleon's famous statement: "Nobody has cause to overthrow a régime where every talent is properly placed." True it is that such right placing of merit, in a sense justifies the Prince who has seen to it, but also it imparts a natural stability to such a "right" structure and therefore limits the ability of the successor Prince to alter it at his whim. The various strongholds have been entrusted to the men capable of holding them: hold them they shall even against the master who wants to take them back.

If this were my subject, I would be moved to discuss the subtle relationship which obtains between "ancient" holders of independent power, and the trend toward the autonomization of powers received as subordinate and dependent: while the newcomers are far the more capable of holding the power entrusted to them, they are fortified in their will to do so by the idea of independent power of which some remnant of ancient holders are the bearers.

Illustrations of the phenomena which I am so roughly sketching will come to every mind. The very simplest illustration is, of course, offered by what happens when "the public sector" of the economy is greatly enlarged: so vast a "Crown domain" naturally breaks up into largely autonomous "duchies." Those "dukes" which so perform as to satisfy their own following and the general public are therefore well able to promote the autonomy of their realm.

All this pushing and elbowing in high places is of itself an unattractive subject. If it fully deserves our interest, it is because of its relevance to our individual liberty. This liberty is as precarious as it is precious. We cannot safely entrust it to any hands. And therefore, as it seems to me, we misread our interest if we give any constant backing to any one contendant. If the "barons" are too well entrenched we need the princely threat to shake them, and we should support the "barons" when the Prince flourishes.

The Manners of Politics

Politics is often called a game, but there is a difficulty in the simile: in a game, a man is free to play or not, and, if he chooses to play, he can limit his stakes. Not so in politics. In a cardroom, a few people can enjoy a game incapable of ruining them or of bringing misery to third parties. But suppose that the rules are changed so that when a newcomer enters the room and raises the stakes the old players cannot refuse the higher stakes and, if they leave the table, the intruder wins by default. This is politics. The "old" parties of the Weimar Republic certainly never agreed to stake civil liberties and the lives of German Jews on a game of dice with Hitler: but that in fact was what they lost. As this instance illustrates, it is not even necessary for the intruder to name the stakes: "You must play with me," says he, "and if you lose, you shall find out in my own good time what you have lost."

The game of politics in its parliamentary guise obtained a good reputation thanks to its manners in nineteenth-century England. Neither the players nor third parties stood to lose from the game. Whatever its fortunes, the governance of England altered very little and always in the direction of improvement. Citizens had no cause for alarm: they feared nothing from government, whatever category they belonged to; neither did they look to government for any sudden change in their condition. The public was not much concerned with politics. In *Principia Politica* Leonard Woolf describes this state of feeling prior to the eighteen nineties:

> In my father's generation, very few people were occupied professionally or permanently with politics. . . . when I was a child, except at the time of Mr. Gladstone's Home Rule Bill, politics were rarely or never mentioned. In those days

politics were something which took place in parliament; it was something carried out by a special class of persons; it entered the life of the ordinary person on very rare occasions, principally when he paid his income-tax (at 6d. on the £) or at the time of a general election. . . .

Anyone who can look back, as I do, to a childhood lived in the eighties, and adolescence in the nineties of the last century, will remember the remoteness of politics to their fathers' generation compared with the nearness, urgency, and devastating impact in the lives of all later generations.

As for the players themselves, mere admission to the playrooms of Westminster was honorable and enjoyable; it committed the entrant to decorous conduct. This was an opportunity to achieve office and distinction, to be useful and to feel important. Defeat was no tragedy: the loss of office was not irrevocable, and even if the player left the scene he was certainly not worse off than on entering it, and that was usually good enough. In *The Prime Minister* Trollope describes a very relaxed participant:

> Throughout his long life he had either been in office, or in such a position that men were sure that he would soon return to it. He had taken it, when it had come, willingly, and had always left it without a regret. As a man cuts in and out at a whist table and enjoys both the game and the rest from the game, so had the Duke of St. Bungay been well pleased in either position. He was patriotic, but patriotism did not disturb his digestion. He had been ambitious—but moderately ambitious, and his ambition had been gratified. It never occurred to him to be unhappy because he or his party were beaten on a measure. When President of the Council, he could do his duty and enjoy London life. When in opposition, he could linger in Italy till May and devote his leisure to his trees and his bullocks. He was always esteemed, always satisfied, and always Duke of St. Bungay.

Trollope used this picture to contrast the attitude of his hero, the Duke of Omnium. Of this latter, we are told:

> But with our Duke it was very different. Patriotism with him was a fever, and the public service an exacting mistress. As long as this had been all, he had still been happy. Not trust-

ing much in himself, he had never aspired to great power. But now, now at last, ambition had laid hold of him, and the feeling, not perhaps uncommon with such men, that personal dishonour would be attached to political failure. What would his future life be if he had so carried himself in his great office as to have shown himself to be unfit to resume it?

As our author has wanted to draw a contrast, it is all the more remarkable that the chapter which describes the fall of the Omnium Cabinet is entitled: "Only the Duke of Omnium" (the same note as "still the Duke of St. Bungay"), and contains this dialogue between Lady Glencora and the defeated Prime Minister:

> *Glen:* Don't you feel like Wolsey, Plantagenet?
> *Duke:* Not in the least, my dear. No one will take anything from me which is my own.

How true! And how right is Trollope to point the lesson by reference to the persecution of the fallen Wolsey! The Duke of Omnium has won and lost the premiership; but as he goes out, he is assured of retaining his liberty, property, and status. And this safety of *res privatae* from the vagaries of politics is enjoyed by every inhabitant of the realm: no one is going to suffer from the fall of the government just as no one suffered from its advent.

To a man of our day, impregnated with class-war concepts, it comes easily to say that politics could well be mild when it was retained in the hands of a very narrow class, with huge vested interests. These happy few had not much to quarrel about; the tone could not help changing with the awakening of the exploited and when their urgent demands would strike fear in the hearts of the privileged: politics then and thereafter, involving high stakes, would become a violent business.

Surely there is truth in this now commonplace view, but far less than one is wont to think. Many instances can be adduced of politics waxing violent in the wake of class demands. But many more instances can be quoted of political violence occurring without any such associations with class conflict.

Social clash can be pointed to as responsible for the climate of violence which colored the last century of the Roman Republic, but thereupon followed well-nigh fifteen centuries of Roman Empire (I count its prolonged existence in the East), replete with political crimes which cannot, by any stretch of fancy, be interpreted as manifestations of class war. A brave and interesting effort has been made to stress the element of social revolt in the German Reformation; the net result of this effort is to show how limited in time and space was the intervention of this factor. Of course each outbreak of political violence affords to some the opportunity of appropriating the belongings of others: but robbery by the few can hardly be represented as falling into the pattern of demands by the many. We have witnessed the advent of brutal politics in Germany where they had been unknown since the Wars of Religion: they were certainly not evoked in the service of the workers against the capitalists, or the other way around.

On the contrary, the land where industrial capitalism and proletariat first expanded, and which Marx regarded as their field of Philippi, has to this day remained free from political violence. Lloyd George was not bludgeoned to death at Westminster for having introduced progressive taxation: no crowd of angry peers surged out from the Upper House with a mob of servants unleashed upon this new Gracchus. Nor have the corpses of beheaded dukes been dragged infamously through the East End. Without any expense of ferocity or anger, what a change has been achieved! Surely it is less a consequence than a cause of such smooth progress that politics has retained its ancient systems of manners: the perfume of eighteenth-century civility clings to Westminster.

It is easy to think lightly of manners. Whoever is so disposed should read what Necker had to say on the subject in 1792. Here is no feather-brained dandy bemoaning lost struts and sweeps of the leg. "Le bonhomme" was all stodgy and virtuous earnestness, quite bereft of sympathy for exquisite futilities. But this essentially good man was deeply shocked by the brutality which developed at an early stage in the course of the French Revolution, however irrelevant to the achievement of its positive reforms. An unimpeachable witness, Necker describes the proscription of civility; he stresses that polite forms forever call to the mind the feelings whereof they bear the outward appearance. He points out that, conversely, a flaunting of brutal language, loutish familiarity, and gross irreverence foster actions of the same ilk: the man who prides himself on not sparing the feelings of his fellows in his language will pretty soon not mind inflicting more concrete injuries.

The subversion of civility in the French Revolution is surely the true explanation of so violent a reaction as Burke's. This subversion came as a staggering surprise to Europe. All expected political change; none expected the new expression on faces, the new tone of voices. Indeed members of what was to be the Constituent Assembly came in no such mood: they were all men of learning, grounded in the classics, whose modes of speech had been shaped by Ciceronian periods. They saw themselves as displaying the *gravitas* of Roman senators, to whose example their minds had been addressed by the reading of the ancients, by the representation of tragedies, and by their early admiration of the robed magistrates who had stood up to the king. Moreover, the lighter literature which they had absorbed, from l'Abbé Prévost, Rousseau, Marmontel, and so many others, was all a display of sensitivity, an invitation to the ready shedding of tears on every occasion.

With such initial inclinations to dignity on the one hand and to the softer emotions on the other, it is indeed a wonder that events should have taken so brutal a course, the more since the reforms they demanded met only with unsubstantial opposition. Episodes are telling: when the mob marched to Versailles and carried the royal family with it by mere pressure of force, when the heads of guards, carried on spears, were kept bobbing up and down at the windows of the Queen's carriage, this outrage, both to formality and to sensitivity, was one which the deputies dared not condemn, and it is apparent in Burke's writing that such a scene and its condoning by the Assembly swayed him altogether.

It has weighed heavily upon the subsequent history of parliamentary government in France that the first National Assembly was incompetent to discipline itself, improvident against lawless behavior at the very time when it sought to be omniprovident in its renovation of all laws, dared not condemn disorderly behavior, allowed itself to be dictated to by bold self-appointed deputations which were forever coming to harangue it, and thus opened the door to a successive coarsening of the public style in the course of the Revolution.

The French Revolution has played no mean part in world history. Whatever boons have been conferred by many of its principles and laws, it has also left another inheritance: it has hallowed violence. The generation of Benjamin Constant and Lafayette, its minds full of memories of howling hordes and recollections of murdered friends, was concerned to separate the positive achievements of the Revolution from its violence; but this attitude was soon regarded as squeamish. "The sound and the fury" came to be regarded not only as inseparable from the tale but as essential to it, and indeed as necessary to make it sublime. The actions of the revolutionary figures came to be admired not in function of their beneficence, or even good intentions, but because they were extreme: this culminated in the idolatry of St. Just.

The history of political messianism has been well written by J. L. Talmon, but we lack a parallel history of the sanctification of political violence. After mature consideration, I would deny that excessive hopes by themselves move men to ferocious conduct: there is some radiancy in hope which does not tend to inspire the inflicting of harm. What most easily moves men to destructive conduct is the unpleasant emotion of fear. At least so it seems for the rabble of followers, though the leaders of violence must have overcome the natural sense that it is wrong. I purposely use the verb *overcome* because it adequately describes the subjective attitude of the man who "elects" violence. He feels that he "rises above" the prejudices of his fellows, defies their vulgar opinion, and, the more difficult and truly sinful feat, does not allow his conscience to "make a coward" of him. This evil attitude is far more harmful than any false ideas: and it is not fostered by intellectual error but by esthetic suggestions: slipping on a ludicrous panoply of "Spartan Brutus," revolutionary leaders saw their cruelty as heroic virtue. And in turn their atrocious deeds provided a new set of pseudoheroic masks to be worn by others.

The new "sublime of extreme actions" has been immortally illustrated by Stendhal in the microportrait, the medallion, of Julien Sorel. What characterizes the hero of *The Red and the Black* is that, in a succession of small incidents, he overcomes both his timidity and his decency, which he satanically confuses, in order to do the bold thing. Faguet acutely remarks that toward the end of this great novel the hero has it in his power to sate all his wants of wealth, title, and position, by marrying the girl he has wanted, humiliated, and won: quite reasonably, Faguet underlines that Madame de Rênal's denunciation of Julien, while embarrassing, does not really alter his prospects; it is therefore incredible, says the critic, that Julien should run off and quite literally lose his head in killing his prior mistress. But if there were no such extreme action at the end, then all the smaller acts of daring with which the novel is strewn would sink to the condition of rational means for a profitable consummation: the story would then carry only a lesson of expediency; it would not be what in fact it is, an apology for criminality for its own sake. Crime its own reward, that is the lesson of *The Red and the Black:* it is in crime that man truly rises above himself, an idea echoed more or less ably by so many others after Stendhal.

Obviously this is no place to sketch out, however roughly, a history of attitudes toward violence, but it would be the height of absurdity not to mention at least George Sorel, who stands—particularly in his *Reflexions sur la Violence*[1]—at the beginning of the twentieth century as its herald. Here the praise of violence is starkly puritan. Violence is not a means to a desirable end, it is not a grand operatic fulfillment, it is an ascetic exercise performed by the chosen to maintain and develop a separateness from the corrupt. There is perhaps no more revealing sentence in the whole book than this: "Let the proletariat shun the evil which befell the Germanic invaders of the Roman Empire! Ashamed to see themselves barbarians, they sought lessons from teachers of decadent latinity: how much better their fate, had they not wanted to be civilized!" Sorel also pours his contempt upon the peacemongers, those who, as he accuses, mediate between the working class and the bourgeoisie, obtaining—now from fear, now from goodwill—this or that advantage. Strangely enough, Sorel is not really interested in the spoils of victory: what obsesses him is the image of the sacred battalion which develops its virtues in the fight—courage, temperance, solidarity. He even goes so far as to hope that the fight will revive some virtue in the opponents. All this would have seemed fantastic to men of the eighteenth century but in the twentieth century there have been bands of "militants" which saw themselves more or less in this posture, however differently they appeared to others.

No deep understanding of the twentieth century is possible, I believe, unless we grasp that violence has received psychological promotion. Basic to the Saint-Simonian idea that the ethos of

1. (Paris: Librairie de "Pages libres," 1908.)

industrial society inevitably outmodes the ethos of military societies are two propositions, one of which is a postulate, the other a historical surmise. The postulate is that violence cannot be anything but a means to the acquisition of material goods, the historical surmise is that such means become increasingly irrational relative to their end.

The historical surmise seems well founded. Within a given society of advancing wealth, the improvement of organization will yield more, over time, to any *large* group than pillage. This finding logically leads to the conclusion that optimal organization of the whole is, in the long run (and not so very long), the best way to advance the material interests of any large section of the public. If so, any rational politician, even if he is wedded only to the interests of a section of the public, provided it be large enough, can logically seek nothing other than optimal organization and policies for the whole. It then follows that the area of conflict about public affairs will be confined to disagreements about optimal organization and policies.

Under such conditions politics must logically be peaceful: my opponent wants the same thing as I want. Optimal management is not so determinate as to remove any occasion for dispute, but it is not so indeterminate as to impede discussion. Where there is full agreement about the purpose, there must be some underlying sympathy between those who pursue it, a conviviality which tempers their disagreements, and their mutual attempts to convert each other take the form of a conversation which can hardly fail to be fruitful. The procedure of settlement of an issue is greatly mellowed by the hope, if not conviction, that some *algorithm* might be found in common, which provides a *certain* answer to the same question which haunts different minds.

A man of our day is entirely justified in stressing optimistically that a large part of public affairs now comes under that description; and strangely enough, the divisions which Madison, after Plato and Aristotle, deemed the most dangerous for the commonwealth seem amenable to such treatment.

The surmise that violence is an irrational way of securing material benefits is, then, probably correct, but the postulate that violence is *nothing but* a means to acquire worldly goods, which is essentially a *bourgeois* postulate, unfortunately is quite unfounded. Innumerable instances can be adduced of men fighting for some material possession, but such instances do not prove that men never fight for any other reason; in fact, innumerable instances can be adduced of violence resorted to where a material possession was not the motivation (even if it was often a by-product).

It is then idle to believe that fighting can be removed as it becomes apparent that there are more efficient ways of achieving material advantages. An ethos of peacefulness has precluded resort to violence where violence would have paid off. A contrary ethos may bring violence where it is not likely to pay off. It seems consonant with observation that only small minorities are apt to have a "militant" ethos (which really means an ethos of war). But that is quite enough, because then the motivation of fear (which is very common) can lead to the intervention of great numbers. Clodius and Milo who brandish swords at one another do not remain alone, because Clodius can convince many that Milo's sword is pointed at them and by the same argument Milo also can rally many around him.

This simple image, which explains the spread of violence, suggests two simple remedies. Let Clodius and Milo fight it out by themselves in general indifference, or disarm them. Neither remedy is easy to apply. You will get general indifference if you can persuade people that whoever wins, the victory will not affect them. This result was pretty nearly achieved in the international affairs of the eighteenth century, when whichever king won a province mattered not at all to the local institutions and the conditions of the people. This gave rise to the expectation that wars could be done away with altogether. The reasoning ran as follows: (1) the people have nothing at stake in our present wars; (2) these are only the wars of kings; (3) therefore do away with the kings and you will do away with the wars. It was stressed in favor of this view that already wars were very tame, which was taken as a clear indication that little remained to be done for their total elimination. All this was quite persuasively stated, but unfortunately the booklet that stated it[2] appeared just as the French Revolution was embarking upon a war which was, with a number of intermissions, to rage for twenty-three years.

2. J. P. Rabaut: *Reflexions Politiques sur les Circonstances Présentes* (Paris, n.d.).

Yet there was much to be learned from the booklet's argument. Its facts were undeniably correct; truly the wars had become tame and truly they were only the wars of kings. But the prognosis derived therefrom was, as events proved, quite unwarranted. Which proves that the facts, however correctly stated, were not understood; a suitable explanation leads to a correct prediction, a blatantly incorrect prediction reveals an inadequate explanation. The people had no stake in wars because the royal governments of the eighteenth century were so alike that it could make no difference to live under one or the other, each of them moreover being a great respecter of existing establishments.

This was true even of that archetype of absolute kings, Louis XIV. A warlike, conquering, overbearing, illiberal monarch—that he was beyond doubt. It is therefore the more striking that annexation of a province to the kingdom of France meant no change for the inhabitants, who were henceforth ruled in the name of a different sovereign but in the same manner, as stressed in a letter from the *intendant* newly installed at Douai to Colbert: "As I understand it to be your intention to bring no change at all to existing usage, be it dangerous. . . ." Now, in sharp contrast, it did make a great deal of difference for the Czechs to come under German "protectorate" in 1939. The European settlers in Algeria cannot regard it as a matter unlikely to bring any change in their lives if the land they inhabit should pass from French sovereignty to the government of the FLN. The inhabitants of West Berlin have displayed great emotion whenever it has seemed to them likely that their city would be absorbed in the Republic of East Germany.

A change of sovereign in the eighteenth century was an affair which interested alternative sovereigns far more than their subjects, because any sovereign would exercise sovereign rights, in fact conceived as very limited, in much the same manner. All this is changed when the emphasis is upon *national* sovereignty; that is, when each national government determines at will the rights of those incorporated in its realm, so that passing from one realm to another means being subjected to quite different rules and bound to quite different manners.

It is ironic that in times when so much is said about an "international community" it should have become a greater hazard than ever to find oneself incorporated in a different parish.

Just as the fear of our fate should the "other" army win is enough, whatever other motives may intervene, to put our hearts in a war as we had no reason of doing in the eighteenth century, in the same manner if a militant band threatens to seize power in our own country, the fear of what we would suffer under its rule is enough to make us respond to the other band which forms against it. We cannot leave them to fight it out "alone" because we are aware that the winner will not leave us alone. It is telling that Cicero himself, hating and dreading the violence of Clodius, to which he had been exposed, welcomed and condoned the mobster's murder by Milo.

When I first mentioned these obstreperous champions, it was suggested either to let them fight it out by themselves (and that, we find, will not do) or to disarm them. Let us turn to the second possibility. The question arises: "Who shall disarm them?" Another man with a stronger weapon? That is the Hobbesian remedy. Let there be one ruler, strong, and quite intolerant of any faction. This is not a pleasant solution; the other that offers itself is that the whole circle of onlookers, a much larger group than the gangs of Clodius or Milo, should intervene to overpower them. However, the chances are that some will be more concerned to disarm Clodius and others Milo, and we are back with a general fray.

It seems therefore that one must make haste to stamp out the fire of angry bellicose politics whenever and wherever it is kindled. The happy combination of security with liberty requires a perpetual intolerance of any displays of violence, indeed of any appeals to violence. Those who "play the game of politics" according to rules must combine without hesitation to quash any departure from the rules. These rules must be understood to apply not only to the acquisition but also to the wielding of authority. If this threatens to be immoderate the contest for it is apt to be irregular. Violent pretensions arouse violent politics on the defensive as well as the offensive. Violent attitudes should bring exclusion from the political arena at their first appearance: there must be an "eternal vigilance" to that effect. Unfortunately, only those who have themselves risen by violence know how dangerous it is to tolerate its appearance, while those who have risen by legitimate means are puzzled by the inception of violent politics, and hesitate to deal with the peril in time: and then . . . "hic exitus illum Sorte tullit."

The Means of Contestation

Power is potentiality: for those subjected to it, it offers the potential for good and for ill and therefore each and everyone is directly concerned with the way in which power is used. On this account we give the subject the name of citizen; for to do so implies a right to influence the use of power, which is his at least theoretically. But it is a hollow right, without substance, if he cannot use it. It is a hollow right if its only manifestation is that the citizen from time to time be invited to vote for the person or persons who will then wield absolute power. In such cases, the choice of the citizen is limited and furthermore he who before his accession may seem most desirable may after it reveal himself to be very bad: one has only to remember that no emperor was more fervently greeted than Caligula.

Power is in daily use: the means by which the citizens react to it must also be daily. But here a distinction must be drawn between means of pressure and means of opposition. It is not right that a league of citizens should be able to force the hand of the prince or magistrate so that he acts against his will; for then there is an act of authority without a responsible author: the perpetrator is neither the prince nor the magistrate, who has acted against his will, nor is it the league which was not entitled to make the decision. A host of examples come to mind: the League at the time of Henry III, the mobs in small American towns who dragged a suspect from the hands of the law in order to lynch him, the self-appointed "delegations of the people" who presented themselves imperiously at the bar of the National Convention during the French revolution and so on.

Means of opposition are altogether a different thing. Strictly speaking, they are means of checking governmental action. And

"The Means of Contestation" is reprinted from *Government and Opposition*, vol. 1, no. 2 (February 1966). Used by permission of the publisher.

although they are open to abuse, their existence is undeniably both right and necessary. It is in fact the definition of a completely absolute and arbitrary government that it cannot be checked. To approve this, is to approve despotism. It is unfortunate that some minds should have been influenced in favor of despotism by the fiction that the government embodies the sovereignty of the people. It is true that no means exist of preventing the action of the people as a united body: this is a very rare occurrence; if one takes the physical capacity of the actual people, so rarely displayed, to endow with an identical legal capacity an ever present government, this is the foundation of despotism.

To identify those who govern with the people is to confuse the issue and no regime exists in which such an identification is possible;[1] it is equally false to state that those who govern are identical with "the majority." The fallacy of this can be demonstrated by the following experiment. Take a representative sample of the electorate and ask its opinion on a definite number of governmental actions during a given period. You will find that many such actions are not approved by a clear majority while in the case of those which are approved the majority is made up of variable elements.

Those who govern are neither the people nor the majority: they are the governors. Their rights over the governed do not stem from what they claim to embody but from the requirements of the function they exercise. And as their function expands and becomes more complex, so will their rights also expand. Possibly this is necessary in order to hasten the progress of society: but one must also realize that if the potential benevolence of power expands, with the growth of power itself, by the same token so does its potential malevolence; and as the fate of individuals comes to depend increasingly on the governors, so the governed must be in possession of the means to contest those actions of the government which are harmful to them.

OPPOSITION AND OPPOSITIONS

What is vital for us is that the action of the government be discussed, criticized, contested, and if need be prevented. Our sub-

1. No one has shown more clearly than Rousseau how impossible this identification is, except in the forms of small and primitive societies.

ject is how this can be done. I do not hold the opinion that one should take as a starting-point the Opposition (with a capital O) as it exists in the United Kingdom. We are tempted to do so, because the United Kingdom offers a valuable example to all political scientists, and rightly so. What other country can we think of which has been free from dramatic upheavals since 1689, while at the same time combining with the nonviolent character of its politics a dynamism in social change which was for a long time more noticeable there than elsewhere?

But natural as it may be to admire the orderly duel to which the party in power and the besieging party challenge each other in the House of Commons, we should still, I think, be wrong to believe that this is the necessary and sufficient condition of a regime in which governmental action is contested. It is not a necessary condition because governmental actions were very effectively—some would even say too effectively—contested under the French Third and Fourth Republics in which, nevertheless, the opposition party as the sole candidate to replace the government was unknown. And the difficulties involved in its constitution appear formidable as the recent attempt by M. Deferre has shown. But neither is the condition itself sufficient: it is easy to see, in countries in which the duality of government and opposition parties holds sway, that opposition to the policy of the government does not always come from the opposition party. In America, it was not in the Republican Party that criticism of the policy of the Democratic President in Vietnam and Santo Domingo was voiced; it was not in the parliamentary opposition that the Labour government met with opposition to its "incomes policy."

I do not mean to underestimate the usefulness of the great Opposition party (with a capital O): but I believe that one must recognize in it the refined product of a system of political conduct in which the right of opposition is inherent. To believe that this habit of political conduct can be created simply by establishing the two-party system is too optimistic and to believe that it can be threatened simply by the elimination of the two-party system is too pessimistic. To illustrate the second point, let us take the British elections of October 1931: only fifty-two Opposition members were returned to the House of Commons (being outnumbered by nine to one). I do not suggest that this numerical weakness was not inconvenient, but it did not weaken political liberty; the crushing of the Opposition (with a capital O) in no way brought with it the stifling of oppositions.

The means of opposition are the infrastructure of a system of political liberty: the party of opposition is simply an element of superstructure. It is valuable to the citizen because it provides him, if I dare to express it so, with a means to intimidate the government. "If your actions do not please me, I shall vote for the Other." At the same time, one must remember that a certain rigidity of attitude, which is natural to a party, makes the transfer of some votes improbable: Let us imagine that I am an English trade unionist and that the Labour government in order to implement its financial policy is forced to encroach upon the trade unions' freedom of action to an extent which seems to me to be intolerable. Am I, as a reprisal, going to vote Conservative? This would be merely spiteful, with no positive result: and consequently it would seem to me far more natural for the time being to oppose the decision of the Labour government in more immediate and local ways, for instance by way of strikes.

In a word, the fact that there exists for all to see a team composed of candidates for power, who form an alternative to the team of present occupants, is a trump card in the hand of the citizen who is dissatisfied with the government's policy. Not to hold this trump is unfortunate, but its possession does not resolve all the questions. And its very existence is in itself something difficult to bring into being.

THE POWER OF PREVENTION

I propose summarily to recall certain characteristics of the different powers of prevention which have existed in various places at various times, in the hope of deducing from them some pointers toward the establishment of the means of opposition. The term *power of prevention* which I have introduced here answers to the simple distinction which was made above: it is usually harmful when some group of citizens can force the hand of the prince or magistrate: on the other hand, it is very dangerous when the hand of the prince or magistrate cannot be stayed at the will of the citizens. It is the workings of this balance that I propose to examine here.

Montesquieu has perfectly expressed the idea which inspired this research:

La démocratie et l'aristocratie ne sont point des états libres par leur nature. La liberté politique ne se trouve que dans les gouvernements modérés. Mais elle n'est pas toujours dans les états modérés; elle n'y est que lorsqu'on n'abuse pas du pouvoir; mais c'est une expérience éternelle, que tout homme qui a du pouvoir est porté à en abuser; il va jusqu'à ce qu'il trouve des limites. Qui le dirait! la vertu même a besoin de limites.

Pour qu'on ne puisse abuser du pouvoir, il faut que, par la disposition des choses, le pouvoir arrête le pouvoir.[2]

The problem is that a power should exist which checks power, without replacing it, for in that case one runs the same risk. It is difficult to study it without examples. We shall see that institutions which have played this role have never originated in theoretical thought, but have been born of circumstances. From each, we shall have something to learn.

THE TRIBUNES

In juridical language, opposition is a procedure which suspends the execution of a sentence. In classical writers the right of opposition does not simply mean freedom to express dissatisfaction and to seek to persuade others to share it,[3] but a formal right to check the action of the government. The term is applied particularly to the *potestas* of the Roman tribunes.

This *potestas* was born, as we know, from social conflict. It

2. Democracy and aristocracy are not naturally free states. Political liberty is only to be found in moderate governments. But it does not always exist in moderate states. It is only present where power is not abused: but it is an eternal truth that every man who possesses power is tempted to abuse it: he does so until he comes up against a limit. And strange as it may seem, virtue itself must be limited.

In order that power should not be abused, things must be so ordered that power checks power. *Esprit des Lois,* Book 11, chapter 4.

3. It is surely unnecessary to underline the fact that this liberty is truly "natural" in the sense that it is innate; this is the ordinary course of events and if the authorities want to curb it, they must possess extraordinary means which were not at the disposal of former governments. One can in fact say with truth that assaults on freedom of speech are a modern phenomenon, arising out of the appearance of vehicles of expression which can be controlled: the printed word. In support of this, one can quote the fact that Venice, where even speech itself was subject to the Inquisition, was regarded as exceptional and was a source of astonishment in this respect.

seems that it was because they were harshly pursued for the repayment of their debts, while their recruitment into the army precluded them from any possibility of paying, that the plebs seceded (*secessio Crustumerina*).[4] This general strike (if one can venture such an anachronism) was settled only through an armistice, the writing off of debts and the recognition of a function of defence (*jus auxilii*) to be exercised by tribunes appointed specially by the assembled plebs. On this subject Bouché Leclercq writes: "The tribunate of the plebs was not originally a magistrature. It was a special function created by the *lex sacrata* which consisted entirely in a negative energy put at the disposal of and for the aid of the plebs (*jus auxilii*): it was an invincible right of opposition to the acts of the normal government, a right guaranteed by the inviolability (*sacra-sancta potestas*) of the persons of the tribunes."[5]

Jean Bodin was referring to the tribunes when he used the term *opposition* as follows: "And even though Caesar usurped a perpetual dictatorship even so he did not take away from the tribunes their right of opposition."[6] Bodin comments on this right by quoting from the jurist Labéo who wrote "that the tribunes were not set up to exercise any jurisdiction, but solely to oppose the violence and abuses of the other magistrates and to give help and aid to plaintiffs who were unjustly treated and to imprison those who would not defer to the opposition."[7] Incidentally when today one mentions the ombudsman one does not envisage extending to him anything like the extensive rights which pertained to the tribunes.

Intercession, to give it its legal name, was an intervention by the tribune which he had to perform in person and which halted the effects of the decisions of the acting magistrate. This intercession could be made by the tribune on his own initiative, or at the request of a plaintiff: and the tribunes had to hold themselves day and night at the disposal of such *appellatio*. Rousseau wrote of this function: "The Tribunate is not a constituent part of the city and should have no share in the legislative or executive power but it is in this that its greatest strength lies; because, being unable to act in anything, it can obstruct everything. As the defender of the laws, it

---

4. Cf. L. Lange: *Histoire Intérieure de Rome,* ed. fr. 1885, t.1., 130f.
5. Auguste Bouché-Leclercq, *Manuel des institutions romaines* (Paris, 1931), 67–68.
6. Jean Bodin, *Les Six Livres de la République,* Book 1.
7. Idem., Book 3, chapter 3.

is more sacrosanct and more revered than the Prince who administers them or the Sovereign who gives them."[8]

I have always thought that when Montesquieu spoke of "the power which checks power" he must have been thinking of the Tribunate, but refrained from quoting it expressly because the Tribunate did not remain a pure "power of prevention" by the tribunes, but gradually used the convocation of the *concilia plebis* to transform them into *comitia tributa* in which they took the initiative in legislation.

Rousseau forcefully denounced this transformation in the role of the tribunes: "It [the Tribunate] degenerated into tyranny when it usurped the executive power of which it was solely the moderator and tried to dispense the laws which it was intended merely to protect."[9] To illustrate the evils which resulted from this, he quotes first the example of the Ephors of Sparta, adding: "Rome perished when it took the same road and the excessive power which the tribunes usurped by decree served in the end, with the help of laws designed to guarantee liberty, to safeguard the emperors who were destroying it."[10]

He was right: the essential value of the Tribunate was that the people were defended by those who did not aspire to become masters. The role of exercising power is widely different from that of combatting abuses: and the two should be kept separate. This is an idea fundamental to the trade unionists who see their function as one of defending and advancing the interests of the workers in a factory and not as one of directing the factory. It is curious that while trade unionism, so aware of this distinction, was developing in the West, the distinction was being eradicated in the political realm.

THE OFFICERS OF THE KING

As a second example of the powers of prevention, I shall take that of the former French *parlements* from 1715 to 1789; I hope I may be forgiven if I recall certain facts, as the institutions of the ancien régime are little known outside France.

8. *The Social Contract,* Book 4, chapter 5.
9. Ibid.
10. Loc. cit. In support of what Rousseau wrote one must note that among the republican magistracies engrossed by the emperor, there was none to which he clung more than the Tribunate.

At that time the name *parlement* was applied to each court of justice "capital and sovereign" in its own geographical domain. Thus, there was the parlement of Toulouse, the parlement of Bordeaux and so on, offshoots of the parlement of Paris, but in no way subordinated to it. Why were these bodies of magistrates called "parlements" and their members "councillors at the parlement"? Because they were said to derive from the *curia regis,* from the court set up by the king to try cases submitted to his judgment. Instead of summoning his councillors and sitting himself, he delegated this function to "officers" or as we should say today "functionaries." According to the phrase used by Louis XV when speaking of the parlement of Paris: "The magistrates are my officers, appointed by me to acquit me of the truly royal duty of rendering justice to my subjects."[11] And whatever else may have been unpalatable to the magistrates in the speech, it was certainly not this phrase. In the doctrinal work which they wrote at the height of their conflict with the royal authority, they stated: "There are two maxims which it would be culpable to question and to which the parlements have always rendered unquestioning homage: 1. That public power lies wholly and entirely in the hands of the king; 2. That the magistrates, his officers, derive from the king all the authority of which they are the depositaries, for under our monarchy no intermediary power exists which is neither subordinate nor dependent."[12]

If I stress that the magistrates saw themselves as mere agents of authority it is to bring out that this subordination did not impede and indeed helped the building of a remarkably efficient power of prevention; a success which is not without lessons for other agents of authority.

It is not surprising that the sovereign courts should have intervened against the acts of the administration and its authors, whenever these acts violated the law; what is more striking is that the parlements should have intervened in the conduct of public affairs. Voltaire gave an extraordinary example of this: it was at the height of the financial adventure of John Law, August 12, 1718: "The

11. Lit de justice of 3 March 1766.
12. *Maximes du droit public français tirées des capitulaires, des ordonnances du royaume et des autres monuments de l'Histoire de France,* 6 vols. (Amsterdam, 1775), t. 6, 74–75.

parlement dared to deny to the receivers of the royal money the right to carry the specie to the bank. It renewed its former decrees against the employment of foreigners in the state finances. Lastly it decreed the personal appearance of Sr. Law and finally his arrest."[13] It is in this way that on occasion legal proceedings were used to check the course of public affairs. But the chief manifestations of the power of prevention arose in a different field: they concerned the prevention of new taxes or new laws by the refusal to enter them in the register of the parlement.

It may be asked how the parlement justified its power of prevention and what circumstances favored its use. Parliamentary doctrine on this subject has been expressed many times in the different "remonstrances"[14] but as the parliamentarians have written an entire work in order to set forth their doctrine we might as well draw upon it:[15]

> The monarchy being unable to exist without them, the laws must be known: one should be able to have recourse to them if need be: they must be placed in a safe depository, where it is easy to consult them. This depository can only be the political bodies which are the intermediary channels in which the power of the sovereign flows and when the prince gives a new law, the political bodies must *examine* it, they must have the right to make *representations* if they find that it is contrary to the code of laws, is harmful, obscure and impossible to execute, or even to *refuse to register* it, if, above all, the law is *contrary* to the established order in the state.[16]

The words underlined are underlined in the text and correspond to the rights claimed by the parlements as attached to their office. Had I underlined any words, they would have been the two key

13. (Voltaire), *Histoire du Parlement de Paris* par M. l'abbé Big . . . (Amsterdam, 1769), 2 vols., t. 2, 158.
14. Those of the Parlement of Paris were published by Jules Flammermont in the collections of *Documents Inédits sur l'Histoire de France* (Paris, 1888–98), published by Auguste Picard.
15. The *Maximes du droit public français* which has already been quoted, and which was composed for the defense of the parlements after their dismissal by Maupéou (See J. Flammermont, *Le Chancelier Maupéou et les Parlements*, Paris, 1885, published by Auguste Picard). The first edition of the *Maximes* appeared in two volumes in 1772. My quotation is taken from the second edition in six volumes.
16. Op. cit., t. 4, 1–2.

terms *depository of law* and *the intermediary channels.* But let us quote further:

> In France the parlements and the sovereign courts[17] are those political bodies which are the depositories of the laws, charged with the examination and verification of any laws which it pleases the king to send to them, to make remonstrances which the interests of the state or the utility of the citizens might render necessary and even to carry their zeal and fidelity so far as to refuse to register a new law, whenever they found that they could not countenance its execution without betraying their trust and their conscience.[18]

We must remember that no general disposition had the force of law until it had been inscribed in the parliamentary registers. This was the old form of "publishing the laws" and the parlement worked this up from the simple keeping of registers to the function

17. The two expressions are used without redundance because there were several sovereign courts which, by reason of historical circumstances or of geographical peculiarities, were never called parlements; the list of them is to be found in the *Dictionnaire* of Moreri.

18. The process is recalled by P. A. Robert in his thesis on *Les Remonstrances et Arrêtés du Parlement de Provence au XVIII siècle,* Paris, 1912.

As soon as he received from Versailles the wishes of the monarch in the form of letters patent, the Procurator-General entered the Great Chamber, declared his mission and asked for them to be registered. At the same time, he placed in the hands of the First President sealed letters, known as *lettres de cachet* which, according to custom had to be addressed to this magistrate, both for his own use and that of the Company. The Procurator then retired and the clerk read aloud the letter and the declaration which accompanied it. If the contents appeared quite normal and contained nothing prejudicial to the interests of the Court or of the Province, it was at once registered. But if, on the contrary, some clauses seemed suspect or dangerous, it was sent back to the commissioners, who met together and proceeded very carefully to a critical study of the letters. After a prolonged delay, they gave their verdict as to whether or not it was a case for remonstrance. Their advice was always accepted. Whenever they pronounced that a remonstrance was necessary, the Court, in full session of all Chambers, often took a preliminary decision, in the form of observations in which the main objections were briefly set forth. On the basis of this pre-arranged plan, the commissioners met once more and put their project before the full assembly of the Chambers. They then deliberated and in the end the Court adopted by unanimous decision the wording submitted to it. The remonstrances were then ready to be sent to the king. Naturally the registration and therefore the execution of the orders remained suspended until the results of the parliamentary protest were known. Op. cit., 38–39.

of examining the laws, which were not to be inscribed until the parlement had "verified" them, this implying judgment upon their substance.

This transformation was so radical that the parlement of Normandy dared to tell the king that "no act has the forms necessary to give it the force of law until it has been verified in your parlements to which belongs the exclusive right of investing the laws with the final form essential to their authority."[19] The language of this statement smacks of novelty. Somewhat earlier a court would not have spoken of its "right" but would have said that it was the "duty" of a parlement never to allow to pass surreptitiously as the will of the king something alien to it since it lacked those characteristics of justice by which the royal will is recognizable.[20]

But how could these magistrates oppose the royal authority? This can be explained by reason of their material independence, their proud demeanor, the support of public opinion and lastly by the legalistic spirit of the age.

First, the magistrate is irremovable: he can neither be dismissed nor displaced nor can his office be suppressed. This permanence is one of the fundamental principles of the royal administration. Jean Bodin tells us that "in order to understand more clearly the difference between the office and the commission, one may put it that the office resembles something lent, which the owner may not reclaim before the fixed term has elapsed; and the commission resembles something which one has on sufferance and precariously and which the overlord can take back whenever it pleases him."[21] Complete the idea that the office cannot be repossessed except at the end of a given term with the idea of perpetuity; it follows that the office cannot be retaken from its holder, which was the principle proclaimed by Louis XI in the ordinance of October 21, 1467. "He ordained in 1467 that henceforth the officers of France could not be deprived of their office without legal forfeiture."[22]

Now since the office could not be withdrawn from the officer, it follows that the latter had a "right in the office . . . incorporeal and fruitful"[23] and this was the direct result of irremovability. The

19. Quoted by J. Flammermont, *Le Chancelier Maupéou*, p. 121.
20. B. de Jouvenel: *Sovereignty (1957)*, part 3, chapter 3.
21. *Les Six Livres de la République*, Book 3, chapter 2.
22. Ch. Loyseau, *Les Cinq Livres du Droict des Offices*, Book 1, chapter 3.
23. Terms used by Loyseau, particularly Book 3, chapter 4.

"venality of office" merely transformed the right of usufruct into ownership. What was established by the edict of Paulet was (in consideration of the appropriate payment) the right to transmit the office.[24] The officer acquired by an annual payment, which soon became known as "la paulette,"[25] the right to resign his office either in favor of his natural heir or some other person (and this would be for payment): a resignation which could take effect at a given time or on the death of the officer. It followed from this that the irremovability of the officers which was established as a tenet of public law was further reinforced by private law: the officer who had legally acquired his office could not be deprived of his property.[26]

By means of these dispositions the right to recruit the officers was lost to the government and one might have expected that a magistrature in which offices were acquired either by inheritance or for money, would have deteriorated in the quality of its officers and in the respect which it enjoyed. But either the incumbents, in choosing their successors, kept certain moral and intellectual qualities in view, or these qualities were developed in the grantees through contact with the manners of the magistrature into which they were received, for the members of the parlements up to the end of the ancien régime inspired respect by their manners and behavior.[27]

24. See in Loyseau the chapter bearing this title, Book 2, chapter 10.
25. I cannot refrain from the pleasure of quoting the vigorous page in which Loyseau expresses his feelings about this institution:

> Au commencement du mois de janvier 1609 pendant les gelées je m'advisay étant à Paris, d'aller un soir chez le partisan du droict annuel des Offices, pour conférer avec lui des questions de ce chapitre. Il estoit lors trop empesché. J'avoy mal choisi le temps. Je trouvais la-dedans une grande troupe d'officiers se pressans et poussans, à qui le premier lui bailleroit son argent: aucuns d'eux estans encore bottés venans du dehors qui ne s'estoyent donné loisir de se débotter. Je remarquai qu'à mesure qu'ils estoient expediés, ils s'en alloient tout droit chez un Notaire assez proche, passer leur procuration pour résigner et me sembloit qu'ils feignoient de marcher sur la glace, crainte de faire un faux pas, tant ils avoient peur de mourir en chemin. Puis quand la nuict fut close, le partisan ayant fermé son registre, j'ouy un grand murmure de ceux qui restoient à depescher, faisans instance qu'on resceut leur argent, ne sçachans, disoient-ils, s'ils ne mourroient point cette nuict.

26. It is unnecessary to recall that the royal authority did not intrude in matters of private law.
27. See for instance de Tocqueville's praise of the intrepidity of the parlements in *L'Ancien Régime et la Révolution,* Book 2, chapter 11.

Fearlessness was at the root of the parlements' prestige and formed the best guarantee of the inviolability of its members. For if the king could not remove from his office a "councillor at parlement," he could order his musketeers to take him to the Bastille or command him to withdraw to his estates. In spite of all his subtlety, Mazarin as a foreigner never understood French customs. Taking advantage of a great victory, he had the Councillor Broussel removed by his musketeers: he reaped the day of the barricades which was followed by the Fronde, in which the monarchy almost foundered as it had done in England. The result of this astonishing attack upon the individual liberty of the magistrates was to strengthen their inviolability.

To ask a magistrate to withdraw for a time to his estates was a mild enough measure, but it often resulted in the withholding of services by his colleagues. What a contrast there is between the relentless defense of their members by the parlements of the eighteenth century and the ease with which the revolutionary assemblies delivered to the power of the moment even the heads of their colleagues!

During the eighteenth century the prestige of the parlements reached its zenith through the contrast which their gravity offered to the frivolity which reigned not only at Versailles but also in the salons of Paris. The public respected in the parlements the majesty and solemnity of the Roman Senate.

I should be happy to praise the fortunate results of this power of prevention: but honesty forbids me. While it has in its favor an attractive doctrine, an honorable attitude, and well-intentioned actions, I find in it a growing obstruction to the necessary administrative and financial reforms. And if the coup d'état of Maupéou against the parlements in 1770 was made for bad motives of expediency, there were nevertheless good basic reasons for it. It roused strong feeling, but only in the salons and not in the streets. The parlements had been bulwarks against ministerial despotism, but now the middle classes and the workers began to ask for whom and why these bulwarks existed. Voltaire expressed this with severity in his *Remonstrances du Grenier à Sel:* "How many fundamental laws crushed at a single blow! The fundamental law of the venality of charges, the fundamental law of spices and vacations . . . to sum up, Sire, the fundamental law which allocates to the lawyers and procurators the substance of the widow and of the orphan."

That Voltaire was right, and not the salons, appeared clearly when Louis XVI, wishing to appear liberal, recalled the parlements. For their first care, so to speak, was to thwart the reforms of Turgot and in particular to send back the very reasonable decree by which the manual labor exacted from the workers for the upkeep of the roads was transformed into a tax on landowners. It was the perfervid opposition of the parlements to taxation of the rich which reduced the ministers of Louis XVI to financial expedients and finally made necessary the convocation of the States-General.

It must then be recognized that the power of prevention which the parlements arrogated to themselves was in the end much abused. But it does not seem to me that this argument is convincing evidence against a power of prevention if it were used, not by men unversed in public affairs and at the same time the natural defenders of vested interests, but by officers engaged on active tasks of administration. If, for example, one studies the correspondence of the intendants, one can see that the objections they put forward to some of the orders which they received from their chiefs were more soundly based than the remonstrances of the magistrates.

THE REPRESENTATIVES

The genius of the English language, it seems to me, allows for ellipses which are impermissible in French; thus one can speak of "free governments" but one must not translate this expression as "*gouvernements libres*" because it is the very nature of arbitrary regimes that the government should be free and that is not what is meant. The listener, then, aware of the sentiments of the speaker, must translate for himself the elided term: it is to the citizen, who is not mentioned, that the attribute of freedom must be applied: and the government in question possesses some virtue relative to that freedom.

Even more dangerous, because the lacuna is here less apparent, is the expression "representative government," which in French is translated *gouvernement representatif*. Here again, the listener, entering into the speaker's feelings, understands that what must be represented are the interests, the sentiments, the opinions of the governed; but he runs a grave risk of understanding that these are to be represented by the government instead of understanding that they should be represented to the government.

Political liberty does not exist unless the rulers are currently faced with and badgered by spokesmen for current discontents. The need for such spokesmen does not arise when governments are evil and disappear if they mean well: nor again does the need arise because the governors are not the people's elect and disappear if they are. No matter the ruler's origin and mode of accession, once installed as supreme commander of the nation, he sees things from headquarters and thinks the thoughts of a general: this is natural and desirable. But he then needs forceful reminders that things are sensed and seen differently from below: such reminders are properly representations, and those whose business it is to formulate them are representatives.

Governors and representatives play quite different roles. It is the moral obligation of governors, under any regime, to make the decisions which are, in their own judgment, best for the people. What constitutes a representative regime is that the rulers are constrained in their course by the current reaction of the subjects: reactions which are different in different sections of the public, and which must all be faithfully represented. It stands to reason that no policy can satisfy everyone; but more than this, it can easily be shown that a most inconsequent and improvident policy would result, if made up of successive decisions, each of which was dictated by the purpose of minimizing current protest. It logically follows that the government cannot, without dereliction of duty, be itself representative; it is only the regime, not the government, which can be representative, and that only in proportion to the fullness of expression afforded to the various reactions of the governed.

This fundamental duality between government and representation is perfectly understood by industrial workers. Imagine that we place before the employees of a great industrial firm the following proposition: "You are to elect for a term of years the board of directors of your company and its general manager. Thus, the government of the company is henceforth representative; therefore also your unions, shop stewards, grievance committees, and so on become redundant, they are abolished and their reconstitution is forbidden." Most workers would without hesitation regard this as a bad bargain and reject it. The bargain is just as bad for the citizen in the political realm, and the risks are far greater. It is then surprising that so many intellectuals should advocate or sanction just this bargain.

The idea of representation was developed to limit the ruler's freedom of action: in many lands it now serves to enhance it. The responsibility for this lies in the fatal delusion that the magic wand of popular suffrage can change the nature of the governor and turn him into a representative. But all that has in fact been accomplished is the transfer to the governor of the credit earned by representation, thus reinforcing his legitimacy and allowing him to put down any representation which might arise to check his course. That a means of checking the active power should be recruited for its reinforcement is no new phenomenon: this is just what Augustus did when he succeeded in having placed in his hands the function of tribune of the people; what could people fear when a tribune was supreme! All the other tribunes could then be reduced to purely decorative roles such as presiding over feasts.

The way to destroy a representative system is not to deny representation, which the people would defend; it is to absorb representation in government, an identification which destroys the dialogue characteristic of the system. Representatives lend themselves to this process if they take over the government, as the course of the French revolution so well displayed, and it is a great merit of Delolme[28] to have shown that the stability of the representative system in England was due to the fact that the representatives resisted such temptation.

But while representatives may lend themselves to their own destruction, much also depends upon the spirit of government. It is obviously fanciful to picture all the governments which have ruled in London over a succession of centuries as in some way one continuing government, and the same for all the governments which have in the meantime ruled from Paris. But no matter how fanciful the conceit, it serves to bring out an all-important contrast. In each capital two opposite tendencies have been continually manifest, intervening at different moments with different weights: the tendency to destroy independent seats of power or influence, the tendency to work through them. If one takes the long view I suggested, nobody, I think, will deny that the tendency to destroy autonomous seats has been far more pronounced in Paris than in London, and the tendency to work through them far more pronounced in London than in Paris.

Parliament indeed developed as an institution whereby a neces-

28. J. L. Delolme: *The Constitution of England* (the original was published in French in 1771).

sitous monarchic government drew private power and influence
into the achieving of the goals of public policy. When something is
to be achieved for the common profit and welfare, it is surely a
wise and prudent procedure to involve all those who, on various
scores, can make specific contributions to the achievement, once
they have been convinced that it is desirable. Call these potential
contributors to discuss the project, let them hear about its advantages, let them formulate their objections: if, at the end of the
session, the project is agreed to, with whatever amendments may
have been necessary to rally their support, there is not only a gain
in prestige for the project from their signatures, but the main thing
is that they are now each committed to it and can be counted upon
to serve its pursuit with their specific power and influence. This is
the only way to get things done if the Crown, of itself, lacks the
means of enforcement; and if it has them, then it is still the best
way to get things done, the least imperative, the most considerate.

French planning, as it developed after the last war, offers a
great kinship to the English Parliament in its early stages. Men of
power are convened, heads of great firms, who by their individual decisions, can commit considerable resources: these can be
compared to the House of Lords. Men of influence are convened,
leaders of trade unions, who can state what their members will or
will not stand for, and who are capable within limits of committing the support of the workers: and these can be compared to
the members of the Commons. What a lesson it is that in societies so far apart a similar political problem has led to similar
political practices!

Mistaken are those critics of French planning who regard this as
a bureaucratic invasion while in fact it is a departure from our
tradition of achieving public objects by means of public servants
and an attempt to get them achieved by cooperation of autonomous forces. Or to take another example, consider George
Brown's attempt in 1965 to bring about the immensely difficult
achievement of an incomes policy: here again we find him seeking
the contribution of those new "Lords" and new "members of the
Commons" who have been so designated above.

When the object is to win the cooperation of these heads of
firms and leaders of trade unions, discussion gains a new preg-
nancy. We take too much for granted when we regard it as wholly
natural that governors should submit to discussion and criticism of
their policy. This is to be regarded as a very good habit, estab-

lished by tradition, sanctioned by belief. But natural it is not! To prove that it is not, all we need do is to point to the practices prevailing in a large business or large labor union. It is not regarded as a moral obligation of the chairman and board of directors of a company to give every facility of access to shareholders, to a rival team desirous of taking over the control of the company, and meetings of shareholders are not so arranged as to give an equal chance to the leader of an opposition; nor is this the custom in a trade union. Generally speaking, holders of power dislike being criticized, attacked, and threatened with supersession. They may be wise enough to invite criticism but they prefer that such criticism be uttered in private without damage to their reputation.

It follows that governors are not apt to favor public discussion unless they have a positive incentive. Such an incentive exists when the discussion is, so to speak, a diplomatic process by means of which the governors can hope to gain auxiliary forces. The incentive is the greater the more important the forces, which those who discuss can bring to the governors. Now if the government is such a violent monopolist that it will allow no building of any power, influence, or prestige other than its own, it consequently feels that it has nothing to gain by allowing or inviting discussion, and much to lose as this affords an occasion for competing leaders to assert themselves.

It is hardly necessary to point out that this is a bad use of political resources. If politics is the art of getting things done, political productivity is the greater the more you get done with a given degree of sheer "command"; and productivity is increased the better you use the "natural resources" which spontaneous positions of leadership afford you; the playwright Becque said that "Business is other people's money"; one might paraphrase this and say that "Good politics is other people's influence." Tapping other people's influence to further a project is good politics, enforcing it by coercion is bad politics. Such bad politics evoke bad means of changing the governors: the more or less bloody coup d'état which seldom changes the regime itself.

Of far greater interest to us is what happens in societies of liberal mores. The test of such mores is that the government allows the emergence of autonomous centers of influence. The problem of the governors is to enlist the support of such centers. This problem is not dealt with nowadays by convening in an assembly called parliament the men who are "representative," meaning here bearers of such influence. Influence in our day is very sharply professionalized: a "name to conjure with" in a given field is practically unknown outside that field. As society is more partitioned into an ever increasing variety of specialities, and as governmental activities are more all-embracing, the government finds it necessary to seek the opinion and enroll the support of men who are "representative" in their specific fields. So called "interdisciplinary problems" give rise to the setting up of councils which bring together qualified representatives. If he attends one, the minister must perforce take a modest attitude, coming as an ignoramus among experts: in the session he learns, from the session he obtains support which otherwise would have been wanting; but more than that, what is decided is to some degree what the representatives think fit, because they alone have ideas on the subject. Now this is very much what Parliament used to be, and no longer is. Because in the sense used above members of Parliament are not "representative." It is not true now that each member comes to the House with his own personal dowry of influence in some part of the country, on some section of the population.

Parliament is not then a "congress of powers," strong in its relation to the nation because it is a gathering of men who were individually trusted before they were convened, strong in relation to the government because it can move the nation as the government cannot. This, as it seems to me, threatens to change Parliament from an efficient to a "dignified" institution, in Bagehot's terms, and an institution therefore which can go on rendering the services of a dignified institution—which are incalculable as Bagehot rightly says—only in countries which sense the value of dignified institutions. Just as ministers may not show disrespect to the Queen so they may not treat Parliament lightly: and this is a great deal. But it crumbles away in nations which regard the loss of decorum as a badge of progress.

There the "disciplined parliamentary majority" makes a mockery of parliament. And I find it baffling that so many of my wise friends should seek the salvation of the parliamentary form of government in what offers a means of turning parliament into a mere body of "yes-men."

If I am right in being worried about the future of parliament— and I hope that I am wrong—what remedies are there? They may be sought in two opposite directions. One is to restore the representativeness of parliament by making it an assembly of those who bring to it some outside influence they already enjoy. This course can, it seems, be recommended to the so-called underdeveloped countries which have before them a difficult task of national integration, for the performance of which the means can be recommended which well served that very purpose in the case of Great Britain. But it is hard to conceive how the more advanced nations could have such a representative body because of the great heterogeneity of the body necessary to reflect the complexity of society and the specificity of influences.

The alternative course is to recognize the new character assumed by Parliament in its country of origin. It is the seat of the ministerial *aristocracy*. About one-sixth of the members of the Commons hold some ministerial office: if an election brings in the other party this means that another sixth sitting at the moment on the opposite benches will occupy executive offices. Thus the probability of occupying executive office is for members of Parliament one in three. This very rough estimate of objective probability could of course be improved: but more significant and a good deal higher, is the subjective probability in the mind of a young man who seeks a seat in Parliament. He is very apt, I think, to regard himself as embarking upon a ministerial career.

In a way then, standing for Parliament is a near equivalent to entering the competition for admission to the École Nationale d'Administration (ENA). The young people who get into the ENA will do more or less well in the upper reaches of the civil service, those who enter the House of Commons will do more or less well in ministerial careers. If one takes this view, one then feels that the character of government hinges largely upon the selection and apprenticeship of the aspiring governors. This then becomes, so to speak, a problem in sociology. Incidentally I have long found it puzzling that sociologists did not recognize Parliament as the most interesting of all *milieux* to be studied.

Thus seen, Parliament is not a representative body: it is a college from which the political managers are drawn and also their fault-finders Currently less than half the members of the college are employed in finding fault with what has been done or left undone. This is in principle extremely useful employment; in contrast one wonders whether the back-benchers of the majority are not rather uselessly employed.

As contestation is our subject here, what matters to us is how well the job of fault-finding is performed and how it can be improved. I must admit that I do not find it impressively carried out. However, the grossest faults are precluded by the very existence of this activity.

CONCLUSION

This is an excessively long study. To round it off, a few words only will suffice. From the Roman Tribunate it seems to me that we should keep the idea of a *jus auxilii,* confined however within strict limits. We should have "social advocates," public officials who are ready to respond to the appeal of the citizens, either in groups or as individuals to whom violence is being done by a governmental act. Such advocates should be able to suspend the execution of the injurious act in much the same way as habeas corpus works. From what was said about the king's officers we can retain that there is merit, but not without its dangers, in the idea that public officers have a responsibility to the public not to lend themselves to the execution of governmental commands infringing certain basic principles. From our summary discussion of representation an idea emerges, which is by no means new, that the representative character belongs to the many voices which speak up for various sections of the public, and not to the voice which speaks down from the seat of power. It is the business of present governors to reconcile as best they can the demands of representatives, it is the business of aspiring governors to achieve or promise a better reconciliation. But those whose business it is to exercise power must be faced by those whose business it is to bring to light the complaints of the people, even if they are not vote-raising issues.

I am aware of the inconvenient elements in each of these means: but I am more aware of the dangers of an unlimited *imperium.* The greater one allows the public power to be, the greater must be the safeguards against the harm which it can do. Do not let us deify power: this has never succeeded with other peoples who also have known freedom.

Translated from the French by
Valence Ionescu

The Team Against the Committee

A certain small group of men (hereafter called "the team") shares an intention, the implementation of which requires at least a once-for-all decision of some public authority.[1] The most obvious procedure is to plead in favor of that decision with the holders (or holder) of the competent authority. The next most obvious is to win over people who have easy and habitual access to the decision maker or makers. These first and second procedures can be practiced under any regime.

In the contemporary United States the first procedure consists in calling upon the president, or appropriate cabinet secretary, or upon senators and congressmen, and expounding the case for the decision desired. The second procedure consists in mobilizing people who "have the ear" of those important people and may bring up the matter. The same methods can be practiced under a despotic regime. The despot is seldom inaccessible: the case can be put to him; also, he lives surrounded by courtiers; and these may mention the request at favorable moments. Of course, some requests have no chance at all of being listened to by the despot: but the same is true in any regime.[2]

Here, the case of moment is that in which the decision makers ("committee") cannot be persuaded directly or swung over by the

"The Team Against the Committee" is reprinted from *The Review of Politics*, vol. 25, no. 2 (April 1963).

1. It may require as much as the complete taking-over of public authority but we begin with the narrower requirement.
2. For example, in the United States: that all unions be dissolved and henceforth illegal, or that all corporations with a capital exceeding a million dollars be nationalized, or that no citizen with a German grandfather be eligible for public office.

mild nagging of their immediate environment. The team then turns to a "third" procedure, the organization of an outside pressure upon the committee. This is a current procedure in a regime of liberty: indeed its legitimacy defines political liberty.

What is this third procedure? Through propaganda, the team recruits partisans of its intention who join with it in demanding the decision. How does this affect the committee? Here two possibilities must be distinguished. A: when the team first expressed its demand, the committee failed to consider it, because of the abundance of other business or sheer negligence. Anyone at all familiar with government knows how often demands fail to pass the threshold of attention. Where such is the case, then the volume of support gathered behind the demand may force it through the threshold; and it may be that the committee, now impelled to pay attention, finds that the arguments advanced in favor of the decision are sound and convincing. But there is a second possibility, B: the committee had seriously considered the request, heard the reasons given in its favor, and had found against the request. Let us concentrate on this latter case. If the decision demanded by the team is "wrong" in the eyes of the committee, it is still wrong now that there is notable support for it. How then may this support swing the decision? In this case the support obtained by the team works as a threat.

First, committeemen may have a selfish regard for their own political future: for example, the calculation, "I might not be re-elected if I antagonized this determined group," may prevail. But, second, they must have a patriotic regard for peace and order, and may dread the trouble which the faction now arrayed in support of the measure is capable of causing.

Thus, to instigate support for the team's intention may well be necessary to force its request through the committee's threshold of attention: if the proposal, then and therefore commanding proper attention, is deemed receivable, well and good, and the mobilizing of support has been effective and salutary. If, however, the committee, having given due consideration to the proposal (whether before or after the mobilization of support) has condemned and rejected the proposal, then support can "swing" the committee only through its nuisance value. This is, then, the next matter for consideration.

To restate the assumptions unmistakably: (1) there is a team which demands of a committee a certain decision; (2) the committee has fully heard the reasons given in favor of the decision, and after deliberation, has found them wanting; (3) the team has mobilized outside support for the decision.

The situation can then evolve in various ways, which I shall classify from the angle of the team, on which my interest centers here.

A: the team is confident that it can muster ever-increasing support, expects that such backing will in time become overwhelming, and is content to await such a favorable development.

In this case, then, the team logically turns its back upon the negative attitude of the committee and addresses its attention solely to generating positive attitudes in the public. It makes converts who then join their voices to those of the team, and clamor in favor of the desired decision grows exponentially.

What is the committee to do? It may stand fast because it forms an estimate of the team's potential support very different from the team's own sanguine expectations. If the latter seem likely to be realized, the committee may suddenly cave in, seized by a fit of political cowardice, or it may stand fast, come what may, and then the surge of public opinion will wash it away. But in any of the eventualities envisaged, the process involves no breach of the peace. This would not ensue under another system of behavior of the team, following from alternative premises.

B: the team regards as unlikely that it can in time mobilize adequate support to secure its goal, the decision, by sheer weight of numbers, or it is unwilling to accept the delay implied, either because the critical date is too distant or too uncertain for its patience, or because the decision called for would be stultified by the passage of time.

Then the team's problem is to overcome, with its present means, a mere minority support, the stubborn refusal of the committee. This is not a matter of winning over indifferent or near-indifferent members of the public but of breaking the deliberate will of men in authority, who enjoy the obedience of agents, and at least the passive support of the majority. How can this be achieved? For the answer only observation is necessary.

In such a position, the team avails itself of its dedicated supporters to generate nuisances for the committee. Nuisance policies are the natural resort of a team which relies upon intensive rather than extensive support. Its efforts are addressed to subverting the committee rather than to converting the people. The word, *nuisance*, is here used relatively to the committee: it is not implied that the actions so denominated are, in themselves, "wrong," but that they are meant to badger the committee. There exists a vast range of nuisance tactics. Ethically speaking, going on a hunger strike and throwing a bomb are poles apart: yet both are demonstrations of intense feeling, meant to break the will of the committee.

All forms of action here dealt with tend to dissolve the assurance of the committeemen, to make them feel insecure in one way or another. The milder forms of action, such as picketing, demonstrations, marches, peacefully conducted, bring home to the rulers that here is discontent: and it must generate in them some doubt whether they have done all they should. A feeling of compassion and possibly shame is excited by the self-inflicted suffering of a hunger striker.

There are many means of pressure which raise a question mark in the minds of the committeemen, without offering them a direct challenge. But it is tempting for the intense team to go further. If its militants turn to obstructive practices, then the committee is forced to choose between enduring the disturbance caused by the team, giving in to the demand backed by the perturbators, or using the means of force at its disposal to put down the perturbation. The first course is acceptable only if the perturbation is limited in time. The government for instance may put up with the blocking of roads by the farmers, if it lasts but a day or two, not if it is kept up. On the other hand, breaking up the barricades by force is also a disturbance, the moral costs of which the government must weigh. Or supposing that a group which petitions parliament mulishly bars access to the capital, the authorities must clear the way but if this clearing is pertinaciously opposed, the clearing can involve considerable moral costs to the committee.

In such cases, much depends on just how far demonstrators are prepared to go. A march peacefully begun may turn ugly. Pressure designed as a show of feeling may evolve into an exercise of power. It is all too readily assumed that an assembled crowd embodies the feelings of the people: this is obviously a confusion. A group quite incapable of mustering an electoral majority can be quite capable of mobilizing a marching crowd at a strategic time and place and to endow it with such impetus as to place the committee between the alternative of shooting or fleeing.

Terrorist strategy unfortunately calls for special mention. It requires only a small number of adepts willing to commit acts of violence to place the committee in a position of extreme embarrassment. Especially when the terrorist blows are delivered at random it almost inevitably happens that reactions go wide of the mark and involve innocent parties. Goading the authorities into hurting innocent bystanders is essential to terrorist strategy. Its efficiency lies mainly in evoking blind anger and blundering retorts: if pea-shooting at a policeman can induce him to run after a harmless little girl, that is farce: on the same pattern, major tragedy can be enacted. A course of terrorism can be guaranteed to call forth reactions which breed a feeling of indignation against those subjected to terrorism, and of guilt in themselves. The trick of combining the manners of gangsters with the moral benefits of martyrdom has been well developed throughout the twentieth century.

This is the century of the terrorist technique, fittingly opened by Sorel's *Reflexions sur La Violence* (1908). If a team feels very strongly about an issue and communicates this strength of feeling to others, there is always a risk that one of the latter will commit an act of violence. Where this happens, those who inspired the feeling should experience a sense of guilt: that is an ancient and natural pattern. Very different is the modern pattern. The acts of violence are positively desired by the team, not only for their immediate impact upon the adversary but for the reactions to which they shall goad him and in view of the harm they shall do to his reputation. Devising such a strategy requires this complete abolition of moral sense which can be obtained in man only if and when he becomes possessed by an *"idée fixe,"* an intention, deemed moral, which he pursues at all costs. The most immoral of all beliefs is the belief that it can be moral to suspend the operation of all moral beliefs for the sake of one ruling, supposedly moral, passion. But this precisely is the doctrine which has run through the century.

It has led to a form of politics which first admits that what is waged is a form of war and second admits that there are no ethical rules in this sort of war. This dreadful evolution has been prepared by the thoughtless admission that politics is institutionalized conflict. If essentially conflict, why respect the institutions?

There are "our people" and "others." With others, we may be

at peace or at war. We Oceanians may be at war with the Ruritanians for a variety of reasons roughly falling into five classes: (1) we want to do them some harm in reprisal for the harm they have done to some of us—this is *avenging warfare* (a very ancient category); (2) we must oppose the present exercise of their power against us—this is *defensive* warfare (and this has also been adjudged a *just* war); (3) we dread, rightly or wrongly, the future exercise of their power against us—this is *preventive* warfare; (4) they stand in the way of something we want (purely and simply, or because we deem ourselves entitled to it) and their opposing will and power constitute an obstacle which has to be overcome—this is *purposeful* warfare; (5) their behavior offends our moral feelings and we must force them to desist from it—this is *moralizing* warfare. I set no great value on this classification, it is nearly expedient for what follows.

No century has been more concerned than ours to do away with war: it has proved signally unsuccessful. All too little attention has been given to the phenomenon (not irrelevant to the preceding observation) that internal politics have become increasingly more warlike.

War is a condition which may obtain with foreigners, but peace is the condition which must obtain between compatriots: that is a most ancient maxim of politics. The idea of peace implies that I wish my neighbor well, rejoice or grieve with him, take notice of his needs and wants, help him to success or out of failure, bear with his faults, am slow to take offense and ready to forgive, do not grudge him his good fortune, do not suspect his intentions, and would rather excuse than condemn his vagaries.

While this peaceful and friendly attitude is unanimously accepted as proper in a private man, strangely enough, as soon as I address other men, all is changed. It is easy to compose a political oration which brings in the five war motives spelled out earlier:

My friends, you are Blues. It would be wrong of you to forget the harm which was done to our fellows by Greens on X day (motive one). This was indeed nothing but an instance of the immoral behavior of the Greens, which cannot be tolerated in a proper City, and must be curbed (motive five). Indeed how can you let them at this very moment exercise their powers in a manner injurious to you (motive two).

Will you then allow them to build up this power still further? Should you not act before it has become irresistible (motive three)? Think of the gain if you constrain these Greens to concede what, on any reasonable view of the matter, should be yours (motive four). Therefore, my friends, awake, rise, etc!

Which of us has not listened many a time to speeches built on this model? We hardly notice that the pale horses of war are evoked therein, being fully confident that the speaker means a great deal less than he says, and that the hearers take it at an enormous discount. It comes as a shock to us that sometimes an orator does mean just what he says and does convey an emotion corresponding to the face value of his utterances. The speaker is not, in that case, using big words to drum up mild support for a mild measure mildly opposed by the Greens, but he is actually mobilizing the Blues for war.

When some part of a people is joined together in a bellicose spirit against some other part, the grouping is called "a faction."[3] All great political authors[4] have condemned "factions" and for an obvious and fundamental reason. What constitutes "a people" is general feeling of amity which faction turns to enmity. Militant

3. For American readers, it may be proper to point out that the present definition is different from Madison's; it is simpler and, I believe, more convenient. Madison wrote: "By faction, I understand a number of citizens, whether amounting to a majority or a minority of the whole, or who are united and actuated by some common impulse of passion, of interest, adverse to the rights of other citizens, or to the permanent and aggregate interests of the community" (Federalist X). I quite agree with Robert A. Dahl in *A Preface to Democratic Theory* (Chicago: University of Chicago Press, 1956) that such a definition is equivocal. Say that I am a member of a group "united and actuated by some common impulse." I shall not grant that our action is directed against "the rights of other citizens" but only against rights abused or usurped, or which, while they may at this moment be positive rights (under present law) have no basis in equity and should "rightly" be cut down by a change in the law. In like manner, I shall not grant that our action is directed against "the permanent and aggregate interests of the community" but only against a caricature of these interests invoked by our opponents. A difference of opinion regarding what rights should be and what are the aggregate interests must then produce a difference in the denomination of our movement, a faction to those who disagree with us, but not to ourselves.

On the contrary, the far simpler definition offered above rests upon two ascertainable facts: that some are banded against others, and that their spirit is bellicose; and, of course, it may be more or less so. This banding and bellicosity is what classical writers have had in mind when speaking of factions.

4. With but one exception, Machiavelli.

members of a faction regard some of their compatriots with "hostility," that is, as strangers.[5] To form a faction is to "estrange" some members of the commonwealth from others and such a feat stands in direct contradiction to the classical understanding of the statesman's function, deemed to be the establishment, preservation, and increase of amity between citizens. Therefore the founder of a faction plays exactly the opposite role from that which legend attributes to mythical founders of states. Hume expresses it very strikingly:

> As much as legislators and founders of states ought to be honored and respected among men, as much ought the founders of sects and factions to be detested and hated; because the influence of a faction is directly contrary to that of laws. Factions subvert government, render laws impotent, and beget the fiercest animosities among men of the same nation, who ought to give mutual assistance and protection to each other. And what should render the founders of parties more odious is, the difficulty of extirpating these parties, when once they have taken rise in any state. They naturally propagate themselves for many centuries, and seldom end but by the total dissolution of that government, in which they are planted. They are, besides, seeds which grow more plentifully in the richest soils; and though despotic governments be not entirely free from them, it must be confessed that they rise more easily, and propagate themselves faster in free governments, where they always infect the legislature itself, which alone could be able, by the steady application of rewards and punishments, to eradicate them.[6]

The urbane Hume speaks here with unwonted and significant intensity. Historical experience entitles him indeed to feel that warring factions first ruin the climate of civility and ultimately bring down the form of government under which they have arisen. Thus did the Roman Republic perish and again the Italian Republics of the Middle Ages. But what can he mean when he calls for their eradication? He is too much of a realist to deny that men are

5. "Hostility" from *hostis* means "enemy" but originally nothing other than "stranger," he who is not one of us.
6. David Hume, *Essays and Treatises on Several Subjects,* vol. 1 (London, 1742), Part 1, Essay 7, 52.

prone to band together for a common purpose, and too far from being an authoritarian to recommend that such banding should be forbidden and contraveners persecuted! What then does he have in mind? The key is given, I believe, in the definition proposed above.

It is natural that men should band together in pursuit of a common intention;[7] it is deplorable that the animus which unites them should turn to "animosity" against those who do not favor their purpose; it is detestable that they should develop "bellicosity" toward these compatriots. If such bellicosity defines the *faction* then what is more reasonable than to desire the eradication of factions. This clearly means that whatever groupings may occur within the people, none should wax bellicose. But how to prevent it?

Hume advances the view that it can be prevented by the legislature through "the steady application of rewards and punishments." The thought is not developed: it might have been of great value to the Weimar Reichstag. To me it is a wholly pleasing principle that a political activity which waxes angry, pugnacious, and threatening, should thereby forfeit its legitimacy, but the principle raises a host of problems. Where is the neutral authority to be found, capable of uttering a fair judgment that a movement behaves in such a way as to be called an enemy to civil peace? Is this not a matter where the party on the defensive will be prompt to condemn? And if this is borne in mind, may not honest leaning backwards favor the increase of the faction? If condemnation is passed, the sentence will not be easy of execution; in fact, it will become a trial of strength. Overcoming the warlike spirit once implanted in politics seems almost impossible: and yet this spirit can be expunged from politics.

I like to ask which of the states enduring to this day has the most lurid record of political violence, the most numerous instances of

7. Action groups such as I have in mind differ essentially from American political parties. The former I picture as a bunching of energies, a kinetic phenomenon, while I regard the latter mainly as a bipartition of the political field, a structuring of space helpful for balancing the "sides" of the chorus. The distinction of American political parties is useful in the same way, though to a much higher degree, as the distinction of the "prompt" side in theatrical performance. To my mind the great merit of American political parties is that they are structural facilities for orderly play, containers rather than expressions of political will.

authority won at the point of the sword, and the longest list of murdered princes and ministers. The answer is: "England!" The frequency of brutality in English convulsions through the Middle Ages and right into the seventeenth century is unparalleled. It is the prodigious achievement of British genius that its tempestuous politics have changed to an exemplary mildness rightly admired throughout the world. This marvelous achievement cannot be adequately appreciated if one assumes that change in political manners must inevitably go in the direction of improvement. This unfortunately is not so. A striking contrast is offered by the history of Rome where political disputes, however vigorous, were for many generations conducted with formality, up to the evil day when raving senators assaulted Tiberius Gracchus and caused the blood of the reelected tribune to be spilled on the Capitol itself. This opened a horrible century, marked by the fury of Marius and the ruthlessness of Sulla. Rent by such ferocity, Rome was to seek peace at the hands of Octavius, but political criminality reappeared at the very court of the emperors. This is classical proof, which may, also, be bolstered by modern instances,[8] that the change in political manners can also occur in the wrong direction.

Words borrow their weight from experiences, which can be very different. The words *overthrow of the government* fall softly upon the ear where they call to mind a defeated president driving to the capitol with his victor, and then retiring to enjoy high moral status, assured that respectful notice shall be taken of his occasional pronouncements. Or again where one pictures the defeated Prime Minister "expelled" from the Treasury bench no further than to the bench opposite, or, in another country "tumbled" from his leadership of the cabinet to the holding of some less important position therein. The man whose memory harbors nothing but pictures of this kind cannot imagine that political defeat may mean exile, imprisonment, execution, or murder.

As subject to government, if he happens to have opposed the winning team, or if he belongs to a category of citizens denounced and reviled in their campaign, he does not feel in jeopardy because of their victory. The "new management" may be less favorable to his interests and more offensive to his feelings than the former, but he will not be despoiled of his property and deprived of his liveli-

8. See my article, "The Manners of Politics," p. 191, this volume.

hood. His liberty, life, and dignity are not at stake. It is to him "unthinkable" that he might be hunted as game, herded as cattle. But to a man who with Tacitus has witnessed *saeva jussa, continuas accusationes, perniciem innocentium,* politics bears quite another figure.

Such contrasting experiences foster opposing views. The man born into mild politics cannot imagine them to be ferocious, and to him historical instances are fantastic tales. But whoever has once seen men unmanned by victory and unmanned by defeat, who has watched blood flushing the face of the one and draining from the face of the other, who has heard the blustering laugh and the piteous cry, such a man feels and recognizes that the mildness of politics is not well assured, that its maintenance must be contrived and worked for, that the maintenance of mildness indeed is the first and foremost of political arts.

A Selected Bibliography of the Works of Bertrand de Jouvenel: 1928–1985

Books

L'économie dirigée: le programme de la nouvelle generation. Paris: Librairie Valois, 1928.

La fidélité difficile, roman. Paris: E. Flammarion, 1929.

L'homme rêvé, roman (avec Marcelle Prat). Paris: E. Flammarion, 1930.

Vers les Etats-unis d'Europe. Paris: Valois, 1930.

Vie de Zola. Paris: Librairie Valois, 1931; Julliard, 1978.

La crise du capitalisme américain. Paris: Gallimard, 1933.

La prochaine, roman (avec Marcelle Prat). Paris: E. Flammarion, 1934.

Le Réveil de l'Europe. Paris: Gallimard, 1938.

D'une guerre à l'autre. 3 volumes. (1) *De Versaille à Locarno.* Paris: Calmann-Levy, 1940. (2) *La décomposition de l'Europe libérale: Oct. 1924–Jan. 1932.* Paris: Librairie Plon, 1941. (3) *La dernière année; chose vues de Munich à la guerre.* Brussels: La diffusion du livre, 1947.

Après la défaite. Paris: Plon, 1941.

Napoleon et l'économie dirigée; le blocus continentale. Paris: Les Editions de la Toison d'or, 1942.

L'or au temps d'Charles-Quint et de Phillipe II. Bertrand de Jouvenel et al. Paris: Sequana, 1943.

L'économie mondiale au XXe siècle. Paris: Presses universitaires de France, 1944.

Du pouvoir: histoire naturelle de sa croissance. Geneva: Editions du Cheval Ailé, 1945; Paris: Hachette, 1972.

Quelle Europe? Raisons de craindre, raisons d'espérer. Paris: Le Portulan, 1947.

Du contrat social de J.-J. Rousseau, ed. Bertrand de Jouvenel. Geneva: Editions du Cheval Ailé, 1947.

Les passions en marche. Paris: Le Portulan, 1947.

L'échec d'une expérience: problèmes de l'Angleterre socialiste. Paris: La Table ronde, 1947.

France: No Vacancies. Irvington-on-Hudson, NY: Foundation for Economic Education, 1948.

On Power: Its Nature and the History of its Growth, trans. J. F. Huntington. New York: Viking Press, 1948; London: Batchworth Press, 1952; Boston: Beacon Press, 1962.

L'Amérique en Europe: le plan Marshall et la coopération intercontinentale. Paris: Plon, 1948.

Problems of Socialist England, trans. J. F. Huntington. London: Batchworth Press, 1949.

The Ethics of Redistribution. Cambridge, U.K.: Cambridge University Press, 1951.

De la souveraineté: à la recherche du bien politique. Paris: M. T. Génin, 1955.

Sovereignty: An Inquiry into the Political Good, trans. J. F. Huntington. Cambridge, U.K.: Cambridge University Press, 1957; Chicago: University of Chicago Press, 1957.

The Pure Theory of Politics. New Haven, CT: Yale University Press, 1963; Cambridge, U.K.: Cambridge University Press, 1963.

De la politique pure. Paris: Calmann-Levy, 1963.

Futuribles: Studies in Conjecture, ed. Bertrand de Jouvenel. Geneva: Droz, 1963.

L'art de la conjecture. Monaco: Editions du Rocher, 1964.

Futuribles. Santa Monica, CA: Rand Corporation Paper, 1965.

Discours sur l'origine et les fondements de l'inégalité parmi les hommes de J.-J. Rousseau, ed. Bertrand de Jouvenel. Paris: Gallimard, 1965.

Problèmes économique de notre temps. Bertrand de Jouvenel et al. Paris: Librairie générale de droit et de jurisprudence, 1966.

The Art of Conjecture, trans. Nikita Lary. London: Weidenfeld & Nicolson, 1967; New York: Basic Books, 1967.

Arcadie, essais sur le mieux-vivre. Paris: SEDEIS, 1968.

Du principat et autres réflexions politiques. Paris: Hatchette, 1972.

Les débuts de l'état moderne; une histoire des idées politiques au XIXe siècle. Paris: Fayard, 1976.

La civilisation de puissance. Paris: Fayard, 1976.

Vers la forêt du 21e siècle. Paris: Genie Rural, 1978.

Les Français: roman. Paris: Julliard, 1979.

Une voyageur dans le siècle: 1903–1945, avec le concours de Jeannie Malige. Paris: R. Laffont, 1978.

Marx et Engels, la Longue Marche. Paris: Julliard, 1983.

Sido, lettres à sa fils; précidé et de lettres inédites de Colette, prefaces de Bertrand de Jouvenel, Jeannie Malige, et Michele Sarde. Paris: Des femmes, 1984.

Essays

"War Debts." *Review of Reviews* (London) 84 (January 1933): 41–42.

"France is Bored with Herself." *Review of Reviews* (London) 84: (August 1933): 57–59.

"Henri de Jouvenel parmi les jeunes." *Revues des Vivants* IX (November–December 1935).

"Leçon d'Espagne." *L'Europe Nouvelle* 19 (September 1936): 945–47.

"Le Parti populaire française." *Sciences Politiques* 52 (October 1936): 363–70.

"La politique étrangère du Parti populaire français." *L'Europe Nouvelle* 14 (November 1936): 1140–41.

"Evolution des partis de gauche en France depuis la guerre; abstract." *Sciences Politiques* 52 (March 1937): 82–83.

"Traditions et progrès s'opposent en la personnes de Chesterton et de Wells." *Les Nouvelles Literaires* 760 (May 1937).

"L'erreur mortelle de la défense nationale." *Revue Hebdomadaire* 15 (April 1939).

"Of Political Rivalry." *Suisse Contemporaine* (February 1943).

"Qu'est-ce que la scïence politique?" *Fédération* 77 (June 1951): 248–54.

"Actualité de Hobbes." *Fédération* 78 (July 1951): 372–84.

"Sur le développement de l'idée de volonté souveraine." *Fédération* 79–80 (August/September 1951): 462–74.

"Le souverain législateur." *Fédération* 81 (October 1951): 567–77.

"Le mythe éqalitaire et la justice sociale." *Nouvelle Revue de l'Économie Contemporaine* 35 (November 1952): 7–11.

"Liberté d'opinion et lumière naturelle." *Fédération* 84 (January 1952): 18–32.

"L'instabilité ministérielle en France." *Fédération* 87 (April 1952): 201–210.

"Réflexions sur la justice sociale." *Nouvelle Revue de l'économie contemporaine* 29 (May 1952): 4–6.

"Les ententes sur le marché mondial du pétrole." *Revue Française de l'Energie* 4 (October 1952): 15–25.

"Le problème du progrès économique en France." *Cahiers économiques* (October 1952): 1–7; also published in *Annales d'économie politique* 7 (1951–53): 29–39.

"L'apport des théories du 'welfare' à la théorie politique normative." *Economie Appliqué* 5 (October/December 1952): 201–210.

"L'époque de la suprématie européene." *Fédération* 97 (February 1953): 115–125.

"Les ressources actuelle et les besoins futurs de l'Europe d'après le rapport Paley." *Revue Française de l'Energie* 4 (February 1953): 147–59.

"Le métabolisme économique de l'Europe." *Nouvelle Revue de l'Économie Contemporaine* 12 (February 1953): 3–9.

"Le miracle de l'Europe." *Fédération* 102–103 (July/August 1953): 581–594.

"A Discussion of Freedom." *Cambridge Journal* 6 (September 1953): 701–724.

"The Factors of Diffusion." *Confluence* 2 (September 1953): 69–81.

"Gibt es Politische Neurosen?" Bertrand de Jouvenel, R. H. S. Crossman, Hans Kohn, and Arthur Koestler. *Monat* 6 (February and May, 1954): 464–85; 140–51.

"The Nature of Politics." *Cambridge Journal* 7 (May 1954): 451–65.

"The Treatment of Capitalism by Continental Historians." In *Capitalism and the Historians,* ed. F. A. Hayek, 91–121. Chicago: University of Chicago Press, 1954.

"Du groupe." *Revue Française de Science Politique* 5 (January/March 1955): 49–62.

"The Mover and the Adjuster." *Diogenes* 9 (1955): 28–42.

"Money in the Market." In *Money and Trade,* ed. Sir Wilfrid Eady. London: Batchworth Press, 1955.

"De l'autorité." *Fédération* 120–21 (January/February, 1955): 5–13.

"Naissance d'une fédération." *Fédération* 122 (March 1955): 101–124.

"Reflections on Colonialism." *Confluence* 4 (October 1955): 249–65.

"Order versus Organization." In *On Freedom and Free Enterprise: Essays in Honor of Ludwig von Mises,* ed. Mary Sennholz, 41–51. Princeton, NJ: Van Nostrand, 1956.

"The Crisis of the Communist Mind." *Orbis* 1 (April 1957): 77–96.

"From Political Economy to Political Ecology." *Bulletin of the Atomic Scientists* 13 (October 1957): 287–91. Reprinted in *Readings in Economics and Politics,* ed. H. C. Harlan, 162–72. New York: Oxford University Press, 1966.

"Woodrow Wilson." *Confluence* 5 (Winter 1957): 320–31.

"Invitation à la théorie politique pure." *Revue Internationale d'Histoire politique et constitutionelle* 25–26 (January/June, 1957): 86–91.

"L'épargne." *Bulletin SEDEIS Etude* (February 1, 1957).

"De l'économie politique à l'écologie politique." *Bulletin SEDEIS Etude* 671 (March 1, 1957): 1–23.

"Nostalgia for the Small Community." In *Documents of Modern Political Thought*, ed. T. E. Utley and J. S. Maclure, 79–81. Cambridge, U.K.: Cambridge University Press, 1957.

"Une science de la politique: est-elle possible?" *Revue des Travaux de l'Académie des Science Morales et Politique* 111, 1er sem. (1958): 51–60.

"Conjoncture internationale." *Bulletin SEDEIS Chroniques d'actualité* Supplement (April 1958): 1–17.

"Thoughts on a Theory of Political Enterprise." *University of Detroit Law Journal* 36 (December 1958): 143–53.

"Authority: The Efficient Imperative." In *NOMOS I: Authority*, ed. Carl J. Friedrich, 159–69. Cambridge, MA: Harvard University Press, 1958.

"Instabilité des régimes." *Tour d'Horizon* 48 (January 1959): 65–76.

"De l'UEP à la convertibilité: l'example brittanique." *Bulletin SEDEIS Etude* (1 January 1959): 1–19.

"What is Democracy?" In *Democracy in the New States* (Rhodes Seminar Papers). New Delhi, India: Office of Asian Affairs of the Congress for Cultural Freedom, 1959.

"Notre commerce extérieur après l'ajustement monétaire." *Bulletin SEDEIS Etude* (15 February 1959): 1–20.

"On the Character of the Soviet Economy." In *The Soviet Crucible*, ed. S. Hendel, 449–54. Princeton, NJ: Van Nostrand, 1959.

"Ego in Otherdom." *Yale Review* 48 (June 1959): 505–14.

"The Political Economy of Gratuity." *Virginia Quarterly Review* 35 (Autumn 1959): 513–26.

"L'idée de droit naturel." *Annales de Philosophie Politique* 13 (1959).

"A Place to Live In." *Modern Age* 4 (Winter 1959/1960).

"L'économie politique de la gratuite." *Economie et Humanisme* 19 (May/June 1960): 25–35.

"Les prévision de croissance." *Bulletin SEDEIS Etude* 758 Supplement (June 10, 1960): 1–23.

"American Policy and the Free World." In *America's Foreign Policy*, ed. H. K. Jacobson, 632–42. New York: Random House, 1960.

"The Treatment of Capitalism by Continental Intellectuals." In *The Intellectuals*, ed. G. B. de Huszar, 385–97. Glencoe, IL: The Free Press, 1960.

"The Pseudo-Alcibiades: A Dialogue on Political Action and Political Responsibility." *Yale Review* 50 (December 1960): 161–71.

"Sur l'évolution des formes de gouvernement." *Bulletin SEDEIS Etude* 875 (April 20, 1961): 1–21.

"A Better Life in an Affluent Society." *Diogenes* 33 (Spring 1961): 50–74.

"Théorie politique pure." *Revue Française de Science Politique* 11 (June 1961): 364–79.

"Investissement et épargne selon les comptes de la nation." *Bulletin SEDEIS Etude* 790 Supplement (June 10, 1961): 1–16.

"The Chairman's Problem." *American Political Science Review* 55 (June 1961): 368–72.

"Political Configuration and Political Dynamics." *Review of Politics* 23 (October 1961): 435–46.

"On the Nature of Political Science." *American Political Science Review* 55 (December 1961): 773–79.

"Les conditions du bonheur." *Les Editions de la Baconniere* (1961).

"Planning in France: Technique and Lessons." *Moorgate and Wall Street* (Autumn 1961): 24–39.

"Rousseau: the Pessimistic Evolutionist." *Yale French Studies* 28 (Fall–Winter 1961–62): 83–96.

"The Manners of Politics." *Yale Review* 51 (March 1962): 414–24.

"On State Expenditure." In *Private Wants and Public Needs*, ed. E. S. Phelps, 74–83. New York: Norton, 1962.

"The Logic of Economics." In *Problems of Communism: Russia Under Kruschev*, ed. Abraham Blumberg, 599–605. NY: Praeger, 1962.

"De la conjecture." *Bulletin SEDEIS* (March 20, 1962).

"Aspects sociaux et politiques du développement économique." *Bulletin SEDEIS* 818 (April 10, 1962): Supplement *Futuribles:* 1–33.

"L'art de la conjecture politique." *Table ronde* 177 (October 1962): 40–48.

"Proposals for a Plan of Study." In *Paths to Economic Growth*, ed. A. Datta, 1–11. New Delhi: Allied Publications, 1962.

"Jean-Jacques Rousseau." *Encounter* 19 (December 1962): 35–42.

"Political Consequences of the Rule of Science." *Bulletin of the Atomic Scientists* 19 (1963).

"On the Evolution of the Forms of Government." In *Futuribles*, vol. 1, ed. Bertrand de Jouvenel, 65–119. Geneva: Droz, 1963.

"The Team Against the Committee." *Review of Politics* 25 (2) (April 1963): 147–56.

"La prévision des idées." *Bulletin SEDEIS* (December 1, 1963).

240   *Selected Bibliography*

"Niveau de vie et volume de consommation." *Bulletin SEDEIS Etude* 874 (January 10, 1964): 2–25.

"Utopia 1980." *The Spectator* (February 14, 1964): 204.

"Surmising Forum." *The Spectator* (June 12, 1964): 787.

"Pre-discussion: the Condition of Democracy." *The Spectator* (July 3, 1964): 7.

"Letter from France." *Bulletin of the Atomic Scientists* 20 (October 1964): 27–29.

"Pourquoi une politique des revenus?" *Bulletin SEDEIS Etude* 902 (November 20, 1964).

"Rousseau." In *Western Political Philosophers,* ed. Maurice W. Cranston, 65–79. London: Bodley Head, 1964.

"Du Principat." *Revue Française de Science Politique* 14 (December 1964): 1053–86.

"Toward a Political Theory of Education." In *Humanistic Education and Western Civilization: Essays for Robert M. Hutchins,* ed. A. A. Cohen, 55–74. New York: Holt, Rinehart & Winston, 1964.

"Conjecture américaine." *Bulletin SEDEIS* (January 1, 1964).

"The Principat." *Political Quarterly* 36 (January–March 1965): 20–51.

"Science politique et tâches de prévision." *Res Publica* 7 (1965): 3–14.

"Political Science and Prevision." *American Political Science Review* 59 (March 1965): 29–38.

"Du pouvoir actif." *Bulletin SEDEIS* (April 10, 1965): *Futuribles* no. 90.

"Sur le financement des investissements." *Bulletin SEDEIS Etude* 920 (May 1965).

"Utopia for Practical Purposes." *Daedalus* 94 (Spring 1965): 437–53. Reprinted in *Utopia and Utopians,* ed. F. E. Manuel, 219–35. Boston: Houghton, 1966.

"The British Parliament." *Government and Opposition* 1 (October 1965): 134–39.

"Prospective économique." In *Problems économiques de notre temps,* by Bertrand de Jouvenel et al. Paris: Librairie générale de droit et de jurisprudence, 1965.

"The Means of Contestation." *Government and Opposition* 1 (February 1966): 155–74.

"Sur la stratégie prospective de l'économie sociale." *Analyse et Prévision* 2 (October 1966): 745–54.

"Tâche de la prévision." *Economie et Humanisme* (November/December 1967): 39–46.

"Sur les rendements sociaux des dépense publiques." *Analyse et Prévision* 4 (December 1967): 879–85.

"The Ethics of Redistribution." In *Inequality and Poverty,* ed. E. C. Budd, 6–13. New York: Norton, 1967.

"Situation des sciences sociale aux Etats-unis." *Analyse et Prévision* 5 (May 1968): 319–28.

"La problématique des actions sociales." *Analyse et Prévision* 7 (October 1969): 629–40.

"Jean-Jacques Rousseau." In *Essays in the History of Political Thought,* ed. Isaac Kramnick. New York: Prentice-Hall, 1969.

"Technology as a Means." In *Values and the Future: The Impact of Technological Change on American Values,* ed. K. Baier and N. Rescher, 217–33. New York: Macmillan, 1969.

"The Drive to Power." In *Peaceful Change in Modern Society,* ed. E. B Tompkins, 33–49. Stanford, CA: Stanford University Press, 1969.

"La thème de l'environnement." *Analyse et Prévision* 10 (September 1970): 517–33.

"The Stewardship of the Earth." In *The Fitness of Man's Environment,* ed. Smithsonian Institution, 99–117. Washington, DC: Smithsonian Institution Press, 1968.

"Efficiency and Amenity." In *Readings in Welfare Economics,* ed. K. J. Arrow and T. Scitovsky, 100–112. Homewood, IL: Irwin, 1969. Reprinted in *Microeconomics: Selected Readings,* 2nd ed., ed. E. Mansfield, 542–65. New York: Norton, 1975.

"Rousseau's Theories of the Forms of Government." In *Hobbes and Rousseau: A Collection of Critical Essays,* ed. Maurice Cranston and Richard Peters. Garden City, NY: Doubleday/Anchor, 1972.

"France: No Vacancies." In *Verdict on Rent Control,* ed. F. A. Hayek, 33–41. IEA Readings, no. 7. London: Institute of Economic Affairs, 1972.

"An Economic View of Marine Problems." In *The Tides of Change,* ed. E. M. Borgese and D. Krieger, 4–32. New York: Mason/Charter, 1975.

"Sur la croissance économique." *Analyse et Prévision* 14 (October 1972): 1143–91.

"The Future of the World Economy" (with Wassily W. Leontief). *Etudes et Expansion* 76 (July/September 1977): 505–32.

"Réflexions prospectives sur la forêt francaise." *Futuribles* 14 (March/April 1978): 201–209.

"Vers la forêt du XXIe siècle: Rapport d'orientation du groupe de travail présidé par le Professeur Bertrand de Jouvenel." *Forêts de France* 215 (April 1978): 17–37.

"Mastering Technology." *Center Magazine* 11 (July–August 1978): 70–79.

"Essai sur la politique de Rousseau." In *Du Contrat Social de J.-J. Rousseau,* ed. Bertrand de Jouvenel, 13–165. Paris: Le livre des poche, 1978.

"Pure Politics Revisited." *Government and Opposition* 15 (Summer/Autumn 1980): 427–34.

"Back to Basics: The Concrete Economy." *The Futurist* 14 (June 1980): 11–15.

Works on Bertrand de Jouvenel

Hannah Arendt. "On Violence." In *Crises of the Republic,* 103–199. New York: Harcourt, Brace, Jovanovich, 1972.

D. W. Brogan. "Power." In *French Personalities and Problems,* 225–36. London: H. Hamilton, 1946.

Michael R. Dillon. "The Sensitive Citizen: Modernity and Authority in the Political Philosophy of Bertrand de Jouvenel." *The Political Science Reviewer* 5 (Fall 1975): 1–46.

Dante Germino. *Beyond Ideology: The Revival of Political Theory,* ch. 7. New York: Harper & Row, 1967.

André Gur. "Bertrand de Jouvenel on le rêve politique d'une generation." In *Mélanges Paul E. Martin.* Geneva: 1961.

Hans Morgenthau. "The Evocation of the Past: Bertrand de Jouvenel." In *Dilemmas of American Politics,* 358–65. Chicago: University of Chicago Press, 1958.

Roy Pierce. "Biography of a Generation." In *Contemporary French Political Thought,* ed. Roy Pierce, 24–48. London: Oxford University Press, 1966.

Roy Pierce. "Bertrand de Jouvenel: Dux, Rex, and the Common Good." In *Contemporary French Political Thought,* ed. Roy Pierce, 153–61. London: Oxford University Press, 1966.

Evelyn Pisier. *Autorité et liberté dans les écrits politiques de Bertrand de Jouvenel.* Paris: Presses Universitaires de France, 1967.

Evelyn Pisier. "Les idées politiques de Bertrand de Jouvenel." *Revue Politique et Parlementaire* (April 1972): 29–42.

Carl Slavin. "Bertrand de Jouvenel: Efficiency and Amenity." In *Contemporary Political Philosophers,* ed. A. de Crespigny and K. Minogue. New York: Dodd, Mead, 1975.

Carl Slavin. "Social Change and Human Values: A Study of the Thought of Bertrand de Jouvenel." *Political Studies* 19 (1971): 49–62.

David Spitz. "Conservatism and the Medieval Mind." In *Essays in the Liberal Idea of Freedom,* 153–61. Tuscon: University of Arizona Press, 1964.

Jean Touchard, *Histoire des idées politiques,* vol. 2. Paris: Presses Universitaires de France, 1962.

Index

Totalitarianism
  genealogy of, xxii–xxiii
  inevitability of, xxvii
Trade Disputes Act of 1906, 61
Trade union movement, American,
  165–66
Treason, 13
Tribunal, political, 56
Tribunes, 206–8, 217, 222
Trollope, Anthony, 192–93
Trotsky, Leon, 181
Turgot, Edicts of, 117n.21, 215
Two-party system, 91
Tyranny, 133, 152
  Bodin on, 171
  caesarism vs., 111–12
  challenge to constitutional democ-
    racy, 111
  Daunou on, 138n.50
  Halévy on, 108

Uncertainty, political, 102, 103
Underdeveloped countries
  personalization of power in, 162
  representative parliament in, 221
Unemployment, 126
Unifying terms, 68
Unions, labor, 61
United Kingdom. *See* Great Britain
United States, 155
  Congress, 128, 130n.39, 178
  Employment Act of 1946, 127
  political parties of, 231n.7
  president of, 168
  team against committee in, 223
  trade union movement in, 165–66
Unity of executive power, 118

Universitas (company of men or social
  formation), 10
Ut actions, 73

Vector, 11
Vedel, Georges, 188
Veto, 130
  of judiciary, French, 115–17
Violence, 231–33
  remedies for, 199
  sanctification of political, 196–99
  spread of, 199
Vis politica, 10
Voltaire, 34–35, 96, 209–10, 214–15
Voting rights, 149–50
Voyageur dans le Siècle, Un (de Jou-
  venel), xiv

Waelder, Robert, 112n.9
Warfare, types of, 228
Washington, D.C., 69
Weak political behavior, 39
Weimar Germany, 151, 191
Welfare state, creation of, xxiv
Western concept of associations, 15–16
Will, fiction of collective, 59
Wilson, Woodrow, 85
Woolf, Leonard, 191–92
Words, power and, vii–viii
World government, 181n.37
World War I, Beneš on results of,
  105–6

Young, Arthur, 171
Young, Michael, 186n.45

Zola, Emile, 5

DATE DUE

oct. 1			